ANIMAL-FR

DATE: 1.6.95

ERS

ANIMAL
FREE
SHOPPER

Compiled by

Keith Bird
Richard Farhall
Amanda Rofe
Julie Whitlock

First published June 1991
Second edition published June 1993
Third edition published April 1995

© The Vegan Society

All rights reserved. No part of this book may
be reproduced or transmitted in any way or by
any means without the prior permission of the
publisher

ISBN 0 907337 19 8

Design by Taylor McKenzie,
30 Britton Street, London EC1

Printed on recycled paper by Litho Techniques
(Kenley) Ltd, 46–50 Godstone Road,
Whyteleafe, Surrey

Illustrations by Suzanne Whitelock

Cartoons by Mark Thatcher

Project Manager: Richard Farhall

Cover 'sheep image' credit: Comstock inc

Published by The Vegan Society,
Donald Watson House, 7 Battle Road,
St Leonards-on-Sea, East Sussex TN37 7AA,
United Kingdom. (Tel. 01424 427393)

CONTENTS

MULTIPLE OUTLET QUICK REFERENCE GUIDE

ASDA 16, 17, 21, 24, 25, 28, 29, 36, 40, 41, 42, 43, 45, 46, 47, 48, 59, 60, 61, 62

Co-op 16, 18, 21, 24, 26, 28, 29, 30, 31, 34, 36, 37, 41, 42, 46, 47, 48, 62, 74, 78, 82, 89, 91, 95, 97, 100, 103, 110, 114, 115, 121, 133, 146, 147, 148, 149, 150, 151, 152, 153

Culpeper 16, 26, 28, 29, 37, 46, 48, 74, 78, 83, 88, 89, 91, 95, 97, 100, 104, 113, 115, 121

Dolland & Aitchison 85

FADS 151

Holland & Barrett 16, 18, 21, 23, 28, 30, 31, 38, 41, 45, 48, 75, 80, 82, 84, 87, 88, 91, 98, 105, 112, 122

Marks & Spencer 16, 19, 21, 24, 26, 29, 31, 33, 38, 42, 43, 45, 46, 50, 60, 63, 141

Safeway 17, 20, 23, 24, 27, 29, 30, 31, 33, 34, 35, 36, 38, 41, 42, 45, 46, 47, 48, 50, 59, 61, 62, 64

Superdrug 17, 76, 81, 82, 88, 90, 92, 96, 99, 107, 113, 115, 117, 128, 134, 147, 148, 149, 150, 151, 152, 153

Thorntons 27, 45

Waitrose 17, 20, 23, 25, 27, 29, 30, 31, 33, 34, 35, 36, 40, 43, 46, 47, 48, 50, 57, 59, 61, 62, 68, 132, 134

Notes

ASDA Details of non-food animal-free products were not received by the deadline.

Body Shop Each branch has access to its 'Product Information Manual' which indicates products suitable for vegans. For a list of products containing animal ingredients contact the head office *(see page 192)* and ask for the current 'Animal By Product List'.

Kwik Save February 1995: No list of animal-free products available

Marks & Spencer No plans to produce a list of animal-free toiletries & cosmetics and household products.

Sainsbury's Its new list of animal-free foods was compiled on the basis that vegans do not eat foods containing additives because they will have been animal-tested at some point!

Consequently, a substantial number of Sainsbury's products believed to meet the *Animal-Free Shopper*'s animal-free criteria have been omitted from its vegan guide. At the time of going to print, an amended list had not been received.

Somerfield/Gateway Due to the consistent unreliability of the information provided, lists of own brand foodstuffs have not been included. Toiletries, cosmetics, household products etc: As at March 1995, no list was available.

Tesco Updated animal-free food list awaiting revision as at March 1995. Intends to compile a list of non-food animal-free products.

Waitrose No plans to produce a list of animal-free toiletries & cosmetics and household products.

The entire range of the company's products is animal-free
*(see **ANIMAL-FREE CRITERIA**, page 164)* √

Some or all of the company's products are available by mail
order *(see **MAIL ORDER ADDRESSES**, page 193)* Ø

The company is an authorized user of the Vegan Society
Trade Mark *(see **VEGAN SOCIETY TRADE MARK**, page 169)* TM

The company has at least one vegan proprietor and its entire
range of products is animal-free §

The finished product is not microbiologically tested using a
technique involving animal derivatives *or*, if after the
company name, all the products listed are not microbiologically tested using techniques involving animal derivatives
*(see **OTHER ETHICAL CONSIDERATIONS**, page 11)* †

The company is a registered user of the British Union for the
Abolition of Vivisection's 'Not Tested on Animals' logo
*(see **ANIMAL TESTING CRITERIA**, page 10)* Δ

The company has a policy of using only ingredients which
have not been tested on animals by, or at the initiative of,
the company and its suppliers since a specified date *(Note: In
the product listings, the year follows this symbol — eg a 1976
cut-off date appears as fcd76). In addition, the company will
not initiate animal tests on its finished products
(see **ANIMAL TESTING CRITERIA**, page 10)* fcd

w = with *(product listings only)*

GUIDELINES

• Although, as far as is practical, the publisher has taken care to ensure the accuracy and reliability of information supplied to it, the reader should bear in mind that manufacturers may make alterations to the constituents, derivation and testing of their products *at any time*. The diligent animal-free shopper always checks a product's ingredients listing (where one is provided) before making a purchase. *(*Note: *A current update slip for this publication may be obtained by sending an SAE marked 'AFS3 Update' to:* The Vegan Society, *Donald Watson House, 7 Battle Road, St Leonards-on-Sea, East Sussex TN37 7AA.)*

• The absence of an (apparently) animal-free product does not necessarily mean it does not meet the Society's **ANIMAL-FREE CRITERIA** *(page 164).* Product categories which are obviously or typically animal-free (eg tinned fruit, tea, coffee, nuts, dried pulses and beans) have been excluded. Additionally, despite repeated approaches, some manufacturers/distributors failed, or simply refused to supply the information requested.

• In order to make effective use of this *guide*, it is suggested that the reader familiarizes him/herself with the location of the **KEY** *(page iii)* and **CONTENTS** *(page i)* — and, at least initially, regularly consults the **INDEX** *(page 200).*

• The inclusion of a product should not be construed as consti-tuting Vegan Society approval for the product, its intended use, or its manufacturer/distributor *(see OTHER ETHICAL CONSID-ERATIONS, page 11).* The listing of products under 'Remedies & Supplements' is not intended to take the place of advice provid-ed by health care professionals.

INTRODUCTION

Welcome to the third edition of the *Animal-Free Shopper* — a regularly-published *guide* to products which are free of animal substances and involve no animal testing. Its publisher, the Vegan Society — an educational charity, has encouraged the development of animal-free — ie *vegan* — products since its inception in 1944. In the last few decades the Society has seen a dramatic expansion in the availability of such products, paralleling the rapid growth of the animal rights, vegetarian/vegan and green movements — and heightened interest in health, diet, nutrition and food processing techniques.

The *Animal-Free Shopper* caters for vegans (estimated number of adult vegans in the UK: 100,000 (1993 Gallup/Realeat Survey into Vegetarianism)); vegetarians seeking to move further along their ethical path; the dairy product intolerant; those recognizing the environmental and resource consequences of livestock farming, and individuals wishing to take the first step towards reducing their dependence on the products of animal exploitation.

WHY ANIMAL-FREE?

Though animal-free shoppers constitute a diverse social grouping drawn from a wide variety of allegiances (and none), and often possess an impressive range of views on every subject imaginable, their principal reasons for adopting an animal-free lifestyle may be categorized loosely as 'animal rights', 'health', 'ecology', 'resource use' and 'spiritual'.

ANIMAL RIGHTS

By far the most prevalent motivation for rejecting animal produce, animal rights is a popular term used to describe those who have moved beyond an animal 'welfare' stance (the amelioration of suffering rather than abolition of the root cause) to a philosophy which, as far as is possible and practical, seeks to enable animals to follow the dictates of nature free from human interference.

All animal (including human) species share similar characteristics — such as the ability to experience pain, fear and hunger. Humankind practices speciesism — that is, discriminating against animals solely because they are not of the same species. Speciesism, like racism, is irrational and perpetuated by ignorance and subtle coercion.

Humankind continues to permit the use of billions of animals for food, science, personal adornment and amusement. Animals are nothing more than commodities — sacrificed in the name of profit, greed and 'progress'. Generations of vegans have shown that it is possible to live healthily without recourse to the tainted 'fruits' of animal use and abuse.

eggs Approximately 86% of Britain's estimated 40 million laying hens are debeaked and crammed 4–5 to a cage measuring 50 x 45cm — up to 30,000 to a 'battery' shed. Wire meshed floors result in foot deformities; close confinement in aggression, feather loss and sometimes cannibalism. Two million die annually in their cages. The survivors are slaughtered after 18–24 months for use in soup, pastes, pet food, stock cubes or baby food. Intensive, semi-intensive and 'free range' systems are all served by hatchery-bred chicks. For each laying hen in Britain, an unwanted male chick was gassed or crushed for animal feed or fertilizer.

The 'humane' veneer of the free range systems is egg-shell-thin — monetary considerations require the culling of poor layers. Around 33% of battery hens and 14% of free range have broken bones before reaching the slaughterhouse.

experimentation In 1993 2,827,745 (1992: 2,928,258) 'scientific procedures' were carried out on living animals — including mice (1,457,292), rats (819,720), rabbits (70,485), primates (4,994), cats (2,916), dogs (8,817), birds (116,434), reptiles & amphibians (17,735) and fish (152,098). 63% were undertaken without anaesthetic.

There were 241,999 (1992: 258,602) 'safety' tests: environmental pollution — 62,892 (1992: 59,192); substances used in agriculture — 67,266 (1992: 76,986); substances used in industry — 80,238 (1992: 91,832); substances used in the household — 2,204 (1992: 2,080); food additives — 7,617 (1992: 6,134); cosmetics and toiletries — 3,826 (1992: 2,164); tobacco — 0 (1992: 157); alcohol research — 7,328 (1992: 1,087); other safety evaluation — 10,626 (1992: 18,970).

Typical safety tests include: LD50/LC50 (1993: 154,880; 1992: 153,222) — in which a group of animals is administered a substance to ascertain the level required to kill half of them, by way of loss of appetite, nausea, convulsions, discharges and diarrhoea; and eye irritancy (1993: 7,208; 1992: 114,145) — in which substances are applied to rabbits' eyes (rabbits have no tear ducts), possibly resulting in swelling, ulceration, haemorrhage and discharge.

fur Around 40 million animals, mainly mink and foxes (but also chinchilla, sable and even wolf) are held captive in row upon row of metal cages, where they are unable to pursue their natural instincts and so resort to fighting, self-mutilation and cannibalism. Death comes by gassing, electrocution, lethal injection or neck dislocation. There are around 11 such farms in Britain (10 mink, 1 fox), imprisoning around 47,000 animals. Trapping accounts for an estimated 10 million animals worldwide, normally by means of steel-jawed leg hold traps (illegal in Britain).

honey The primary food and energy source of adult bees, honey is removed from hives and, in commercial production, is substituted with a nutrient-deficient sugar solution. Worker bees fly the equivalent of six orbits of the earth to produce 1kg honey. Bees are frequently crushed during hive manipulation, the queen's wings are clipped to prevent 'swarming', and hives may be destroyed before the non-productive winter months. Queens are also subjected to artificial insemination and transit in the post. Bee sperm is obtained by decapitation, sending an electric impulse to the nervous system which causes sexual arousal.

Other bee products include propolis, royal jelly (bee milk) and venom — all *claimed* to have medicinal qualities.

leather The profitability of the meat industry depends significantly on the sale of hides, which are tanned to produce leather. The hide of a slaughtered animal is worth around 10% of the total carcase value. In 1991 the United Kingdom's leather sales totalled £430 million (1987: £705 million).

Although the hides of sheep, pigs and goats are an important source of 'raw material' for tanners, cattle hides and calf skins account for most footwear and leather goods produced in the UK. The softest leather is obtained from the dairy industry's unwanted calves. The softest of all comes from the unborn calf of a pregnant cow.

Speciality leathers are made from deer, alligators, lizards, sharks, snakes, crocodiles, kangaroos, ostriches and other 'exotic' species.

meat Over 700 million cattle, sheep, pigs, chickens, turkeys, ducks, geese and rabbits are slaughtered annually in Britain (and 60–80 million tonnes of fish asphyxiated worldwide) in horrific circumstances to satisfy our (waning) appetite for decaying animal flesh and to provide a wide range of commercially valuable 'by-products' — including bone, hides, skins, hair, bristles, feathers, fur, blood, bone meal, hoof & horn meal, and fats. Millions of animals fail to make it to the slaughterhouse or trawler — dying of neglect, exposure, disease, starvation, deformity, drug side effects or pollution.

The majority of food animals — primarily poultry (especially egg laying and broiler chickens), but also pigs and rabbits — are selectively bred and reared for a fraction of their natural lifespans in cramped, dimly-lit, disease-conducive 'factory farm' conditions — suffering not only physical injury but stress and psychological trauma. Like cattle and sheep, pigs and poultry are subjected to stock operations such as teeth-grinding and debeaking – to prevent them injuring their equally frustrated 'cell' mates.

milk The modern dairy cow is nothing more than a milk machine: artificially inseminated (60–75%), milked 2–3 times a day, and for 6–7 months each year milked *whilst pregnant*. Instead of producing 3 litres of milk a day for her calf, she produces 30. Her full udder can weigh up to 50kg (the equivalent of 50 bags of sugar). Unsurprisingly, every year 20% of dairy cows go lame, while 25% suffer infections such as mastitis.

Her natural life span is 20 years or more but, pushed beyond her limits, is worn out due to disease (36%), poor yield (28%) or inability to calve (36%) and so is slaughtered for burgers at 3–7 years.

The inevitable result of humankind's bizarre desire to drink the milk of another species, the calf, is allowed to suckle for no more than a few days before it is prevented from consuming 'too much' of its mother's milk by being put on milk substitutes. Naturally, they would suckle for 6 months.

Only 20–25% of calves go on to provide milk. The remainder are exported to continental veal crates (where they are confined in narrow crates, unable to turn around and fed an iron-deficient liquid diet); killed at 2 weeks for pies, rennet for cheese-making and calf skin; or reared for beef (60–70% of beef in the UK originates from, and helps make profitable, the dairy herd).

By 30 September 1994, 140,000 cattle had died of the brain disorder bovine spongiform encephalopathy (BSE). Researchers have identified two new viruses in cattle: bovine leukaemia – cancer of the lymph tissue, and bovine immunodeficiency (BIV).

silk The breeding of the silk worm (the larva of the silk moth) and the production of silk employs 2.5 million farmworkers in 30 countries. Using a substance produced from glands in its mouth the larva makes 300,000 figure of eight movements to spin a cocoon. The industry 'must' unravel the cocoon in a continuous strand and so before the moth can emerge from its chrysalis stage it is killed by baking, steaming or electrocution. It takes 1,500 silk worms to produce 100g silk.

wool Though reared mainly for their coats, sheep also provide mutton, lamb, leather, milk, lanolin and vitamin D_3. Genetic engineering has turned a once wild, agile creature into an over-fleeced, disease-prone monstrosity. Without human meddling sheep would produce just enough covering to ensure survival. Soon after the frequently bloody process of shearing, thousands of sheep die of cold. Millions die annually of exposure, disease, injury and pregnancy complication.

Sheep are subjected to a range of unanaesthetized mutilations including ear tagging, tail docking and castration. Perhaps the most appalling is 'mulesing', carried out on the Australian Merino. Purposely engineered to have extra folds of skin and so a larger fleece, the Merino is consequently susceptible to blowflies which lay their eggs in the folds. Mulesing involves the hacking away of wool and skin from the hindquarters — resulting in a bloody wound which, if uninfected, takes 3–5 weeks to heal. One-third of Britain's wool is obtained from the slaughterhouse floor.

HEALTH

The human digestive system and dental structure, like that of the higher primates, is designed to grind and digest high fibre, moderate protein plant foods. An essentially *wholefood* animal-free diet is low in cholesterol, high in fibre, high in vitamins and minerals, low in saturated fat, low in sodium and contains all human nutritional requirements. Meat, dairy products and eggs contain no dietary fibre, are the principal sources of saturated fat and cholesterol in the British diet, and are responsible for most incidents of food poisoning — harbouring salmonella, listeria and campylobacter. The Communicable Diseases Surveillance Centre recorded 68,590 *(provisional)* incidents of food poisoning in 1993 (1989: 52,557).

Research involving human 'guinea pigs' has shown that an animal-free diet can be beneficial in the treatment of high blood pressure, angina, atherosclerosis, kidney disease, diabetic neuropathy, rheumatoid arthritis and asthma. Additionally, it is believed that such diets can reduce the risks of contracting certain diseases/conditions including: constipation, irritable bowel syndrome, varicose veins, haemorrhoids, diverticular disease, duodenal ulcers, gallstones, coronary heart disease and cancers of the bowel, breast, womb, prostate and pancreas.

Allergy to cow's milk is the most common food allergy in childhood, causing diarrhoea, vomiting, persistent colic, eczema, urticaria, catarrh, bronchitis and asthma. Milk and other dairy products account for about half the saturated fat intake of UK omnivores. A number of studies have directly implicated cow's milk consumption in heart disease and juvenile-onset diabetes.

ECOLOGY

Animal-based agriculture is a major contributor to environmental destruction.

acid rain Animal wastes are suspected of contributing to acid rain — a term used to describe the fallout (via rain, snow or fog) of industrial pollutants which react with water and sunlight to form sulphuric and nitric acids. Acid rain has rendered lakes devoid of fish life and has led to the death of millions of trees.

Nitrogen in animal waste is volatized to form ammonia. In the industrialized countries ammonia is the greatest single cause of acid rain. In the Netherlands, half of the 250,000 tonnes emitted each year comes from liquid manure being spread on fields, 80,000 tonnes wafts out of stock housing, and 30,000 tonnes from grazing animals.

deforestation The large-scale felling of trees for livestock allows wind and rain to remove valuable nutrient-rich topsoil, increases the risk of flooding and drought, and causes climatic imbalance. The roots of trees and the debris on the forest floor soaks up rain and prevents it rushing unchecked down slopes, carrying topsoil. Trees also help protect soil from desiccating winds. Exposed, mainly dry areas, where rainfall is occasional and heavy, degenerate rapidly into dust bowls.

Over 150 acres of tropical rainforest are cleared every minute, much of it for cattle grazing, beef production and soya — used primarily for animal feed. The rainforests help regulate the world's oxygen supply and maintain a rich diversity of plant and animal life; yet one species is extinguished *every* day.

Grazing animals, principally cattle, contribute directly to soil erosion and imbalance; devouring tree seedlings, compacting the surface, and depositing considerably more waste products than would wild animals under natural conditions.

global warming The greenhouse effect, caused by rising levels of greenhouse gases, describes the gradual warming of the earth — threatening widespread flooding and crop failure. Cattle, sheep and other ruminants are one of the main sources of the greenhouse gas methane, considered to be 20–25 times as potent as carbon dioxide, the chief global warming culprit. A typical cow belches out 200 litres daily. The cattle population has reached 1.3 billion — one cow for every four humans.

The greenhouse effect is aggravated greatly by the burning of vast tracts of rainforest for livestock grazing, releasing millions of tonnes of carbon dioxide into the atmosphere.

tanneries An application to Milton Keynes Borough Council for authorization under Part 1 of the Environmental Protection Act 1990 to operate "Leather Finishing Processes" at a tannery lists the following as "Chemicals Potentially Capable of Causing Emissions": formic acid, hydrochloric acid, sodium hydrogen sulphide, sodium hypochlorite, sulphuric acid, caustic pearl soda, ammonia 0-88 solution, ammonium chloride, ammonium sulphate, Purgatol substitute, sodium carbonate, hydrated lime, sodium sulphide, Derugan 2000, Irgatan LU Liquid, dyestuffs, liquids, powders, Meritose and potassium dichromate!

water pollution Animal farming is probably *the* major source of water pollution. British farms produce 200 million tonnes of excreta — containing nitrates, antibiotics, parasites (including cryptosporidium, a micro-organism which has found its way into tap water and causes a particularly nasty form of diarrhoea) heavy metals, and pesticides — each year, three times as much waste as humans. A 1992 National Rivers Authority survey of farmers in England and Wales found that nearly half were polluting the water supply with manure, fertilizers and pesticides.

Slurry enters water courses, contributing to fish deaths, deoxygenation and algae blooms. Cattle slurry is 20–40 times more potent at removing oxygen from river water than untreated human sewage.

In 1992 Taiwan's pig population topped 10 million, one pig for every two people. Each pig produced 3.5kg of manure and urine a day. 35,000 tonnes daily poured into the country's lakes and rivers, turning them black and devoid of oxygen.

RESOURCE USE

Animal farming represents a squanderous misuse of scarce natural resources. Farm animals compete with us for land, water, fuel and consume 5–10 times as much primary plant food as humans. Approximately 38% of the world's food grain is fed to livestock yet 15 million children die from malnutrition every year and over 500 million individuals are severely malnourished. The EEC imports 50 million tonnes of plant food annually to feed animals of which 60% is produced by the 'Third World'. Around 80% of the UK's agricultural land is used for grazing or to grow animal feed — yet it has been estimated that only 25% would be required to supply the British population with an animal-free diet. Passing plant matter through animals is grossly inefficient — only about $1/10$ of the plant protein consumed is converted into animal protein.

The animal farming industry makes heavy use of both fossil fuels and water. It takes an estimated 78 calories of fossil fuel to produce one calorie of beef; 36 for one calorie of milk; and 2 for one calorie of soyabean protein. Farm animals account for 80% of water supplies worldwide. In the UK, livestock husbandry is the single largest user of water. Approximately 70 litres of water per day per head of livestock are needed for cleaning and cooling. The production of 1lb of wheat requires 60 gallons of water; meat can require up to 6,000 gallons.

SPIRITUAL

Central to the beliefs of many of those following an animal-free lifestyle is the conviction of harmlessness or reverence for life, embodied in the spirit of *ahimsa* — the Sanskrit word for non-killing and non-injury popularized by Mahatma Ghandi.

Though some animal-free shoppers are allied to a particular church — such as the pacifist Society of Friends (Quakers); or a particular faith — especially Buddhism; or empathize with paganism; many consider that their animal-free lifestyle — its 'rules', practical application, and sense of inner peace — provides for most of their spiritual needs.

The liberation of animals from human tyranny, health advantages, ecological, resource and spiritual considerations, are five very good reasons for adopting an animal-free lifestyle. Animal farming serves the world ill on all counts; its widespread rejection is not only an urgent necessity, it is fast-becoming inevitable.

ANIMAL TESTING CRITERIA

The animal protection movement and toiletries & cosmetics industry abound with variations on the 'not tested on animals' theme. Depending on where one's priorities lie, all have their strengths and weaknesses.

The criterion used to compile the *Animal-Free Shopper (see page 165)* recognizes that most substances have been, and some may continue to be, animal tested and requires simply that a product's manufacturer, or 'related' company, has not initiated testing on either the finished product or, where applicable, the ingredients.

For those readers who prefer to patronize companies using other popular criteria, the publisher asked those it surveyed to indicate whether they adhered to either of the criteria described below.

5-year rolling rule Neither the finished product nor its ingredients have been tested on animals by the company, or at its initiative, within the last 5 years. In addition, the company will not initiate animal tests on its finished products. The best-known proponent of this criterion is the British Union for Abolition of Vivisection (BUAV). In the product listings, authorized users of the BUAV's 'white rabbit' logo are indicated by '∆'.

fixed cut-off date The company has a policy of using only ingredients which have not been tested on animals by, or at the initiative of, the company and its suppliers since a specified date. In addition, the company will not initiate animal tests on its finished products. In the product listings, the specified date (year) follows 'fcd'.

Further Information: 'Guide to Products Not Tested On Animals', Research Animals Department, RSPCA.

OTHER ETHICAL CONSIDERATIONS

To qualify for inclusion in the *Animal-Free Shopper* a product need only be free of animal ingredients and animal testing. However, whilst avoiding products having *direct* animal involvement is a coherent and far-reaching ethical stance in itself, requiring considerable commitment, many animal-free shoppers choose to make purchasing decisions based on a wide range of additional ethical considerations pertaining to humans, animals and the environment. The following are common (indirect) 'animal' areas of concern:

- **company ownership** Some animal-free shoppers prefer to patronize those companies which are wholly or partly owned by vegans *(see KEY, page iii)*;
- **product range** Many companies manufacture/distribute both animal and non-animal products. Given the choice, many animal-free shoppers prefer to buy from those companies whose entire range is animal-free *(see KEY, page iii)*;
- **company activities** A number of companies manufacturing/distributing animal-free (and animal) products are involved directly in animal abuse — such as the meat and dairy industries;
- **company connections** Some seemingly innocuous companies have parent, sister or subsidiary companies which are involved directly in animal abuse;
- **company affiliations** Possible manufacturer/distributor animal use affiliations include: The British Industrial Biological Research Association (BIBRA), Research Defence Society (RDS), British Field Sports Society (BFSS), Game Conservancy;
- **company sponsorships & donations** Common areas of sponsorship and donations include animal-connected medical research and sporting events;
- **organized boycotts** Even large multi-national companies have ceased an objectionable activity when threatened with, or subjected to, a boycott campaign. Though not always successful, it is argued that boycotts are, nevertheless, a useful means by which to heighten public awareness;
- **microbiological testing** In order to ensure the safety of their products, and to forestall damaging law suits which might arise following the discovery of a defect, many manufacturers test batches

of their products for the presence of bacterial contaminants. The nutrient media 'fed' to the bacteria (in order to identify them) are commonly derived from the slaughterhouse or the dairy industry. Virtually all foodstuffs, and most toiletries & cosmetics products are subject to testing techniques involving the use of animal derivatives. However, a number of microbiological laboratories have developed and validated 'stage one' animal-free tests for use on *toiletry and cosmetic* products.

Unfortunately, animal-free shoppers cannot avoid microbiologically-tested foodstuffs, which not only include processed foods but also unprocessed fruits and vegetables — and even drinking water!

The *Animal-Free Shopper* identifies products that are not microbiologically tested using a technique involving animal derivatives *(see KEY, page iii)*.

Recognizing that human and animal rights are inextricably linked and that all life is dependent upon the well-being of the planet, the animal-free shopper might also wish to avoid companies involved in/with: cash crops, environmentally damaging practices, irresponsible marketing, land rights, low wages and poor conditions, and oppressive regimes.

further information

The Ethical Consumer Research Association, 16 Nicholas Street, Manchester M1 4EJ. 0161 237 1630. Publisher of *The Ethical Consumer Guide to Everyday Shopping*; and *The Ethical Consumer*, a magazine providing information on companies behind brand names across a range of ethical issues — including 'Animal Testing', 'Factory Farming' and 'Other Animal Rights'.

APPLE JUICE & BETA-CAROTENE

apple juice Gelatine *may* be used to clarify apple (and possibly also pear and grape) concentrate. Apple concentrate is used in the production of fruit juices, soft drinks and 'healthy' products requiring a non-sugar sweetener — including confectionery, soya milks and fruit spreads.

The British Fruit Juice Importers Association, and a number of major UK importers/suppliers of fruit juices and soft drinks, have stated that the use of gelatine as a clarifier is now rare — cheaper, animal-friendly 'ultra-filtration' being the preferred method.

All soya milks containing apple juice would appear to be free of a gelatine connection — as are Whole Earth products.

beta-carotene Gelatine *may* be added to orange-coloured drinks to stabilize beta-carotene, which is used as a colouring agent.

Note: The publisher of the *Animal-Free Shopper* did not have sufficient time to check every juice- and beta-carotene-containing product listed in this guide. Where it has documentary or firsthand evidence that gelatine has been used, the products affected have been omitted.

ACKNOWLEDGEMENTS

Thanks to Erik Millstone for his invaluable advice on additives.

LOOKING AHEAD . . .

Please send your comments and details of new product discoveries to: *The Vegan Society*, Donald Watson House, 7 Battle Road, St Leonards-on-Sea, East Sussex TN37 7AA. To receive a current update slip for this publication, send an SAE marked 'AFS3 Update' to the same address.

FOOD

BISCUITS

ASDA

Barnstormers, Bourbon Creams, Coconut Crumble Creams, Fruit Barnstormers, Fruit Shortcake, Ginger Nuts, Ginger Thins, Lemon Shortcake, Morning Coffee, Nice, Rich Tea (Fingers, Rounds)

BORDER BISCUITS

Dark Coated Ginger Crunch, Ginger

BRAYCOT FOODS

Half-Coated Cookie, Hazelnut Crunchy, Mountain Cookie, Oat Nuttie, Tea Crunch

BURTON'S BISCUITS

Country Snapjacks, Fruit Snapjacks, Rich Tea Biscuits

CRAWFORDS

Bourbon Creams, Butterpuffs, Marie, Morning Coffee, Thin Arrowroot, Wafers

CO-OP

Bourbon Creams, Chocolate Cookies *w* Choc Chips, Citrus Fruit Crunch, Coconut Crumble Creams, Country Crunch, Digestive Wheatmeal, Fig Roll, Fruit Country Crunch, Fruit Shortcake, Ginger Thins, Ginger Nuts, Lemon Puff, Lincoln, Morning Coffee, Plain Chocolate Ginger Rings, Plain Chocolate Rich Tea, Plain Chocolate Wheatmeal, Rich Tea, Royal Duchess, Thin Arrowroot

CULPEPERøfcd76

Hand Made: Aniseed, Clove & Lemon, Treacle & Spice, Scottish Marmalade, Stem Ginger

DOVE'S FARM√ø

Organic Digestives; *Organic Cookies:* all

FOX'S BISCUITS

Classic Biscuit *(uncoated)*, Coconut Crinkle Crunch, Ginger Snaps, Original Thick Tea

GRANOVITAø

Wafer Rolls: Hazelnut Cream, Peanut

HOLLAND & BARRETT

Digestive, Fruit Shortbread, Shortbread

HOPPERS

Apricot Oat Slice

JACOB'S

Fig Roll, Shortcake

MARKS & SPENCER

Butter Puff, Digestives, Fruit Cookies, Ginger Snap, High Fibre Digestives, Plain Chocolate Ginger, Rich Tea, Rich Tea Finger, Stem Ginger

MOTHERS PRIDE

Plain Cookies

PATERSON ARRAN

Bronte Apple, Raisin & Cherry Hex Pack; *Bronte Country Cooking:* Oatcrunch, Peanut, Shortcake, Walnut; *Paterson Bronte Giant Cookies:* Choc Chip, Fruit, Double Choc Chip, Ginger, Peanut, Oat; *Paterson Bronte Minipacks:* Golden Crunch, Shortcake; *Paterson Bronte Twin Giants:* Fruit; *Paterson's:* Oat Fingers, Rough Oatcakes, Scottish Oatcakes

PENNYWISE

Bourbon Creams, Finger Nice, Rich Tea, Rich Tea Finger, Shortcake

POTTERS

Cookie Malt; *Gluten-Free:* Fruit & Nut, Plain

RAKUSEN'S™

Digestive, Fruit Shortcake, Nice, Shortcake, Viennese Star

SAFEWAY

Bourbon Creams, Coconut Crumble Creams, Coconut Rings, Fig Rolls, Fruit Shortcake, Ginger Nuts, Lemon Puffs, Morning Coffee, Oaten Crunch, Orange Finger Creams, Plain Chocolate Ginger Crunch, Plain Chocolate Orange Crunch, Plain Chocolate Rich Tea, Rich Tea, Rich Tea Fingers, Shortcake, Syrup Crunch

SIMMERS

Macvita

SNOWCREST

Chocolate Coated Fingers: Mint, Plain; *Wafers:* Chocolate, Lemon, Orange, Raspberry

SUPERDRUGfcd87

Bourbon Creams, Custard Creams, Oat Crunch, Round Rich Tea

WAITROSE

Breaktime Plain, Coconut Crumble Creams, Digestive Sweetmeal, Fruit Shortcake, Morning Coffee, Plain Chocolate Ginger, Plain Chocolate Orange Crunch, Plain Wafer Fingers, Rich Tea (Finger, Biscuit); *Cookies:* Choc/Orange, Crunchy

WHOLE EARTH†

Organic Cookies: Russian, Waffle

BREADS, ROLLS ETC

ALLIED BAKERIES

Hovis Loaf

ALLINSON

Wholemeal: Family Soft Sliced, Malt Loaf, Rolls, Sliced, Stoneground Baps, Stoneground Sliced

ANDUTRA

Mestemacher Breads: Farm, Muesli, Organic Sunflower Seed, Organic Wholemeal Rye, Pumpernickel, Rye, Wholemeal

ASDA

Bread from Instore Bakery: Bloomer (Sunflower & Sesame, Seeded, Unseeded), French Whirl, French White Baguette (Seeded, Unseeded), Granary Baguette, Granary Loaf, Hedgehog (Sunflower & Sesame), Hi-Bran Loaf, Large Oven Cake, Multi-Grain, Onion & Rye, Soft Danish Loaf, Sunflower & Sesame Whirl, Stottie (White, Wholemeal), Sunflower & Sesame Cluster, Tin Loaf (Granary, White, Wholemeal), White Farmhouse Loaf; *Continental Breads from Instore Bakery:* Boccacini, Cholla, Ciabatta, Daktyla, Hellesroggenbrot, Parisienne, Veneziani, Vielsaatbrot, Vine Fruit Plait, Zweibelbrotchen; *Continental Rolls from Instore Bakery:* Daktyla, Hellesroggenbrot, White; *Morning Goods from Instore Bakery:* Bun Loaf, Combicorn

Baguette, Combicorn Schnecken, Fruit Teacakes, Muffins (White, Wholemeal), Pitta Bread (Large & Mini: White, Wholemeal), Potato Cakes, Scotch Crumpets, Scotch Fruit Crumpet, Sliced Baps (White, Wholemeal), Victoria Fruit Teacake, White Crumpets, White Spice Batch; *Pre-packed Breads:* Brown Medium Sliced, Granary Medium Sliced, Hovis Wheatgerm Medium Sliced, Softgrain Medium Sliced, White (Medium, Thin, Thick Sliced), Wholemeal (Medium, Thick Sliced); *Rolls & Baps from Instore Bakery:* Baps (White, Sunflower & Sesame Wholemeal), Continental Rolls (White, Seeded, Combicorn), Crusty Rolls (Granary, Sunflower & Sesame, White), Finger Rolls (White, Wholemeal), French Rolls, Large Baps (White, Wholemeal), Scotch Morning Rolls (Plain, Wholemeal), Soft Rolls (White, Wholemeal), White Crusty Cobs, White Sesame Baps, White Vienna Rolls (Seeded, Unseeded), Yorkshire Breadcakes (White, Wholemeal); *Take & Bake:* White Baguette, White Rolls

BRITISH BAKERIES

Daisy Fresh Nutty Brown Bread, High Fibre White Bread, Seeded Burger Buns; *Dinky Rolls:* Brown, White; *Family Value:* Brown Baps, Brown Rolls, Soft Brown Rolls, White Baps, White Rolls; *Farmstead:* Brown Baps, White Baps; *Fruit Buns:* Spiced Fruit, Wholemeal Fruited; *Rolls:* Sunday, White Morning, White Sandwich, Wholemeal Morning; *Take & Bake:* Crusty Cobs, Garlic Baguettes, Granary Batons, Granary Petite, Granary Rolls, Mini Loaves, Variety Brown Rolls, White Petite

CARLEYø

Breads: all — **except** Cheese & Onion, Herb

CO-OP

Crumpets, Fruited Teacakes, Soft White Finger Rolls; *Baps:* Goodlife Wholemeal, Soft White; *Bread:* Goodlife Sliced Wholemeal (Medium, Thick), Sliced Brown (Medium), Sliced White (Medium, Thick, Thin); *Frozen:* 3 Baguettes, 6 Petit Pain

CROFTERS KITCHEN

Oatmeal Bread

DAYOFRESH

White Sliced Bread; *Rolls:* Brown, White

DE RIT

Waffles: Hazelnut, Malt Syrup

FOODWATCH√ø

Versaloaf Breadmix

GENERAL DIETARYø

Ener-G Yeast-Free Brown Loaf; *Ener-G Bread:* Brown Rice, Tapioca, White Rice

GOSWELL BAKERIES

Bagels; *Bread:* Light Rye, Polish Rye, Prewetts Wholemeal

HEINZ

Weight Watchers Danish Bread: Brown, Malted Softgrain, Oat, White; *Weight Watchers Soft Rolls:* Brown, White

HOLLAND & BARRETT

Multigrain Cob

HOVIS

Baps: Stoneground Wholemeal, Wholemeal; *Bread:* Countrygrain Wholemeal, Family Wheatgerm, Golden Oatbran

Brown, Goldenbran Brown, Handy Wheatgerm, Malted Brown, Malted Soft Brown, Mildbake Brown, Premium White, Stoneground Wholemeal, Wholemeal; *Mini Loaves:* White, Wholemeal; *Mini Rolls:* White; *Rolls:* Cobble, Granary Malted Brown, Multigrain Wholemeal, White, Wholemeal Long, Wholemeal Scotch, Wholemeal Snack

INTERNATIONAL HARVEST

Pitta: White, White Mini, Wholemeal

KINGSMILL

Rolls: White, Wholemeal & Wheatgerm; *Sliced Bread:* White, Wholemeal & Wheatgerm

MANNA FOOD CO

Bread: Fruit, Multi-Grain, Onion

MARKS & SPENCER

Bread: Allinson Sliced, Allinson Unsliced, Barmbrack, Batch, Brown Batch, Ciabatta, Granary, Harvest Brown, Hi Bran, Hovis, Light Rye, Lite Wholemeal, Morning Loaf, Multi Grain, Oatmeal, Premium (Medium, Sandwich Medium, Thick), Rich Fruit Loaf, Sandwich Medium, Square Loaf, Sundried Tomato Bread, Walnut & Sultana Loaf, Whiskey Loaf, Wholemeal Sandwich Medium; *Rolls etc:* 4 Granary Rolls, 6 Potato Farls, Breakfast/Morning Rolls, Finger Rolls, Muffins, Old Eng/Scot Rolls, Pikelets, Potato Scones, Soft Wholemeal Rolls, Waffles, White Split Rolls; *Ready to Bake:* Ciabatta, Ciabatta Rolls, Half Baguettes, Olive Ciabatta, Tomato Ciabatta, White Rolls

MIGHTY WHITE

Mighty Munchers, Mighty White Sliced

Bread, Plain Loaf *(Scotland only)*

MOTHERS PRIDE

Potato Cakes; *Baps:* Burger Buns, Premium Soft White, White Burger, White Sandwich; *Bread:* Champion Softgrain White, Crusty White French Bread, Danish White, Long White Loaf, Traditional White; *Crumpets:* Fingers, Plain, Premium, Square; *Family Bakery:* Wholemeal Rolls; *Fruit Buns/Teacakes:* Currant Buns, Family Value Teacakes, Fruited Teacakes, Fruit Loaf, Mini Fruit Buns, Northumbrian Teacakes, Selkirk Bannock, Small Fruit Loaf, Teacakes Economy; *Muffins:* Plain, Wholemeal; *Rolls:* Brown, Family Value Long White, Family Value Soft White, Family Value White, Hamburger, Long White, Multigrain Sandwich, Scotch Finger, Soft Round, White Bridge, White Crusty Ploughman, White Onion Hot Dog, White Scotch, White, White Mini, White Morning, White Snack, White Split; *Take & Bake:* Assorted Rolls, Crusty Rolls, White Batons

NAPOLINA

Pizza Bases: Deep Pan, Mini, Standard

NEW YORK BAGEL COMPANY√

New York Bagels: Cinnamon & Raisin, Onion, Plain, Poppy

NIMBLE

Bread: White, Wholemeal

RAKUSEN'S™

Frozen: Bagels, Garlic Bread

RUSHALL FARMSø

Bread, Rolls: all — **except** Cheese & Herb Loaf

FOOD

SAFEWAY

Crumpets, Pizza Bases, Potato Scones; *Bake At Home Bread:* Granary Baguettes, White Baguettes; *Baps:* Bran, Burger, Granary, Sliced Wholemeal, Stoneground Wholemeal, White, Wholemeal; *Bread:* 100% Wholemeal, Bran, Brown, Danish Toaster White, Hovis, Premium White, Soft Grain White, White Sliced, Wheatgerm, Wholemeal Thin; *Finger Rolls:* White, Wholemeal; *Fruited Buns/Teacakes:* Currant Buns, Fruit Teacakes, Spiced Fruit Buns; *Petit Pains:* Granary, White; *Pitta:* Garlic & Herb, Sesame Seed, White, Wholemeal; *Muffins:* White, Wholemeal; *Rolls:* Stoneground Wholemeal, White Soft Snack, Wholemeal Morning

SNOWCREST

Pittas: Mezonath, Regular

SOYFOODS√™

Breads No Yeast: 80% Campagne, Wheat 100%, Wheat & Mixed Seed, Wheat & Rice, Wheat & Sprouted; *Breads No Yeast/Gluten:* Chick Pea, Grain Free, Soya; *Breads No Yeast/Wheat:* Barley 100%, Rye 100%, Rye & S/Corn; *Bread Yeasted:* 80% Unbleached, Ale, Herb, Six Grain, Spelt 100%, Wheat 100%, Wheat & Mixed Seed; *Yeasted Rolls:* Plain, Seed

SUNBLEST

Brown Sliced, Danish Toasting, Danish White, English Toasted Crumpets, Lunchbox White, Pikelets, Standard White Muffins, Sunmalt Loaf, White Unsliced; *Baps:* Farmhouse; *Fruited Buns/Teacakes:* Currant Buns, Fruited Teacakes; *Rolls:* Crusty Cob, Morning, Scottish Morning, Seeded Burger, Soft Brown, Soft White Batch; *Scotland only:* Farmhouse White Sliced Loaf, Scottish Plain White Bread; *White Sliced:* Medium, Thick, Thin

SUNNYVALE√ø

Fruit-T Loaf, Malt Loaf, Mixed Grain Gluten Free Bread, Rye & Onion Bread, Rye Sourdough Bread, Spicy Onion Bread, Wheat Sourdough Bread; *Sprouted Wheat Breads:* Date, Fruit & Almond, Onion, Plain, Raisin, Stem Ginger, Sunseed

VITBE

HiBran Sliced, HiGrain Sliced, HiLite Bran Sliced, Wheatgerm Sliced

WAITROSE

Crumpets; *Bread:* 100% Rye, Black Rye, Brown w Malted Wheat Grains, Ciabatta, Focaccia, Granary w Sesame Seed, Grand Rustique, Greek Style Daktyla, Greek Style Wholemeal, Heyford Premium Wholemeal, Light Rye, Malted Granary Brown Tin, Malted Wheat Brown Sliced, Malted Wheat Sandwich, Organic Wholemeal Wrapped, Paesano, Pane di Olive Ring, Poppy Seeded Knot, Pugliese, Rye, Seeded Gallego, Seedless Light Rye, Small Tin, Soft White, Stoneground Organic Wholemeal, Tomato Ciabba, Traditional White, Traditional Wholemeal, White Farmhouse Sesame, White Bloomer Seeded, White Organic, White Poppy Seeded Bloomer, White Poppy Seeded Finger, White Poppy Seeded Knot, White Sliced (Medium, Thick, Thin), Wholemeal Sliced (Medium, Thick), Wholemeal w Oats, Wholemeal Farmhouse Tin, Wholemeal Long Tin, Wholemeal Sandwich, Wholemeal Sliced; *Bagel:* Onion, Plain, Poppy Seeded;

Baguette: French Styled, Plain; *Baps:* Floured, Granary, White Floured, Wholemeal; *Cob:* Malted Brown Granary; *Muffins:* White, Wholemeal; *Part Bake:* 3 Small Baguettes, 6 Petit Pain, Frozen Petit Pain; *Pittas:* White Traditional, Wholemeal, White Picnic, Wholemeal Picnic; *Ready To Bake:* Assorted Rolls, Baguettes, Petit Pain;

Rolls: Bridge, Ciabatta, Cocktail Selection, Focaccia, Granary Long, Granary Malted Brown, Malted Granary, Heyford Premium Wholemeal Rolls, Organic White, Petit Pains, Petit Parisienne, Poppy Seeded Finger Roll, Soft Cottage, Soft White Finger, White Cob, White Crusty, White Cottage, White Finger, White Soft, White Vienna, Wholemeal, Wholemeal Crusty; *Stick:* Mini White, Rye, Rye w Onion, White Poppy Seeded

WARBURTON'S SOREEN

Lincolnshire Plum Loaf

BREAKFAST FOODS

ASDA

Fruit & Fibre Muesli, Golden Puffs; *Whole Wheat:* Cereal, Muesli

CO-OP

Bran Flakes, Fruit w Fibre, Wholewheat Cereal Biscuits, Wholewheat Muesli; *Goodlife:* Fruit & Bran Muesli, Muesli, Oat Bran Flakes

DOVE'S FARM√ø

Organic Cornflakes

EARLSTREE FOODS

Country Home Bran Flakes

GRANOVITAø

Whole Bran Fibre

HEINZ

Perfect Balance Breakfast Cereal

HOLLAND & BARRETT

Mueslis: Base, Deluxe, Fruit & Nut, Gluten Free, High Fibre

JORDANS

Mueslis: Crispy, Natural Country

KELLOGG'S

Banana Bubbles, Bran Buds, Frosties, Ricicles

MARKS & SPENCER

Cereals: Luxury Fruit & Flake, Luxury Muesli, Strawberry, Banana Flake, Lite Crunchy; *Mueslis:* Unsweetened

MORNING FOODSø

Mornflake: Bran & Apple Crunchy, Chocolate Fruit & Nut Crunchy, Chocolate Squares, Crunchy w Malt & Vine Fruits *(no sugar/salt)*, Hawaiian Crunchy, Oatbran & Nuts Crunchy, Orange & Lemon Crisp, Orange & Walnut Crunchy, Peanut & Maple Crisp, Raspberry Crisp, Strawberry Crisp, Sultana & Apple Crunchy, Toasted Oatbran Crunchy, Treasure Crunchy

QUAKER OATS

Oat Bran Crispies, Oat Krunchies, Puffed Wheat, Quaker Oat Bran, Quaker Oats

PREWETTS

Natural Wheatbran, Oatbran & Oatgerm, Wholewheat Flakes

QUEENSWOOD NATURAL FOODS

Mueslis: Apple & Apricot, Bumbles Breakfast, Country, De Luxe, De Luxe Date, Dietary High Fibre w Chopped Fruit, Dietary High Fibre w Whole Fruit, Fig & Date, Gluten Free, Hazel Malt Crunch De Luxe, Organic De Luxe, Original, Standard Base, Sultana Crunch, Super De Luxe

RYVITA

High Fibre Cornflakes

SAFEWAY

35% Fruit & Nut Muesli; *Whole Wheat:* Breakfast Biscuits, Flakes

SILBURY

Organic: Silbies, Cereal Crisps

SUNWHEEL

Special DeLuxe Muesli

WAITROSE

Wheat Flakes, Wholewheat Cereal Biscuit; *Muesli:* Fruit & Fibre, Fruit & Nut, Luxury

WEETABIX

Alpen Nutty Crunch, Bran Fare, Crunchy Oat & Wheat Bran, Frosted Chex, Ready Brek, Weetabix, Weeta Flake

WHOLE EARTH†

Breakfast Crunch Cereals: Almond, Orange

'BURGERS', 'SAUSAGES' ETC

CAULDRON FOODS

Burgers: Chilli Tofu, Mixed Vegetable, Savoury Tofu, Spicy Bean

DIRECT FOODS

Sizzles

DRAGONFLY FOODSø

Tofu Burgers: Fresh Vegetable Organic, Fruity Curry, Herby Mushroom, Saucy Tomato, Savoury Nut, Spicy Bean

GOODLIFE

(Chilled & Frozen:) Herb Bean Bangers, Spicy Bean Burgers; *Cutlets:* Mexican, Nut, Tandoori, Vegetable

GRANOSE

Rissolnut, Sausalatas, Sausfry, Vegelinks

GRANOVITAø

Savour Burga Mix, Vegetarian Sausage Mix

HOLLAND & BARRETT

Vegetable Mix: Burger, Sausage

IMPULSE FOODS√

Circles Tempeh Burgers: Savoury Garlic & Coriander, Smokey

LINDA McCARTNEY

Farmhouse Sausages, Sausage Rolls, Southern Fried Grills, Traditional Sausages

PLOUGHSHARES√ø

Vegan Sosrolls; *Burgers:* all

REALEAT

Fishless Fish Cake; *Vegebanger:* Herb, Spicy; *Vegeburger:* Chilli, Herb & Vegetable, No Salt

REDWOOD

Vegetarian Rashers; *Cheatin':* Chicken, Garlic Sausage, Ham

SAFEWAY

Nut Cutlet *(chilled)*

SOYFOODS√™

Rissoles; *Burgers:* Bengal, Herb, Nut, Mexican

SUNRISE√ø

Vegetarian Burgers

VEGETARIANS CHOICE

Frozen: Vegetable Protein Burgers, Vegetable Protein Sausages; *Mixes:* Vegetable Protein Sausage

VEGGIES√ø™§

Veggies Mixes: Burger, Sosage

WICKEN FENø

Sausages: Chestnut & Orange, Herb, Mushroom & Garlic, Mushroom & Tarragon, Tomato & Garlic

CAKES & CAKE MIXES

ASDA

Bramley Apple Pies

BRITTONS

Dutch Apple Pie

CARLEYø

Variety of cakes

CO-OP

Rock Cake Base Mix

EMMA'S

Eccles Cakes

GRANOVITAø

Rich Dark Fruit Cake, Wholesome Oat Brans

LYONS

Apple Mini Pies, Assorted Mini Pies, Blackcurrant & Apple Pies

MARKS & SPENCERS

Chorley Cakes, Lattice Fruit Pie Selection

MR KIPLING

12 Fruit Pies & Tartlets Selection, Apple & Blackcurrant Pies — **except** large individuals, Bramley Apple Pies, Fruit Pies Selection — **except** large individuals, Glazed Fruit Tartlets (Fruits of the Forest), Glazed Fruit Tartlets (Summer Fruits), Jam Tarts Selection, Treacle Lattice Tart

PLOUGHSHARES√ø

Bakewell Tart; *Cakes:* Carob & Nut Fridge, Carob & Raisin Fridge, Ginger, Rich Fruit

SAFEWAY

Frozen Strudel: Apple, Country Fruits; *Pudding Club:* Spotted Dick

SAKER FOOD CO

Cakes: Apricot & Almond, Banana & Walnut, Carrot & Sultana

SNOWCREST

Apple Strudel; *Pies:* Apple, Apricot, Blackcurrant, Cherry

SOYFOODS√™

Strudel; *Fruit Pies:* Fruit, Fruit & Ginger

SUNNYVALE√ø

Cakes: Cherry Genoa, Choc 'N' Cherry, Choc 'N' Orange, Date & Pecan, Fig & Orange, Rich Fruit, Rich Plum, Stem Ginger

WAITROSE

Summer Pudding

'CHEESE' & 'CHEESE' SPREADS

BUTE ISLAND FOODS†

Scheese (hard 'cheese'): Cheddar, Cheddar w Chives, Cheshire, Edam, Gouda, Hickory Cheddar, Mozzarella, Stilton

PLAS FARM

('Cheese-type' spreads:) Creme de Cajou: Coriander & Lemon; *Soho Soft:* Plain, Garlic & Herb

PLAMIL√§

Veeze (spread): Garlic, No Added Flavour

PLOUGHSHARES√ø

Soya Cream Cheese

REDWOOD

Tofucheese (hard 'cheese'): Red Cheddar, White Cheddar

CONFECTIONERY & SNACKS — SWEET

ANIMAL AID√ø§

Handmade Vegan Chocolate Selection

ASDA

Barley Sugar, Sherbert Fruits; *Crystal:* Clear Mints, Fruit Drops

BENDICKS

Bittermints, Chocolate Ginger, Mayfair Mints, Mint Crisp, Mint Hearts, Sporting & Military Mildly Bitter

BERRYDALESø

Dairy Free Chocolate Novelties: Bar, Bear, Bunny & Flowers, Elephant, Monkey

BLACKFRIARS BAKERYø

Flapjacks: Apple & Sultana, Apricot, Cherry & Coconut, Date & Walnut, Fruit, Plain

BRITTONS

Carob Choc Flapjack, Crunchy Mince Slice

BUXTON FOODS

Stamp Collection Chocolate

CADBURY

Fry's Cream: Chocolate, Orange, Peppermint

CO-OP

Clear Mints, Fruit Drops, Fruit Jellies

CULPEPERøfcd76

Crystallised Ginger, Stem Ginger in Syrup; *Mint Cakes:* Aniseed, Peppermint, Spearmint; *Natural Sweets:* Aniseed & Coltsfoot, Liquorice Sticks *(wooden)*, Original Barley Sugar, Treacle & Peppermint, Victorian Sweet Assortment

DR HADWEN TRUST√ø§

Vegan Chocolate

DORCHESTER CHOCOLATESø

Bittermints, Chocolate Mint Rounds, Chocolate Slim Mints, Coffee Cremes, Orange Cremes, Plain Chocolate Bars, Vegan Assorted Chocolates

EQUAL EXCHANGE TRADINGø

Latitudes: Dark Chocolate w Brazil Nuts; *Mascao:* Coconut, Dark Chocolate, Orange

FOODWATCH√ø

Whizzers Chocolate Beans

GEORGE PAYNE & CO

Plain Chocolate Ginger

GEORGE SKOULIKAS√

Sunita: Halva, Sesame Bar

GOODNESS FOODSø

Apricot Chunky-Jack, Coffee & Walnut Chunky-Jack Flapjack, Date & Walnut Chunky Jack

GRANOVITAø

Castus Bars: Date, Date/Apricot, Date/Nut, Raisin/Date; *Castus Sandwich Slices:* Fig, Nut

HANDMADE FLAPJACK CO

Flapjacks: Apricot, Californian, Cherry, Chocolate, Chocolate Special, Date & Walnut, Fruit, Ginger, Muesli Fruit & Nut, Nut Cluster, Plain, Raspberry

HOLDSWORTH CHOCOLATES

Mint Crisps; *Carres:* Extra Bitter, Lime, Mint, Mocha, Orange

HOLLY MILL

Dairy Free Carriba; *Jumbo Jacks Flapjacks:* all

ITONA

Westmoreland Chocolate Hollow Rabbit

LEAF UK

Parkinson's: Chocolate Limes, Fruit Choc Bon Bons, Fruit Thins, Jolly Rancher, Mint Choc Bon Bons

LINDT & SPRUNGLI

Plain Chocolate: Excellence, Surfin, Thins

MARKS & SPENCER

After Dinner Mints, Assorted Fruit Rocks, Chocolate Crisp Pieces, Lollipops, Mint Crumbles, Pear Drops, Sherbert Lemons; *Tino Sweets:* Apple, Grapefruit, Lemon

OKANAGAN

Natural Fruit Snacks: all

PANDA√

Licorice: Comfits, Cuts; *Licorice Bars:* Blackcurrant, Licorice, Raspberry

PLAMIL√§

Carob Bars: Hazelnut, No Added Sugar, Orange, Plain; *Chocolate Bars:* Martello, Plain, w Hazelnut, w Mint; *Organic Chocolate Bars:* Mint, Orange, Plain

PLOUGHSHARES√ø

Flapjacks: Apricot & Almond, Date & Walnut, Plain, Seed & Raisin; *Slices:* Date & Fig Apricot, Orange & Ginger Raw Nut

POTTERS

Beanmilk Dairy-Free Nutty Bar, Decaffeinated Chocolate Bar; *Granymels Caramels:* Liquorice, Mint, Plain, Treacle

RESPECT FOR ANIMALS√ø§

Vegan: Chocolate Selection, Mint Creams

RAKUSEN'S™

Fruit Flapjack

SAFEWAY

Clear Mints, Jelly Babies, Jelly Drops, Plain Chocolate Brazil Nuts, Sugared Almonds

SHEPHERDBOY√

Fruit & Nut Bars: Apple, Banana, Coconut, Ginger, Fruit, Organic w Sunflower, Tangy, w Sunflower Seeds; *Just So Carob Bars:* Crispy, Ginger, Orange, Peppermint

SNOWCREST

Nut Crunch Bar

SUFFOLK BAKERY

Range of Flapjacks and Fruit Slices

TERRY'S SUCHARD

1767 Bitter Bar, Sugared Almonds

THORNTONS

Hardboiled sweets: Acid Lemon Slices, After Dinner Mints, Fruit Selection, Lemon Lolly, Orange Lolly, Strawberry Lolly, Sugar Free Fruit Drops, Sugar Free Mints, Tropical Fruits; *Jellies:* Fruit *(all)*, Fish, Mouse, Crocodile, Bat, Welly, Dinosaur *(all)*, Spider, Kiss; *Travel sweets:* Barley, Blackcurrant, Citrus, Fruits; *Misc:* Mince-Meat, Orange Lolly, Sugar Cone

TREBOR BASSETT

American Hard Gums, Assorted Fruit Jellies, Bubbly Bubble Gum, Chocolate Orange Creams, Chocolate Strawberry Creams, Coolmints, Flying Saucers, Mint Creams, Peanut Brittle; Boiled sweets — **except** Frosties, Everton Mints, Humbugs, Kola Drops and Kola Kubes, Kopp Kops, Toffee Crunch, Pascalls Buttermints, Sherbet Pips; *Fruit flavoured Lollipops:* all — **except** Toffee; *Sherbert Products:* all — **except** Sherbert Fountain

VIVA!√ø§

Selection of vegan chocolates

WAITROSE

American Hard Gums, Bitter Chocolate, Chocolate Coffee Cremes, Chocolate Ginger, Chocolate Limes, Chocolate Peppermint Cremes, Clear Fruits, Clear Mints, Fruit Humbugs, Fruit Jellies, Jelly Babies, Jelly Beans, Mint Imperials, Plain Chocolate, Plain Chocolate Brazil Nuts, Plain Chocolate Ginger; *Chocolate Bar:* Hazelnut Filling, Mint Filling, Strawberry Filling; *Flapjacks:* Apple & Sultana, Chocolate Chip, Flapjack

FOOD

WHOLEBAKE

Cherry & Coconut Giant Cookie; *Flapjacks:* Apricot, Apricot Low Fat, Fruit & Nut, Ginger Low Fat, Maple Low Fat, Tropical Low Fat Flapjack; *Slices:* Apple & Cinnamon, Apricot & Apple, Date, Fig, Pineapple & Almond (Carob Coated), Pineapple & Almond (Chocolate Coated), Plum

WRIGLEY

Doublemint, Freedent, Juicy Fruit, Orbit, PK; *Hubba Bubba:* Cherry Cola, Cream Soda, Lemon Lime; *Wrigley's:* Extra, Spearmint

COOKING AIDS — SAVOURY

ASDA

Instant Mashed Potato; *Sauce Mixes:* Bread, Parsley, White

BUITONI

Pasta Sauces in Jars: Mushrooms, Peppers, Traditional

CAMPBELLS

Tastes of the World Cook-In Sauces: Chinese Sweet & Sour, French Chasseur, French Provençal, Mexican Chilli

CARLEYø

Organic Sauces: Pasta, Pesto

CHILTERN HOUSE

Chiltern Herb Stuffing: Country, Sage & Onion

CO-OP

Bread Sauce Mix, Golden Breadcrumbs, Pizza Base Mix; *Casserole Seasoning Mixes:* Beef Bourguignon, Chicken Provencale, Chilli Con Carne, Farmhouse Sausage, Lamb Ragout, Madras Curry; *Savoury Rice:* Beef, Chicken, Golden, Mild Mixed Vegetable, Mushroom; *Speciality Stuffing Mixes:* Country Herbs, Chestnut, Garlic & Herbs; *Stir Fry Savoury Rice:* Chinese, Indian, Mediterranean, Sweet & Sour

CROSSE & BLACKWELL

Simply Fix: Beef Goulash, Black Bean, Chicken Chasseur, Chicken Provençale, Lamb Ragout, Lemon Chicken, Beef Satay, Oriental Beef, Oriental Chicken, Sausage & Beans, Sausage & Tomato, Spaghetti Bolognese, Sweet & Sour Chicken, Sweet & Sour Pork

CULPEPERøfcd76

Spice Purées: Coriander, Fenugreek, Garlic, Garlic Ginger & Chilli, Ginger

GRANOVITAø

Wholemeal Garlic Croutons

HEINZ

Cooking Sauce: Chinese Szechuan, Italian Tomato & Onion, Mexican Chilli *w* Kidney Beans, Oriental Sweet & Sour; *Salsa:* Medium Hot, Mild Medium

HOLLAND & BARRETT

Savoury Soya: Chunks, Mince; *Unflavoured Soya:* Chunks, Mince

JUST WHOLEFOODS√øt

Vege Ren *(rennet); Vegetarian Stuffing*

Mixes: Country Style, Sage & Onion

MARKS & SPENCER

Mushroom Pasta Sauce

PATAK'S

Curries: Masala Sabzi Vegetable, Potato & Pea, Sabzi Tarkari Vegetable

PREMIER BRANDS

Smash Instant Potato; *Pomme Maison:* Country Herbs, Onion

PROTOVEG

Smokey Mince Snaps; *Chunks:* Beef Style, Natural Unflavoured; *Mince:* Beef Style, Natural Unflavoured

REALEAT

Veggie Mince *(frozen)*

RUSHALL FARMSø

Garlic Croutons

SAFEWAY

Basil Pasta Sauce, Pasta Sauce, Sage & Onion Stuffing Mix; *Canned Sauces:* Chilli Cooking, Curry, Sweet & Sour Cooking, Tomato Onion Cooking; *Packet Mixes:* Beef Bourguignon, Bolognese, Bread Sauce, Sausage Casserole, Sweet & Sour Sauce, Traditional Beef

SNOWCREST

Eggless Soya Mince Mix, Soya Mince Mix

VAN DEN BERGH

Pasta 'N' Sauce; *Beanfeast:* Bolognese Style, Mexican Chilli, Savoury Mince; *Ragu:* Traditional

VEGETARIAN WORLD

Santini Marettimo Pesto; *Santini Pasta Sauces:* Pomodoro, Siciliana, Veronese

WAITROSE

Natural Breadcrumbs, Lightly Salted Croutons, Toasted Croutons; *Italian Pasta Sauces:* Arrabbiata, Funghi, Napoletana; *Stir Fry Sauces:* Mexican, Thai

WHOLE EARTH†

Pasta Sauces: Italiano, Organic Italiano, Organic Italiano *w* Mushrooms

ZEST FOODS

Pasta Sauces: Basil & Oregano, Hot & Spicy, *w* Mushroom & Green Pepper, *w* Mushroom & Smoked Garlic

COOKING AIDS — SWEET

ASDA

Marzipan (Golden, White), Plain Chocolate Chips

CO-OP

Assorted Jelly Diamonds, Custard Powder, Cut Mixed Peel, Glace Cherries; *Food Colour:* Green, Red, Yellow; *Food Flavourings:* Almond, Brandy, Lemon, Peppermint, Rum, Vanilla; *Fruit Pie Fillings:* Apple & Blackberry, Apple Fruit, Blackcurrant, Red Cherry, Spiced Apple & Raisin; *Marzipan:* Golden, White

CULPEPERøfcd76

Natural Flavours: Bitter Almond, Lemon

FOOD

Oil, Sweet Orange, Vanilla

DE RIT

Organic Unsweetened Apple Purée

G R LANESø

Gelozone *(gelling agent)*

JUST WHOLEFOODS√ø†

All Natural Custard Powder

HEINZ

Apple Sauce

HOLLAND & BARRETT

Cut Mixed Peel, Natural Cherries

RAYNER

Culinary Essences: all

RAYNER BURGESS

Topping Syrups: all

SAFEWAY

Apple Sauce, Cocktail Cherries, Custard Powder, Cut Mixed Peel, Glacé Cherries, Marzipan; *Essences:* Almond, Peppermint, Vanilla

SNOWCREST

10 litre Snowshake, Baking & Cooking Chocolate; *10 litre Syrup:* Chocolate, Strawberry, Vanilla

STUTE FOODS

Handy Apple Dessert Apple Sauce, Apple Dessert *(jars)*

MERIDIAN†

Malt Extract, Molasses; *Syrups:* Date, Maple

WAITROSE

Cut Mixed Peel, Marzipan; *Cherries:* Cocktail, Glace, Natural; *Marzipan:* Golden, White

YORK FOODS

Chocolat Patissier Menier: Dark Cooking Chocolate

CRACKERS, CRISPBREADS ETC

BN

French Toast: Plain, Wholemeal

CARR'S

Table Water, Table Water *w* Sesame

COMMUNITY FOODSø

Sanchi Japanese Five Flavour Arame Rice Puffs; *Sanchi Japanese Rice Crackers:* Brown, Nori Maki

CO-OP

Water Biscuits, Wholemeal Thins; *Crackers:* Cream, Harvest Grain, Savoury Wheat, Traditional

DE RIT

Organic Sesame Rice Cakes

FOODWATCH√ø

Crispbreads: Corn, Rice & Garden Herb, Rice & Millet, Rice & Pepper

G R LANESø

Vessen Organic Oatcakes: all

HOLLAND & BARRETT

Ginger Wafer; *Rice Cakes:* Salted, Unsalted

JACOB'S

Water High Bake; *Crackers:* Brown Wheat, Cream, Original Ritz

MARKS & SPENCER

Delicracker, Scottish Oat Cakes

NAIRNS

Traditional Oatcakes

RAKUSEN'S™

Crackers: 99% Fat Free, Hilo; *Matzos:* Crackers, Tea, Traditional, Wheaten

RYVITA

Crisp Rolls: Cracked Wheat, Garlic; *Ryvitas:* Dark, Oat Bran, Original, Sesame

SAFEWAY

Rough Oatcakes, Water Biscuits; *Crackers:* Cream, Low Fat Cream, Savoury Wheat, Sesame; *Thins:* Poppy & Sesame, Wholemeal

SHIPPAMS

Old El Paso: Nachips, Jalapenos, Taco Dinner Kit, Taco Shells

SIMMERS

Fine Highland Oatcakes

SNOWCREST

Mazon Crispbreads: Extra Thin, Harvest, Muesli, Nutty

SUMA™

Organic Rice Cakes

VAN POULLES

Gluten Free Wafers: Clergy, Communion

WAITROSE

High Bake, Rough Gridle Oatcakes; *Breadsticks:* Garlic, Plain, Sesame; *Thins:* Onion & Sesame, Poppy & Sesame

CREAM REPLACERS

GRANOSE

Soya Creem

PROVAMEL

Soya Dream

RICH'S

Whip Topping; *Whip Toppings:* Base, European Style

SNOWCREST

Big Top Parev Cream Whip (Sugar, Sugar-Free), Passover 5 Litre Parev Whip, Passover Snowwhip Topping; *Snowwhip Toppings:* Big Top, Unsweetened

DESSERTS

CO-OP

Co-op Syrup Sponge Pudding; *Frozen Strudel:* Apple, Summer Fruit

GRANOVITAø

Dessert Mix: Citrus Fruit & Nut, Tropical Fruit

HEAVEN'S DELIGHT

Desserts: all

JUST WHOLEFOODS√øt

Vegetarian Jelly Crystals: Lemon, Raspberry, Strawberry, Tropical Fruits

MAXIM PHARMACEUTICAL√™§

Weikfield Jelly Crystals: Cherry, Mango, Orange, Pineapple, Raspberry, Strawberry

PLAMIL√§

Rice Pudding w Sultanas: Sugar Free, Sweetened

PROVAMEL

Yofu Exotic Dessert; *Soya Desserts:* Carob, Chocolate, Vanilla

ROWNTREE

Ready to Eat Jelly

SNOWCREST

Apple Blintzes, Italian Trifle, Passover Chocolate Dessert, Unflavoured Diet Jelly, Unflavoured Pure Diet Jelly; *Catering Jelly Crystals, Diet Jellys, Natural Jellys, Original Jelly Crystals, Passover Jellys:* all

DIPS & DRESSINGS

GRANOVITAø

Egg & Dairy Free Alternative to Mayonnaise: Chilli, Garlic, Lemon, Plain

CROSSE & BLACKWELL

Waistline Dressings: Cocktail for Seafoods & Salads, Oil Free French, Oil Free Vinaigrette

HEIDELBERG

Balsamic Vinaigrette, Greek Dressing

HEINZ

Low Fat Dressing, Vinaigrette

LEA & PERRINS

Vinaigrette Maker: Classic French, White Wine & Garlic

MARKS & SPENCER

Lemon & Coriander Dressing

PLAMIL√§

Egg-Free Mayonnaise: Chilli, Garlic, Plain, Tarragon

SAFEWAY

Dressings: French, Garlic, Italian, Mustard, Reduced Calorie Vinegar & Oil

SARSONS

Sarsons for Salads

SUNRISE√ø

Egg Free Dressing

WAITROSE

Dressings: Apple & Walnut, French

WHOLE EARTH†

Salad Dressings: Lemon & Garlic, Oil Free Vinaigrette, Thousand Island

EGG REPLACERS

GENERAL DIETARYø

Ener-G Egg Replacer

FOOD

NUTRITIA DIETARY PRODUCTS

Loprofin Egg Replacer, Rite-Diet Egg White Replacer

VAN DEN BERGH

Oxo Vegetable Stock Cubes

WAITROSE

Vegetable Stock

GRAVIES & STOCKS

CO-OP

Gravy Browning, Rich Brown Gravy Mix

CPC

Knorr Vegetable Stock Cubes

CROSSE & BLACKWELL

Gravy Browning

FOODWATCH√ø

Gravy Mix

G R LANESø

Vecon Stock Paste

JESSUP MARKETING√ø

Naturally Good Vegetable Gravy Powder

JUST WHOLEFOODS√ø†

Vegetarian Stock Powder

MAGGI

Vegetable Bouillon

MARIGOLD

Reduced Salt Vegan Bouillon

RAYNER BURGESS

Gravy Browning

SAFEWAY

Vegetable Stock Cubes

HAMPERS

VEGETARIAN HAMPER COø

Vegan Hamper

'ICE CREAMS', SORBETS ETC

ALLIED FROZEN FOODS

Vive Non Dairy Frozen Dessert

BIRDS EYE WALL'S

Boomy, Jurassic Park, 'Orrible Ogre; *Calippo:* Lemon & Lime, Orange, 'Sport'; *Flintstones:* Barney Rubble, Fred Flintstone; *Mini Juice:* Apple, Orange; *Sparkles:* Lemonade, Orangeade

CO-OP

Ice Lollies: Assorted, Real Orange, Rocket

DAYVILLES ™†

N'Ice Day Non Dairy Alternative: Chocolate, Pistachio/Almond, Strawberry, Vanilla

GENICE√

Ice Delight Cones: Raspberry Ripple, Strawberry, Vanilla; *Maranelli Ice Supremes:* Chocolate, Raspberry Ripple, Vanilla

LYONS MAID

Water Ices: Lipsmacker, Mr Men Real Fruit, Orange Maid, Rowntree Fruit Pastille Lolly

MARCANTONIO

Ice Cream Cones

RAKUSEN'S™

Chocolate, Mint Choc Chip, Strawberry, Vanilla, Vanilla Block; *Choc Ices:* Mint 'n' Vanilla, Vanilla; *Dessert Ices:* Chocolate, Strawberry, Vanilla; *Sorbets:* Lemon, Orange

SAFEWAY

Orange Lollies; *Sorbets:* Lemon, Mango, Peach Melba

SNOWCREST

10 litre Mint Choc Chip, Bulk Plain Ice Cream Cones, Carnival Cups, Everest Lolly, Frosty Caps, Lemon Sorbet Bombe, Neapolitan, Parev Dessert, Parev Individuals, Parev Strawberry Disks, Parev Vanilla Heart Shapes, Parev Walnut & Chocolate Brick, Pistachio, Plain Empty Ice Cream Cones, Praline w Raspberry Sorbet, Real Fruit Sorbet Half Pineapple, Snowcrest Ice Cream Wafers, Undecorated Praline Bombe; *1 litre:* Chocolate & Orange Sorbet, Luxury Lemon Sorbet, Luxury Orange Sorbet, Luxury Raspberry Sorbet, Coffee Choc Chip, Mint Choc Chip, Orange Choc Chip, Parev Strawberry, Praline, Tutti Frutti, Rum & Raisin; *2 litre Parev:* Chocolate, Strawberry, Vanilla; *4 litre Parev:* Chocolate, Lemon Sorbet, Strawberry, Vanilla; *6-cup Passover Sorbets:* Lemon, Orange, Raspberry; *6-pack Sorbets:* Lemon, Orange, Raspberry; *10 litre Parev Sorbet:* Passion Fruit, Regular Mango; *10 litre Sorbet:* Lemon, Orange, Pineapple, Raspberry, Real Blackcurrant, Real Kiwifruit, Real Mango, Real Melon, Real Pistachio; *10 litre Parev:* Chocolate, Coffee, Praline, Strawberry, Vanilla; *10 litre Parev Regular:* Blackcurrant, Kiwi Fruit, Pistachio; *12 Individuals:* Blackcurrant, Lemon, Raspberry; *Catering Blocks:* Parev Vanilla, Praline, Strawberry Ripple; *Chocolate Bombes:* Rose, Vanilla, Undecorated Chocolate; *Choc Rings:* Orange, Rum & Raisin, Undecorated; *Filled Real Sorbets:* Lemon, Orange; *Parev Choc Ices:* Mint, Pistachio, Strawberry/Vanilla, Vanilla; *Parev Family Bricks:* Chocolate, Coffee, Strawberry, Vanilla; *Parev Push Ups:* Chocolate, Strawberry, Vanilla; *Parev Snowcones:* Chocolate, Strawberry, Vanilla; *Parev Vanilla Rings:* Decorated, Undecorated; *Vanilla:* Brick, Handy Pack, Tubs; *Whirls:* Chocolate Rum, Pistachio

SO GOOD

Tofu Delights

SUNRISE√ø

Carob Ices, Iced Yoghert; *Ice Dream:* all

TOFUTTI

Lite Lite: Chocolate Fudge, Coffee Marshmallow, Passion Island Fruit, Peach Mango, Strawberry Banana; *Supreme:* Better Pecan, Chocolate, Chocolate Cookie, Vanilla, Vanilla Almond Bark, Vanilla Fudge, Wild Berry

WAITROSE

Lollies: Assorted, Orange Flavour; *Sorbets:* Blackcurrant, Blueberry, Lemon, Mango, Orange, Tropical Fruit

FOOD

WINNER(UK)√

Swedish Glace Frozen Dessert: Chocolate, Mocha Swirl, Raspberry Ripple, Strawberry, Vanilla

MARGARINES, FATS ETC

BROADLAND FOODS

Broadland Vegetable Suet

CO-OP

Soya Margarine

GRANOSE

Margarines: Soya, Sunflower, Vegetable; *Spreads:* Diet Half Fat

GRANOVITAø

Non-Hydrogenated Low Fat Spread; *Margarines:* Non-Hydrogenated Sunflower Vegetable

MATTHEWS FOODS™

Pure Dairy Free Margarine

MERIDIAN†

Sunflower Spread

RAKUSEN'S™

Tomor Margarine

SAFEWAY

Margarine: Baking, Salt Free Sunflower, Soya

SNOWCREST

Simulated Chicken Fat; *Margarines:* Baker's Parev Vegetable, Creaming & Baking, Parev Block, Passover Creaming & Baking, Sunflower

SUMA™

Margarines: Low Fat Non-Hydrogenated, Soya, Sunflower

WAITROSE

Vegetable Suet; *Margarines:* Soya Soft, Sunflower

WHOLE EARTH†

Superspread

PASTRY

JUS-ROL

Chilled: Fillo, Puff, Shortcrust, Vol-Au-Vents; *Frozen:* Fillo, Puff, Shortcrust, Vol-Au-Vents

HOPPERS

Quiche Base Multi Grain *w* Herbs, Sweet Pastry Shells

SNOWCREST

Puff, Shortcrust, Strudel/Fillo, Unsweetened Shortcrust

PICKLES, SAUCES, VINEGARS ETC

ASDA

Piccalilli, Pickled Vegetables, Tomato Ketchup, Vinegar; *Jellys:* Mint, Redcurrant; *Sauces:* Bramley Apple, Brown, Mint

ASPALL

Organic Cyder Vinegar

BAXTERSø

Beetroot in Tomato & Basil; *Chutneys:* Alberts Victorian, Spiced Fruit, Tomato, Red Pepper, Cucumber, Onion & Chive, Sweetcorn & Red Pepper; *Jellys:* Mint, Wild Rowan; *Sauces:* Creole Pour Over, Mint

CHALICE FOODS√

Condimento: Arrabbiata, Artichoke, Black Olive & Walnut, Sun-Dried Tomato; *Olives:* Kalamata, Traditional Greek Marinade, Traditional Provençale Marinade; *Tapenade (paste):* Black Olive & Herb, Green Olive

COMMUNITY FOODSø

Sanchi Japanese Soy Sauce: Shoyu, Tamari

CO-OP

Piccalilli, Sweet Pickle, Sweetened Piccalilli, Tangy Pickle Spread, Whole Baby Beetroot; *Beetroot:* Crinkle Cut, Sliced; *Pickled:* Onions (Strong), Onions (Sweet), Onions in Brown Vinegar, Onions in Clear Vinegar, Red Cabbage, Silverskin Onions; *Relishes:* Barbecue, Hamburger, Mild Chilli, Mild Mustard, Onion, Sweetcorn; *Sauces:* Bramley Apple, Brown, Fresh Garden Mint, Fruity, Mint, Mint Jelly, Piccalilli, Reduced Sugar & Salt Tomato Ketchup, Tomato Ketchup; *Vinegars:* Distilled Malt, Malt

CROSSE & BLACKWELL

Bonne Cuisine Sauce: A La Orange, De Paris; *Branston Pickle:* Original, Sandwich Pickle; *Branston Sauce:* Fruity, Spicy; *Ketchup:* Tomato, Disney Tomato

CULPEPERøfcd76

Chutneys: Hot Mango, Sweet Mango; *Pastes:* Black Olive, Green Olive; *Pickles:* Chilli, Combination, Lime *(in oil)*; *Sauces:* Aioli *(garlic)*, Barbeque, Béarnaise, Horseradish, Lemon Mayonnaise, Mayonnaise, Pesto (Natural Basil), Tartare

DADDIES

Sonic The Hedgehog Tomato Ketchup

DE RIT

Silverskin Onions; *Bio-Dynamic Pickled Preserves, Bio-Dynamic Vegetable Preserves:* all

DUFRAIS

Bistro Chef; *Vinegars:* all

FLETCHERS

Tiger Sauce

FULL OF BEANS

Barley Pickle

GRAMMA'S√ø

Concentrated Herbal Seasonings: Hot & Spicy, Original; *Pepper Sauces:* Concentrated Herbal, Extra Hot, Hot, Mild, Super Hot

HEINZ

Silverskin Onions; *Ketchup:* Medium Hot Style, Mild Medium Style, Tomato, Tomato Hot; *Ploughman's:* Ideal Sauce, Pickle; *Sauces:* Chilli, Smokey Barbeque, Spicy Pepper; *Speciality Pickle:* Mild Mustard, Piccalilli, Tangy (Sandwich, Tomato)

HENDERSONS

Relish *(thin brown sauce)*

FOOD

HOLLAND & BARRETT

Cyder Vinegar

HP

Sauces: Curry, Fruity Barbecue, Fruity, HP, Mint, Original Barbecue, Rich Jamaican Barbecue, Spicy Tomato

KTC

Tane Soy Sauce

LEA & PERRINS

Curry Concentrate, Ginger Tomato Ketchup *w* Mild Curry Spices, Italian Vinaigrette Maker, Soy & Five Spice, Sweet Peppers *w* Chilli Sauce; *Sauces:* Chilli & Garlic, Fruit, Garlic & Spring Onion, Ginger & Orange, Hot Pepper, Hot Pepper & Lime, Jalapeno Pepper, Mustard & Peppercorn, Plain

MARKS & SPENCER

Mango Chutney, Mixed Pickle, Pickled Onions, Quattro Form Pasticcio, Tomato Ketchup, Traditional Fruit Chutney, Sliced Beetroot; *Olives:* Kalamata, Queen Green; *Sauces:* Cumberland, Italian Tomato, Neapolitana Tomato, Tomato Mascarpone,

MERIDIAN†

Soya Sauce: Shoyu, Tamari

MARTLET NATURAL FOODS

Martlet Vinegars: Cider, Dill, Garlic, Raspberry, Red Wine, Tarragon, White Wine

PATAK'S

Chutneys: Hot Mango, Major Grey Mango, Sweet Chunda, Sweet Mango, Tropical Fruit & Nut; *Pickles:* Brinjal, Chilli, Lime Pickle Hot, Lime Pickle Mild, Mango & Chilli, Mango & Lime, Mango Pickle Hot, Mango Pickle Mild, Mixed, Sweet Lime, Sweet Mango

PAUL CHAPLIN√ø§

Ginger Miso Relish, Miso Mustard, Wild Horseradish

RAKUSEN'S™

Sauces: all

RAYNER BURGESS

Mushroom Ketchup, Sweet Pickle; *Chutneys:* Goodfare, Mango; *Jellys:* Mint, Redcurrant; *Relishes:* Barbecue, Hamburger; *Sauces:* Barbecue, Brown, Mint *(all varieties)*, Tomato

SAFEWAY

Beetroot, Cocktail Onions, Continental Style Mixed Peppers, Crinkle Cut Beetroot, Pickled Gherkins, Pickled Onions, Pickled Red Cabbage, Silver Skin Onions, Sliced Beetroot, Sliced Cucumbers, Sweet Pickle, Sweet Picked Onions, Tomato Ketchup; *Piccalilli:* Mustard, Sweet; *Relish:* Corn, Mustard, Tomato, Tomato & Chilli; *Sauces:* Brown, Fruity, Mint; *Vinegars:* all

SARSONS

Soy Sauce; *Vinegars:* all

SHIPPAMS

Green Chili in Brine; *Old El Paso Picanti Salsa; Old El Paso Sauces:* Extra Hot, Hot Taco, Mild Taco

SNOWCREST

Passover Tomato Ketchup, Tomato Ketchup, Xtra Strong Horseradish & Beetroot

FOOD

STUTE FOODS

Gherkins: Sliced, Whole

VEGETARIAN WORLD

Madhurs Curry Sauces: Korma, Madras, Moglai, Rogan Josh, Vindaloo

WAITROSE

Cocktail Onions, Pickled Onions, Sweet Pickle; *Beetroot:* Baby, Sliced, Sliced w Vinegar; *Chutneys:* Apple & Walnut, Apricot Ginger & Garlic, Curried Fruit, Date Apricot & Orange, Hot Mango, Mango, Spiced Peach; Gherkins: Cocktail, Plain, Whole; *Jelly:* Cider & Sage, Kalamata Black, Large Green, Mint, Redcurrent; *Olives:* a la Greque in Brine, Almond Stuffed, Black Queen, Cocktail Black, Garlic & Chilli, Mixed Stuffed in Brine, Pimento Stuffed Queen, Pitted Black in Brine, w Orange, w Oregano; *Piccalilli:* Mustard, Sweet; *Sauce:* Apple, Chilli Masala, Caribean Creole, Fruit, Mint, Reduced Calorie Tomato Ketchup, Satay, Spicy, Tomato Ketchup; *Vinegars:* Garlic, Malt, Mixed Herb, Tarragon Wine, White Wine

WHOLE EARTH†

Kensington Sauce, Organic Ketchup; *Relishes:* Corn, Real Piccalilli, Tomato

ZEST FOODS

Sauces: Dill, Hoisin, Mexican Chilli, Pesto Basil, Satay, Sweet & Sour

PIES & PASTIES

BRITTONS

Pasties: Curry, Jamaican, Vegetable

FULL OF BEANS

Tofu Pasties

GOODNESS FOODSø

Pasties: Curried Vegetable, Mushroom, Vegetable

LINDA McCARTNEY

Deep Country Pies, Ploughmans Pasties

SAKER FOOD COMPANY

Pasties: Curry Dhal, Nut & Mushroom

SNOWCREST

Minceblintz Savoury Rolls

SOYFOODS√™

Arame Pasty, Mushroom Pie, Mushroom Rolls, Vegetable Pasty

READY MEALS

ASDA

Canned Ready Meals — World Bistro: Vegetable Chilli; *Chilled Ready Meals:* Gobi Aloo, Indian Pilau Rice, Vegetable Chilli, Vegetable Rogan Josh; *Longlife Ready Meals — World Bistro:* Vegetable Chilli w White & Wild Rice, Vegetable Curry

BERRYDALESø

Home Bake Ready Meals: Basmati & Wild Rice Pilaff, Butter Bean Bourguinon, Chilli Con Noces, New Orleans Chilli Jambalaya, Parsnips and Spinach in Ginger & Apple Sauce, Parsnip Corn & Tomato Bake, Pasta Rusticana, Vegetable Couscous

CARLEYø

Frozen Meals: Adzuki Pumpkin & Rice Bake, Almond Loaf, Chick Pea & Adzuki Bake, Spicy Lentil Cottage Pie

CO-OP

Onion Bhajis, Vegetable Samosas, Vegetable Spring Rolls

HEINZ

Weight Watchers Frozen Ready Meal: Vegetable Hotpot

PLOUGHSHARES√ø

Meals: Goulash, Lasagne, Ratatouille, Shepherds Pie, Vegetable Crumble; *Curries:* all

SAFEWAY

Chilled Ready Meals: Basmati Rice, Brocolli Pakora, Gobi Aloo Saag, Onion Bhajia, Onion Pakora, Vegetable Chilli, Vegetable Ratatouille, Vegetable Rogan Josh, Vegetable Samosa; *Frozen Ready Meals:* Vegetable Chilli, Vegetable Dhansak *w* Mushroom Pilau Rice

SAVOURIES — CANNED

ASDA

In Tomato Sauce: Spaghetti, Spaghetti Loops, Teddy Bear's Picnic Shapes; *Reduced Sugar Reduced Salt in Tomato Sauce:* Baked Beans, Spaghetti

CO-OP

Medium Hot Vegetable Curry; *Spaghetti In Tomato Sauce:* Numbers, Plain Spaghetti, Reduced Sugar & Salt, Rings

GRANOSE

Bologna, Lentil & Vegetable Casserole, Meatless Savoury Cuts, Mock Duck, Nut Loaf, Nuttolene, Tender Bits

GRANOVITAø

Chilli Con Carne, Nut Luncheon, Vegetable Hot Pot, Vegetable Ravioli

HEINZ

Baked Beans: Barbecue, Curried, Mixed Chilli; *Pasta In Tomato Sauce:* Flintstones, Noddy, Noodle Doodles, Spaghetti Hoops, Spaghetti, Super Mario World, Thomas The Tank Engine; *Weight Watchers:* Baked Beans In Tomato Sauce No Added Sugar, Italiana Vegetable Ravioli *w* Tomato Sauce, Spaghetti In Tomato Sauce No Added Sugar

HOLLAND & BARRETT

Tarka Dhal, Vegetable Curry, Vegetable Sweet & Sour; *Vegetable:* Bolognese, Chilli, Curry Madras, Curry Mild, Sweet & Sour

PLAMIL√§

Pease Pudding *w* Mace

POTTERS

Ready Cooked Casserole

RAKUSEN'S™

Baked Beans *w* Vegetarian Sausage

SAFEWAY

Mixed Beans Salad; *Beans:* Chilli, Curried, Reduced Sugar/Salt Baked; *In Tomato*

Sauce: Spaghetti, Spaghetti Rings, Wholemeal Spaghetti

SUMA™

Baked Beans, Beans: all

TRS

Patra, Sarson Ka Saag, Undhiu *w* Muthia

VEGETARIAN WORLD

Madhurs: Chenna Dhal, Curried Chick Peas, Curried Whole Moong, Curried Whole Urid, Tarka Dhal, Vegetable Curry; *Quintesse:* Bean & Mushroom, Chilli Con Tofu, Moglai Curry, Tofu Casserole, Tofu Goulash

WHOLE EARTH†

Baked Beans: Campfire, Organic

SAVOURIES — CHILLED/FRESH

ANIMUS/FRUITS OF THE EARTH√§

Creamed Coconut Curry, Indonesian Groundnut Casserole, Mexican Chilli Pancakes, Redwine Moussaka, Spinach & Tofu Gnocchi, Sweet & Sour Chick Peas

ASDA

From Delicatessen: Onion Bhaji, Vegetable Samosa; *From Salad Bar:* Chinese Style Pasta, Fruit Coleslaw, Garlic Mushrooms, Yellow Rice; *Salads from Salad Bar:* Bombay Potato, Corn, Dry Florida, Fruited Pasta, Italian Pasta, Mexican Style Rice, Spicy Rice; *Pre-packed Savoury Snacks:* Onion Bhajis, Vegetable Samosas, Vegetable Spring Rolls; *Tub Salads:* Italian Pasta, Mexican Style Corn, Spicy Bean, White & Wild Rice

BRITTONS

Bhajis, Chilli Pinto Slice, Mexican Bean Slice, Nut & Vegetable Flan, Samosas

CO-OP

Ambient Ready Meal Vegetable Curry, Carrot Nut & Sultana Salad, Three Bean Salad

DALOON

Vegetable Samosas

DRAGONFLY FOODSø

Tofu Roasts: Fresh Vegetable Organic, Herby Mushroom, Saucy Tomato, Savoury Nut, Spicy Bean

FULL OF BEANS

Savoury Seitan

GOODLIFE

Falafels

MARKS & SPENCER

Onion Bhajies, Potato Sag, Stuffed Vine Leaves, Vegetable Balti

PLOUGHSHARES√ø

Stuffed Peppers; *Curries:* all; *Quiches:* Onion, Sweetcorn, Tofu & Mushroom

SAFEWAY

Carrot & Nut Salad

SNOWCREST

Falafel Balls, Mushroom Blintzes

SOYFOODS√™

Aburage, Ganmodoki, Mochi, Nut Roast, Samosa

WAITROSE

Almond Pilau & Masala Dal, Bombay Potatoes, Crunchy Vegetables in Vinegar, Lemon Pilau, Lemon Rice, Masala Dal, Mini Vegetable Spring Rolls, Onion & Spinach Bhaji, Pilau Rice, Tabouleh, Vegetable Curry, Vegetable Samosa; *Salad:* Bombay Potato, Carnival, Carrot & Nut, Chinese Pasta, Greek Style, Indian Style Bean, Indonesian, Mushroom Rice, Onion, Pasta a la Grecque, Spicy Bean, Spicy Pasta, Wild Rice, Yellow Rice

SAVOURIES — DRIED

ASDA

Golden Savoury Rice

CROSSE & BLACKWELL

Rice & Things: Mexican, Mushroom, Peppers, Thai, Vegetable

DIRECT FOODS

Speciality Rices: Country Wild, Quinoa, Wild

GOLDEN WONDER

Pot Lights: Chinese Chicken, Italian Chicken; *Pot Noodles:* Beef & Tomato, Chow Mein, Nice 'N' Spicy, Spicy Curry, Sweet & Sour; *Pot Pasta:* Savoury Beef; *Pot Rice:* Chicken Curry

GRANOSE

Roast Mixes: Brazil Nut, Cashew, Lentil, Mexican Corn, Nut, Sunflower & Sesame

GRANOVITAø

Rice & Bean Chilli, Vegetable Bolognese, Vegetable Curry, Vegetable Shepherd's Pie; *Loaf Mix:* Cashew Nut, Nut & Herb, Vegetable

HEINZ

Lunch Bowl: Country Vegetable Casserole

HERA

Vegetable: Bolognese, Casserole, Chilli, Curry, Goulash, Stew & Dumplings

SAVOURIES — FROZEN

BIRDS EYE WALL'S

Alphabites, Potato Croquettes, Potato Edgers, Potato Waffles, Vegetable Chilli *w* Rice

GOODLIFE

Falafels

KITCHEN RANGE FOODS√

Crispy Crummed Garlic Mushrooms, Letterbites, Mini Potato Waffles, Nobblies, Potato Thins, Potato Waffles, Round-A-Bites

K K WHOLEFOODS

Lentil Hazelnut & Mushroom *w* Garlic Pâté, Vegetable Spice Chille

MARKS & SPENCER

American Potato Skins, Baby Rosti, Duchesse Potatoes, Potato Mushroom & Onion, Spicy Fries

RAKUSEN'S™

Potato Croquettes; *Latkes:* Mini, Potato

REALEAT

Chilean Bolognese

SAFEWAY

Hash Browns, Potato Croquettes, Potato Crunchies, Potato Waffles, Southern Fry Griddles, Southern Fry Potato Wedges

SEASONAL FOODS

ALLINSON

Wholemeal Hot Cross Buns

ASDA

Cranberry Sauce, Fresh Apple Mincemeat; *Morning Goods from Instore Bakery:* Hot Cross Buns (White, Wholemeal)

BAXTERSø

Cranberry Sauce

BERRYDALESø

Dairy Free Chocolate Novelties: Carob Easter Eggs, Christmas Novelties, Easter Eggs

BRITISH BAKERIES

Family Value Hot Cross Buns

HOLLAND & BARRETT

Mincemeat, Mince Pies; *Xmas Puddings:* all

HOPPERS

Single Mince Pies

HOVIS

Wholemeal Hot Cross Buns

ITONA

Chocolate: Box of Five Animal Squares Decorated w Easter Chicks & Bunnies, Granny Ann Foil-wrapped Chunky Mini Eggs

MACSWEENSø

Vegetarian Haggis

MARKS & SPENCERS

Cranberry Sauce, Luxury Mincemeat

MOTHERS PRIDE

Hot Cross Buns, Mini Hot Cross Buns

MR KIPLING

6 Mince Pies

PLAMIL√§

Eggs: Carob, Chocolate

POTTERS

Beanmilk Dairy-Free Chunky Eggs

RAYNER BURGESS

Cranberry Sauce

SAFEWAY

Bread Sauce, Cranberry Sauce, Mince Pies; *Hot Cross Buns:* Extra Spicy, White, Wholemeal; *Mincemint:* Standard, w Almonds & Brandy, w Cherries & Hazelnuts

SUNBLEST

Hot Cross Buns

THORNTONS

Hardboiled sweets: Xmas Design Lolly

FOOD

WAITROSE

Cranberry Sauce; *Mincemeat:* Special, Traditional

SNACKS — SAVOURY

ASDA

Potato: Chips, Sticks; *Ready Salted:* Crisps, Crunch Sticks, Potato Rings

BENSONS

Crisps: Genuine Hand Fried, Jacket Fried Lightly Salted, Ready Salted

BETTY CROCKER

Bacos

BUXTON FOODS

Stamp Collection Chips: Sweet Potato, Vegetable

COMMUNITY FOODSø

Chips Crisps: Hot & Spicy Wasabi, Sea Vegetable, Vegetable

CO-OP

Dry Roasted Peanuts

CULPEPERøfcd76

Bombay Mix, Cheewra, Chick Peas, Crispy Mix

DRAGON

Ready Salted Crisps

GOLDEN WONDER

Crunchy Fries: Salt & Vinegar; *Golden Lights:* Lightly Salted; *Groovers:* Ready Salted, Tomato Sauce; *Nuts:* Dry Roasted; *Potato Crisps:* Ready Salted, Tomato Sauce; *Rileys:* Ready Salted, Tomato Sauce, Roast Beef; *Ringos:* Salt & Vinegar; *Snakebites:* Salt & Vinegar; *Supernaturals:* Salt & Vinegar, Tomato; *Wheat Crunchies:* Bacon, Worcester Sauce; *Tortilla Chips:* Tomato Salsa

HIGHLANDERø

Premium Crisps: Sea Salt

KP

Crisps: Beef Flavour, Ready Salted, Ready Salted Lower Fat Crinkled Crisps (Solos), Salt & Vinegar Flavour; *Frisps:* Ready Salted; *Hula Hoops:* Original, Salt & Vinegar Flavour; *Minichips:* Ready Salted, Salt & Vinegar, Barbecue Beef Flavour; *Nuts:* Dry Roasted Peanuts, Brannigans Beer Nuts; *Original:* McCoys, Roysters; *Skips:* Hot From Rio Flavour

MARKS & SPENCER

Deltas, Dry Roasted Extra Large Peanuts, Indian Snack Mix, Potato Rings, Premium Snack Mix, Reduced Fat Potato Rings, Salt & Vinegar Chiplets, Sticks, Squares; *Crisps:* Apple, Barbeque, Ready Salted, Ready Salted Crinkle, Reduced Fat Crinkle Ready Salted, Spring Onion, Sweet & Sour; *Tortillas:* Extra Strong Chilli, Light Chilli

SAFEWAY

Crisps: Crinkle Cut Ready Salted, Ready Salted; *Sticks:* Ready Salted Crunchy, Ready Salted Potato, Salt & Vinegar Crunchy; *Squares:* Ready Salted Crispy, Salt & Vinegar

SEABROOKø

Smokey Bacon Crinkle Cut; *Original Crisps:* Crinkle Cut, Ripples, Straight Cut

SILBURY

Apache Bio Tortilla Chips: Blue, Sesame, Yellow

SNOWCREST

Extra Large Bags Potato Crisps, Passover Super Six Crisps, Passover Extra Large Potato Crisps, Salt & Vinegar Super 6 Crisps, Small Crisps, Super Six Crisps

WAITROSE

Dry Roasted Peanuts, Lower Fat Crinkles, Salt & Vinegar Potato Twirls; *Crisps:* Jacket Light Sea Salt, Lightly Salted, Low Fat Crinkle, Low Fat Low Salt, Potato, Ready Salted, Salt & Vinegar; *Rings:* Beef, Ready Salted; *Sticks:* Potato, Ready Salted, Salt & Vinegar Savoury, Salt & Vinegar Potato

WALKERS

Beef Burger Monster Munch, Double Crunch Original, Ready Salted Chipsticks, Ready Salted French Fries; *Crisps:* Beef & Onion, Ready Salted, Tomato Ketchup

SOUPS

ASDA

Canned: Thick Country Vegetable, Vegetable

BAXTERSø

Carrot, Onion & Chick Pea

CAMPBELLS

Bumper Harvest: Vegetable; *Condensed:* Lentil, Tomato & Onion w Garlic, Vegetable; *Grannys (Scotland only):* Potato & Leek, Tomato, Vegetable

CO-OP

Canned: Mexican Chilli, Thick Farmhouse Vegetable; *Goodlife (canned):* Farmhouse, Lentil & Sweetcorn, Tomato & Lentil; *Packet:* Minestrone, Spring Vegetable

CROSSE & BLACKWELL

Box Soups: Country Tomato, Minestrone, Spring Vegetable

HEINZ

Ready To Serve Soups: Vegetable; *Wholesoups Ready To Serve:* Country Vegetable, Lentil, Tomato & Lentil, Winter Vegetable; *Weight Watchers Soups:* Country Vegetable, Lentil & Carrot, Wholesome Spicy Bean & Vegetable, Wholesome Winter Vegetable

RAKUSEN'S™

Carrot & Lentil, French Onion, Thick Pea, Thick Vegetable

SAFEWAY

Canned: Country Vegetable, Gazpacho, Minestrone; *Dried:* French Onion, Minestrone; *Instant:* Minestrone, Slim Soup Tomato

SUMA™

All

WAITROSE

French Onion, Soupe Au Pistou, Vegetable

FOOD

SOYA MILKS & DRINKS

ASDA

Soya Milk: Sweetened, Unsweetened

CO-OP

Soya Milk: Sweetened, Unsweetened

GRANOSE

Soya Milk

GRANOVITAø

Calcium Enriched, Chocolate, Organic Sugar Free, Organic Sweetened *w* Apple Juice, Sojagen *(soya protein food powder)*

HOLLAND & BARRETT

Unsweetened Soya Milk

PLAMIL√§

Calcium & vitamin-enriched: Concentrated (Sugar-Free, Sweetened), Ready-to-Use Sugar-Free

PROVAMEL

Chocolate, No Sugar No Salt *(organic)*, Strawberry, Vanilla, *w* Calcium, *w* Wheat Syrup *(organic)*

SAFEWAY

Soya Milk: Sweetened, Unsweetened

SUNRISE√ø

Soya Milk Powder; *Flavoured Soya Drinks:* Banana, Chocolate, Strawberry; *Soya Milk:* Malt, Sweetened, Unsweetened

VITASOY

Carob Supreme, Creamy Original, Rich Cocoa, Vanilla Delite

WAITROSE

Soya Milk: Calcium Sweetened, Sweetened, Unsweetened

SPICES

ASDA

Curry Powders, Spices: all

BART SPICES√

All

CO-OP

Chilli Powder, Cinnamon, Garlic Salt, Ginger, Mixed Spices, Nutmeg, Paprika; *Madras Curry Powder:* Hot, Mild

CULPEPERøfcd76

Natural Curry Powder; *Herb & Spice Blends for Cooking, Selected Spices Whole & Ground, Spice Blends for Indian & Oriental Dishes:* all

SHIPPAMS

Seasoning Mixes: Chili, Taco

SPREADS — SAVOURY

CARLEYø

Organic Pâtés: Carrot, Hazel, Houmous, Sunflower & Onion

CAULDRON FOODS

Vegetable Pâtés: Herb, Mushroom, Red Pepper

CO-OP

Houmous

FOOD

CHALICE FOODS√

Kalamata Olive Pâté

CPC

Marmite

GEORGE SKOULIKAS√

Sunita: Olive Pâtés, Tahini

GRANOVITAø

Tofu and Peppercorn Pâté *(yeast-free)*; *Vegetarian Yeast Pâtés:* Herb Provençe, Original, Paprika, Wild Mushrooms; *Vegetarian Yeast Spreads:* Herbs Provençal, Mushroom, Olive, Original

G R LANESø

Tartex Pâtés: Herb, Herb & Garlic, Mushroom, Pepper, Plain

MARKS & SPENCER

Houmous

MERIDIAN†

Yeast Extract

NATEXø

Yeast Extract: Low Salt, Original

PLOUGHSHARES√ø

Mushroom & Tofu Pâté

SAFEWAY

Houmous, Savoury Spread

SHIPPAMS

Chili Bean Pâté

SUMA™

Hummus, Tahini; *Pâtés:* Herb, Mushroom,

Paprika, Vegetable

UNICORN FOODS√

Hummus; *Pâtés:* Chestnut, Hazelnut, Spicy Bean, Spicy Chickpea

VESSENø

Pâtés: Herb, Herb & Garlic, Mushroom, Pepper

WAITROSE

Houmous, Savoury Spread

WHOLE EARTH†

Houmous, Organic Houmous

SPREADS — SWEET

PLAMIL√§

Carob: Sugar-Free, Sweetened

PREMIER BRANDS

Original Chocolate Spread

SNOWCREST

Chocky Nut, Chocolate, Hazelchoc

SUMA™

Pear & Apple Spread

SUNWHEEL

Pear Spreads: n' Apple, n' Apricot, n' Raspberry

TOFU, TEMPEH ETC

CAULDRON FOODS

Tofu: Marinated, Marinated Pieces, Origi-

So why should you join The Vegetarian Society?

- **Because** we've been working on behalf of vegetarians for nearly 150 years

- **Because** it's kinder to animals, to people, to the world in which we live

- **Because** you'll be entitled to discounts at hundreds of restaurants and health food stores throughout the country as well as 10% discount on all our Cordon Vert cookery courses

- **Because** you'll receive 4 issues of *The Vegetarian* magazine per year, packed with advice and information from the experts

- **Because** we receive no government funding and rely on your support to help finance our programme of education and campaigning

Act now Fill in the coupon below, or ring Janet on **0161 928 0793** with your credit card details

---

Yes I'd like to join The Vegetarian Society and help support its vital work

12 month membership of The Vegetarian Society
❏ Adult £15 ❏ Student/unwaged £12 ❏ Family membership £20 ❏ Junior £5
Annual fees include 4 quarterly issues of *The Vegetarian*

For overseas membership please **add** £7 for Europe
or £10 for countries outside Europe

I enclose a cheque for £ _____ made payable to *The Vegetarian Society*

Name: ....

Address: ....

....

Postcode: .... Tel: ....

Return to: The Vegetarian Society, **Freepost**, Altrincham, Cheshire WA14 2BR
Tel: 0161 928 0793

A registered charity

nal, Smoked

COMMUNITY FOODSø

Sanchi Japanese Tofu; *Sanchi Japanese Misos:* Genmai (Brown Rice), Hatcho (Soya Bean), Mugi (Barley), Mugi Organic (Barley), Shiro

CULTURE FOODS√§

Tempeh: Blocks, Crunchy Fingers, Loaves

DRAGONFLY FOODSø

Tofu: Deep Fried, Handmade Organic, Naturally Smoked

FULL OF BEANS

Miso, Tofu; *Tempeh:* Garlic & Coriander Deep Fried *(chilled)*, Marinated & Deep Fried Tempeh in Ginger Sauce *(chilled)*, Plain *(frozen)*

IMPULSE FOODS√

Smoky Slices *('bacon' alternative)*, Chopps *(ready cooked tempeh portions)*; *Chilled Tempeh:* Plain; *Frozen Tempeh:* Herb & Garlic Flavours, Plain

MARIGOLD

Braised Tofu

MURPHY & SON

Tempeh Starter Culture

PAUL CHAPLIN√ø§

Misos: Amakuchi Mugi, Koji *(miso & amasake starter)*, Mellow Brown, Mellow Barley, Field Bean Barley, Sweet Brown

PLOUGHSHARES√ø

Tofu

SOYFOODS√™

Nigari Tofu

WHITENERS

ELIKO

TamTov Coffee Whitener

SNOWCREST

Snowwhite: Coffee Whitener, Parev Coffee Whitener

'YOGHURTS'

GRANOSE

Soya Yogerts: all

SO GOOD

Yogerts: Black Cherry, Peach & Passion Fruit, Strawberry

Notes

- **apple juice** The apple juice in Meridian's fruit spreads has been clarified with gelatine *(see APPLE JUICE & BETA-CAROTENE, page 13)*.
- **apples & citrus fruits** Both may be coated with shellac, beeswax or other animal/vegetable-derived waxes. Washington Red apples are commonly coated with shellac.
- **baked beans** HP contains skimmed milk powder.
- **banana chips** May be dipped in honey.
- **bread** Most large producers use vegetable-based emulsifiers (E471, E472 etc). A few local bakers may still grease tins with animal fat.
- **cereals** The vitamin D in fortified cereals is commonly the animal-derived D_3.
- **chocolate** Plain Bounty has never been animal-free. Jameson Ruffles and Ruffle Bars contain carmine. Do not assume that plain chocolate is always animal-free. For UK-produced chocolate, reading the ingredients listing is not always sufficient; continental plain chocolate is less likely to contain animal substances.
- **crisps** Whey, and any one of thousands of (possibly animal-derived) processing aids, may be used as a flavour carrier.
- **lecithin** Mainly obtained commercially from soyabean, peanut and corn but can be derived from eggs.
- **processing aids** May be animal derived. There is no statutory requirement for these to be listed on products.
- **sugar (brown)** May not be entirely free of animal involvement. Although the white sugar produced by the largest UK supplier, British Sugar (trading under the Silver Spoon label), is now animal-free at every stage of production, the company cannot guarantee the same for its brown sugars. "The raw sugars and cane molasses... originate from numerous small factories around the world many of which may use *[as a decolourant]* bone char or char of mixed origin, and the type used may vary from country to country, year to year, factory to factory." It is claimed that the charcoal does not end up in the final product.

With the exception of Ready to Roll Icing, all sugars produced by the UK's second largest sugar supplier, Tate & Lyle are free of animal substances at all stages of production — as are those produced by Billingtons.

Manufacturers commonly purchase their raw ingredients from the cheapest source. In the case of brown sugar-containing products, most companies are unable to provide guarantees that the sugar used is, or will always be, free of a bone char connection. Given that brown sugar is neither wholly nor partly derived from animal products, for the present, it has been decided to continue to list all brown sugar-containing animal-free products presented for inclusion in this guide.

- **vinegar** Although malt and spirit vinegars (mainly used in pickles, relishes etc) are generally animal-free, the production of wine, cider and sherry vinegars may involve the use of a fining agent of animal origin.

DRINK

DRINK

BEERS

BLACK SHEEP

Black Sheep Ale [bottle]

CALEDONIAN BREWERY

Golden Pale Organic Ale

CARLSBERG-TETLEY

National: Long Life [can/keg], Lowenbrau Strong Lager [can/keg], Lowenbrau Pils [bottle/can], St Christopher [bottle]; *North:* Tetley Special Pale Ale [bottle/can]; *Scotland:* Alloa Export Ale [bottle/can/keg], Alloa Original Light [keg], Alloa Special 70/- [can/keg/tank], Alloa Sweet Stout [bottle]; *South:* Barleycorn Pale Ale [keg], Benskins Pale Mild [keg]

COURAGE

Budweiser, Holsten Pils

FELINFOEL BREWERY

Double Dragon Ale [can/keg]

GEORGE BATEMAN

Indian Pale Ale, Nut Brown, Valiant, Victory Ale, XXXB Export

GROLSCH

Premium Lager [bottle/can/keg]

HALL & WOODHOUSE

Best Bitter [can/keg], HLB [keg], Hofbrau Export Lager [keg], Malt-House Bitter [can/keg], Oasthouse Bitter [can], Royal Hofbrau Export Lager [keg], Royal Hofbrau Lager [keg], Skona Lager [can]

HOP BACK BREWERY

Entire Stout [cask]

ISLE OF MAN BREWERIES

Okells Beer [keg]

JOSEPH HOLT

Brown Stout [bottle]

LINFIT BREWERY

Linfit Mild [Draught], English Guineas Stout [Draught]

MORRELLS BREWERY

Brewery Gate Bitter [bottle/keg], Castle Ale [bottle], College Ale [bottle], Friars Ale [keg], Graduate Bitter [bottle], Harp Extra Lagers [keg], Harp Standard, Light Ale [bottle]

OAKHILL BREWERY

Black Magic Stout, Mendip Tickler,, OakHill Best Bitter, Somer Ale, Yeoman 1767 Strong Ale

SAMUEL SMITH

4X Best Ale [can/keg], Dark Mild [can/keg], Light Ale [bottle], Nut Brown Ale [bottle], Old Brewery Bitter [can/keg], Old Brewery Strong Pale Ale [bottle], Pale Ale [bottle], Pure Brewed Lager [can/bottle], Sovereign Best Bitter [can/keg], Strong Golden Ale [bottle], Tadcaster Bitter [can/keg], Taddt Brown Ale [bottle], Yorkshire [can/keg]; *Ayingerbräu:* D Pils [bottle/draught], Lager [draught], Prinz Strong Lager [draught], Very Strong [bottle]

SCOTTISH & NEWCASTLE

Becks Beer [bottle/can/keg], Coors Extra Gold Lager [bottle/can/keg]

SEDLESCOMBE VINEYARD√ø™

Bucher Bavarian Pilsner Lager *(organic)*

SHEPHERD NEAME

Kingfisher Indian Lager [draught], Steinbock Lager

THE VEGAN WINE CLUB√ø§

#8 [bottle]

TRAQUAIR HOUSE

Traquair House Ale [bottle]

VINCEREMOSø™

Bottle Green Organic Lager, Original Flag Porter, Original Norvig Ale; *Pinkus Muller:* Alt Lager, Special, Weizen Wheat Beer

VINTAGE ROOTSø

Beers, lagers: all

VAUX BREWERY

Extra Special [cans], Labatts Canadian Lager [bottle/can/keg], Labatts Strong Lager [bottle/can/keg], Norseman Lager [can], Scorpion Dry Lager [bottle/can]; *Vaux Products:* all — **except** cask

WHITBREAD

Heineken Export Lager, Kaltenberg Pils; *Newquay Steam:* Bitter, Lager

WAITROSE

Beer: Hofmark; *Bitter:* Midland, Wessex; *Lager:* Czech, Danish, Dutch, English, French, German, Strong German

CIDERS

ASPALL

Still Cyder

AVALON VINEYARDø

Organic

BIDDENDEN√ø

Bushels, Monks Delight, Special Reserve; *Strong Kentish:* Dry, Medium, Sweet

DUNKERTONS√ø

Cir, Perry

JAMES WHITE√ø

Dry, Extra Strong [bottle/draught], Special Edition October Gold

MERRYDOWN

Ciders: Original Dry, Original Gold, Original Vintage, Pulse White

SEDLESCOMBE VINEYARD√ø™

Traditional Extra Strong *(organic)*

VINCEREMOSø™

Dunkertons Herefordshire Ciders, Perry: all

VINTAGE ROOTSø

Ciders, Perry: all

WAITROSE

Medium Dry, Medium Sweet [canned], Mousseux, Premium, Strong Dry, Traditional Medium Sweet

WESTON & SONS

Country [bottle]: Dry, Medium; *Double M [bottle]:* Dry, Medium; *Extra Strong*

Draught: Dry, Medium; *Extra Strong Scrumpy [draught]:* Dry; *Henry Weston Vintage [bottle]:* Dry, Medium; *Oak Conditioned [bottle]:* Dry, Medium; *Old Rosie [draught]:* Extra Strong; *Original Extra Dry [bottle]:* Dry; *Perry [bottle]:* Dry, Medium, Sweet; *Scrumpy Supreme [bottle, keg]:* Extra Strong; *Stowford [bottled]; Stowford Press [bottle, keg]:* Dry, Medium; *Traditional Draught:* Medium, Sweet; *Vintage Dry [bottle, draught]:* Extra Strong; *Vintage Sweet [bottle, draught]:* Extra Strong

WHITBREAD

Newquay Steam Cider

HOME BREW KITS

YOUNG'S HOMEBREW√

Harvest: Bitter, Lager, Mild, Yorkshire Bitter

'HOT' DRINKS

ASDA

Drinking Chocolate, Fat Reduced Instant Drinking Chocolate Granules

GRANOVITAø

Carob Cup

INTER-MEDICS√

Pioner Coffee Substitute

MAHARISHI AYUR-VEDø

Raja's Cup *(coffee substitute)*

PREWETTS

Instant Chicory Drink

SAFEWAY

Drinking Chocolate

SNOWCREST

Instant Hot Chocolate Mix

VECONø

Country Cup

WHOLE EARTH†

Wake Cup Instant Hot Drink *w* Guarana

LOW & NON-ALCOHOLIC

EISBERG

Alcohol-Free Wines: French, German, Peach

SAMUEL SMITH

Ayingerbräu: Low Alcohol [draught/bottle]

SHEPHERD NEAME

Birell Low Alcohol Lager, Pilgrims Low Alcohol Bitter

WAITROSE

Low Alcohol Cider

SOFT DRINKS

7UP

Cherry, Diet, Regular

DRINK

APPLETISE

Appletise, Appletise Light, Grapetise, Orangetise

ASDA

Carbonated, Dilute to Taste, Juice Drinks, 'C' Drinks: all

BRITVIC

Orange Squash; *55:* Apple, Orange, Pineapple, Tropical; *Cordials:* Blackcurrant, Lime; *Mixers:* American Ginger Ale (Reg & Low Cal), Indian Tonic (Reg & Low Cal), Soda Water

CITRUS SPRING

Lemon, Lime, Orange

COCA COLA

Cherry Coke, Coca Cola, Diet Cherry Coke, Diet Lilt Mango & Mandarin, Diet Sprite, Fanta Orange, Sprite, Tab Clear; *Diet Fanta:* Apple, Orange, Raspberry; *Five Alive:* Citrus, Citrus Lite, Mediterranean, Tropical; *Lilt:* Diet Pineapple & Grapefruit, Mango & Mandarin, Pineapple & Grapefruit

CORONA

Cherryade, Limeade, Orangeade

CRESTA

Apple, Lemonade, Low-Calorie Lemonade, Orange, Polar Brew, Strawberry

IDRIS

Traditional Style: Cream Soda, Dandelion & Burdock, Lemonade [bottles]

KIRI

Diet Kiri, Kiri, Kiri White Grape

KTC

Caribbean Cool Soft Drinks: Mango & Orange, Passion Fruit & Tangerine, Pineapple & Grapefruit, Tropicana

LIBBY'S

Libby's C Drinks, Um Bongo Drinks: all

MARKS & SPENCER

Applesparkle, Bucks Fizz, Ginger Beer, Herbal Fruit Spring Water, Jaffa Orange, Jaffa Orangeade, Jaffa Orange Dilute Drink, Lemon & Lime Dilute Drink, Pina Colada, Reduced Sugar Jaffa Orange, Spice Drink, Traditional Cola, Traditional Lemonade; *Low Calorie Crush:* Caribbean, Lemon & Lime, Orange; *Sparkling Water:* Black Cherry, Elderflower, Peach, Pear, Raspberry; *Still Water:* Black Cherry, Elderflower, Peach, Pear, Raspberry

NESQUIK

All Nesquik Powders

ORCHID DRINKS

Aqua Libra, Dexters Low Calorie Sports Drink, Jive, Purdeys; *Amé:* Red, Rosé, White; *Monsoon:* Elderflower, Kiwi & Lime, Orange & Passionfruit; *Orchid Fruits:* Blackcurrant, Cherry, Peach, Raspberry

PEPSI COLA

Caffeine Free Diet Pepsi, Diet Pepsi, Pepsi Cola, Pepsi Max, Pepsi Strawberry Flavour Cola, Pepsi Tropical Flavour Cola

QUOSH

Apple & Blackcurrant (Reg & Low Cal), Lemon, Lemon & Lime, Lemon Barley Water, Low Calorie Apple & Strawberry;

Cordials: Blackcurrant Flavour, Lime Flavour

RAYNER BURGESS

Crusha Milk Shake Syrups, Rayner Thick Shake Syrups: all

ROCK'S COUNTRY WINESø

Elderflower Cordial

ROWNTREE

Fruit Juice Drinks: all

SAFEWAY

Fizzy Drinks, Squashes: all

SARAH'S

Fruit Crush Drinks: Apricot, Guava, Mango, Peach, Pear

SCHWEPPES

Gini: all; *Kia-Ora Carbonated Drinks:* Cherry, Lemonade, Orange, Pineapple & Grapefruit, Tropical Orange; *Kia-Ora Tetrapak Cartons:* all; *Kia-Ora Bottles:* **except** No Added Sugar Orange, No Added Sugar Orange & Pineapple, Orange, Orange & Pineapple; *Roses, Schweppes, Sunkist:* all

STUTE FOODS

Nectar: Apricot & Orange, Blackcurrant

TANGO

Apple, Blackcurrant, Diet Apple, Diet Lemon, Lemon

TOP DECK

Cherryade, Dandelion & Burdock, Orangeade

WAITROSE

American Ginger Ale, Bitter Lemon, Diet Tonic Water, Dry Ginger, Ginger Beer, Lemonade, Lime Juice Cordial, Old Fashioned Lemonade, Soda Water, Still Lemonade, Tonic Water; *Crush:* Blackcurrant, Melon; *Drink:* Apple & Strawberry, Blackcurrant, Citrus, Diet Lemon, Diet Orange, High Juice Orange Squash, Lemon & Lime, Lemon Juice, Orange, Orange & Apricot, Orange Juice, Orange Lemon & Pineapple, Soda Water, Strawberry, Tonic Water, Tropical, Whole Grapefruit; *Sparkling Juices:* Red Grape, White Grape, Whole Lemon, Whole Orange; *Low Caffeine:* Cola, Diet Cola; *Low Calorie:* American Ginger, Bitter Lemon, Lemonade, Tonic; *Squash:* High Juice Lemon, Lemon, Orange

WHOLE EARTH√†

Sparkling Herbal Drinks: Gusto, Gusto Lemonade; *Sparking Soft Drinks:* Cola w Guarana, Orange Soda, Real Lemonade

SPIRITS & APERITIFS

ASDA

Cognac 3 Star, Gin, Malt 10 Year Old; *Whisky:* 3 Years Old, 10 Years Old Single Malt

INTERNATIONAL DISTILLERS

Amaretto di Saronno, Archers Peach County Schnapps, Black Velvet Canadian Whisky, Bombay Gin, Cockspur Rum, Cointreau, Crocker, Croft Sherries, Croft Vintage Port, Daintons Lemon Cut, Gilbeys

DRINK

Gin, J&B Whisky, Jack Daniels, Jose Cuervo Tequila, Malibu, Metaxa Brandy, Popov Vodka, Rumpleminz Schnapps, Sambuca Romana, Sapphire Gin, Singleton Whisky, Smirnoff Vodka, Southern Comfort, Stubbs Rum

ROCK'S COUNTRY WINESø

Damson Gin

SAFEWAY

Fortified Wine: Fonseca Guimaraens Vintage 1976 Port

VINCEREMOSø™

Flor de Cana Nicaraguan Rums, Lheraud Cognacs

VINTAGE ROOTSø

Cognacs, Liqueurs, Pineau, Calvados: all

WAITROSE

Armagnac VSOP, Cognac, Cognac VSOP Reserve, Fine Ruby Port, French Brandy, Gin, Ginger Wine, Grain Gin, Medium Amontillado, Vodka, West Indian Rum; *Sherry:* Cream, Cream Montilla, Medium Montilla, Pale Cream Montilla, Pale Dry Montilla

Vermouth: Bianco, Dry, Extra Dry, Rosso; *Whisky:* Blended Scotch, Islay Malt Scotch, Pure H/D Malt Scotch, Scotch, Speyside Scotch

WESTBAY DISTRIBUTORS

Asti Martini, Bacardi Rum, Glenmorangie Malt Whisky, Martini Brut; *Martini:* Anytime Rosso & Tonic, Bianco, Ex Dry, Rosé, Rosso

WINES

ASDA

Bordeaux Dry, Bordeaux Medium Dry St Foy, Bourgogne White, Chablis, Champagne Rosé, Chilean Sauvignon Blanc, Cotes de Duras Sauvignon, Cotes du Ventoux Rouge, Gewurtztraminer, Pinot Blanc, Rosé D'Anjou, Soave, South Eastern Australian Semillion Chardonnay, Sparkling Saumur, Vin de pays Coteaux du Libron (White, Red), Vin de Pays Cote de Gasgogne Blanc; *Hungarian:* Cabernet Sauvignon, Chardonnay, Kekfrancos, Merlot, Muscat, Pinot Blanc

AVALON VINEYARDø

Gooseberry, Organic Apple, Organic Grape, Strawberry

BIDDENDEN√ø

Red/Rosé: Biddenden Table Medium Dry, Biddenden Quality Dry Sparkling 1990, Cardinal 1990, Chalice 1990; *White:* Biddenden Table Medium Dry, Huxelrebe 1991 Full Medium Dry, Muller Thurgau 1993 Medium Dry, Noble Oast, Schonburger Medium, Ortega 1993 Medium

CO-OP

Beaujolais, Bordeaux Medium Sweet, Cape Red, Claret, Cotes du Rhone, Herault Rouge, Hock, Laski Rizling, Liebfraumilch, Muscadet, Premier Cotes de Bordeaux, Nierstein Gutes Domtal, Piesporter Michelsberg, Principato Red, Rose D'Anjou, Sicilian Red, Tempranillo, Valle de Monterrey; *Australian:* Red, White; *Bulgarian:* Cab Sav, Merlot Kadarka; *California:* Colombard, Ruby; *Hungarian:*

Red, White; *Valencia:* Red, White; *VdT:* Dry White, Medium White, Red

DISOSø

Pure French: Red, White

MARKS & SPENCER

Beaujolais Villages, French Chardonnay, Georges Duboeuf Chardonnay, Georges Duboeuf Cabernet Sauvignon

ORGANIC WINE COMPANYø†

Champagne & Sparkling Wine France: Champagne Blanc Brut — Jose Ardinat, Chateau des Hautes Combes — Brut Bordeaux AC Methode Traditionelle EARL Garcia Freres, Chateau des Hautes Combes Rosé Bordeaux AC Methode Traditionelle EARL Garcia Freres, Bossard Thouaud — Vin Mousseux Methode Traditionelle — Guy Bossard, Clairette de Die AC — Brut Methode Traditionelle GAEC Achard Vincent, Clairette de Die AC — Demi-sec Tradition GAEC Achard Vincent

Chateau du Puy: Chateau du Puy — Bordeaux Supérieur AC 1990 — Robert Amoreau

Chateau Rocher du Puy: Loire: Vin de Pays des Marches de Bretagne — Cepage Cabernet — Guy Bossard; *Cotes du Rhone:* Cotes du Rhones AC 1992 — Michel Delacroix, Domaine Saint — Apollinaire — Cotes du Rhone AC Cuvee d'Apolline SCA Daumas 1990, Domaine Saint Apollinaire — Cotes du Rhone AC Cuvee de Cépage Syrah SCA Daumas 1990

Red France: Vin de Pays: Albaric — Vin de Pays du Gard — Hoirie Albaric, Domaine de Petit Roubie — Vin de Pays des Cotes de Thau — Olivier Azan, Michel Delacroix — Vin de Pays du Gard, Michel Delacroix — Vin de Pays du Gard — Cabernet; *Bordeaux:* Chateau des Hautes Combes — Bordeaux AC 1993 EARL Garcia Freres, Chateau la Croix Simon — Bordeaux AC 1990, Chateau des Hautes Combes — Ste Foy Bordeaux AC 1993 EARL Garcia Freres, Chateau Cotes des Caris — Bordeaux Superieur AC 1989 Vielli en futs de Chene — Christian Guichard, Chateau des Hautes Combes — Ste Foy Bordeaux AC 1989 Vielli en Futs de Chene — GAEC Deffarge Garcia

Rosé France: Vin de Pays: Michel Delacroix — Vin de Pays du Gard — Michel Delacroix

White France: Bordeaux: Chateau des Cotes des Caris — Bordeaux Blanc Sec AC 1993 — Christian Guichard, Chateau des Hautes Combes Ste Foy Bordeaux AC Sauvignon Blanc 1993, Chateau la Croix Simon — Entre Deux Mers AC 1993 — Jean Gabriel Yon; *Loire:* Muscadet de Sevre et Maine AC 1993 — sur lie Domaine de la Parentiere, Gros Plant du Pays Nantais VDQS 1993 — sur lie Guy Bossard, Muscadet de Sevre et Maine AC 1993 — sur lie Hermine d'Or — Guy Bossard, Sancerre AC 1993 — Nicole et Christian Dauny; *Cotes du Rhône:* Cotes du Rhône AC 1992 — Michel Delacroix, Domaine St Apollinaire — Cotes du Rhone AC 1987 — Vingnier Daumas; *The Midi:* Picpoul de Pinet — Coteaux du Languedoc AC 1993 — Olivier Azan; *Vin de Pays:* Domaine de Petit Roubie — Vin de Pays des Cotes de Thau — Olivier Azan; *Vin de Table:* Blanc de Blanc — Selection Menager — Domaine de ia Parentiere, Cuvee de la Marouette — Blanc de Blancs — Olivier Azan

DRINK

White New Zealand Gisborne Poverty Bay: Gisborne Chenin Blanc — Barrel Fermented 1992 — Millton Vineyard, Gisborne Sauvignon Blanc — Barrel Fermented 1992 — Milton Vineyard

ROCK'S COUNTRY WINESø

Elderberry Wine Punch, Rich Elderberry, Sparkling Gooseberry; *Dry Table:* Damson, Green Gooseberry; *Medium Dry:* Blackberry, Elderflower, Raspberry; *Medium Sweet:* Plum, Strawberry

ROWENDEN VINEYARD√

Rowenden: Huxelrebe, Reichensteiner, Rivaner

SAFEWAY

Australia: Red: Hardys Barossa Valley Cabernet Sauvignon, Hardys Barossa Valley Shiraz, Orlando RF Cabernet Sauvignon 1990 SE Australia, Wolf Blass Yellow Label Cabernet Sauvignon, *White:* Eileen Hardy Chardonnay, Hardys Barossa Valley Chardonnay 1993

Champagne & Sparkling: Lindauer Brut, Safeway Chardonnay Spumante Brut

Eastern Europe: Red: Young Vatted Merlot Russe; *Rosé:* Safeway Cabernet Sauvignon Rose 1992 Nagyrede; *White:* Czech Pinto Blanc 1992 Moravia, Nagyrede Reserva Sauvignon, Szech Sauvignon Blanc, Safeway Dry Muscat 1992 Nagyrede, Safeway Laski Rizling, Seewinkler Impressionen Ansbach 1991 Neusidlersee

England: Elmham Park 1991 Medium Madelaine Angevine/Kerner

French: Alsace White: Gewurstraminer

d'Alsace 1992, Pinto Blanc d'Alsace 1992/93; *Bordeaux & Atlantic Red:* Chateaux Larouche Viella 1988/89 Madiran, Chateaux Le Truche de Reignac Bordeaux Superieur Oak Aged Claret; *Bordeaux & Atlantic White:* Chateaux de Plantiers Entre Deux Mers 1993, Domaine de Malardeen 1993 Cotes de Duras, Domaine de Rey 1993 VdP des Cotes de Gascogne Vegetarian Wine, La Coume de Peyre 1993 Vin de Pays des Cotes de Gascogne, Mouton Cadet 1992 Bordeaux, Safeway Oak Aged Blanc de Bordeaux 1993 Bordeaux, Safeway Vin de Pays des Cotes de Gascogne 1993; *Burgundy White:* Meursault, Safeway Bourgogne Blanc 1992 Aged in Oak, Safeway Chablis Premier Cru Fourchaume/Les Vaillions, Safeway Nuits St Georges; *Loire White:* Domaine des P'tits Perriers 1991/2 Sancerre

Germany White: Hugh Ryman Riesling 1993 St Ursula, Hugh Ryman Scheurebe/ Rivaner 1993 St Ursula, Rulander Kabinett 1990 Ibringer Winklerberg, Safeway Bereich Nierstein, Safeway Hock Deutscher Tafelwain, St Ursula Morio Muskat 1992 Rheinpfalz, St Ursula Scheurebe 1992 Rheinhessen Organic

Greece Red: Xinomavro Naoussis 1990 Macedonia

Italy: Red: Antica Sangiovese di Romagna, Montepulciano d'Abruzzo 1992; *White:* Riva Trebbiano di Romagna 1993, Safeway Chardonnay del Triveneto 1993, Safeway Orvieto Classico Secco 1993, Safeway Lambrusco Light, Safeway Pinot Grigio del Triveneto 1993

New Zealand: Red: Cooks Pinot Noir &

Cabernet Sauvignon 1990; *White:* Montana Chardonnay 1992, Montana Sauvignon 1992/3 Marlborough South Island

Portugal Red: Quinta de Pancas 1990 Vinho Maior da Reserve Alenquer; *Rosé:* Safeway Vinho Rosado

Rhone & Mediterranean: Red: Chateauneuf du Pape La Source Aux Nymphes 1990/92, Safeway Corbieres, Safeway Chateau de Caraquilhes 1990 Corbieres Organic, Safeway Cotes du Ventoux 1993, Safeway Fitou, Safeway Minervois, Safeway Vin de Pays de Vaucluse 1993; *Rosé:* Cotes de Luberon Rosé 1993; *White Dry:* Domaine de Rivoyre Chardonnay 1992 Vine de Pays d'Oc, James Herrick Chardonaay, J & F Larton Sauvignon VdP d'Oc 1993, Safeway Corbieres 1993 Blanc de Blancs, Safeway Vin de Pays de Vaucluse 1993, Sainte Marie 1993 Cotes du Rhone

Spain Red: Senorio de Nava Crianza 1987 Ribera de Duero

SEDLESCOMBE VINEYARD√ø™

Organic: Late Harvest Dry White, Rivaner Medium Dry White, Sparkling Brut, Sparkling Brut Rosé, Special Reserve Medium Sweet White; *Organic Country Wines:* Apple Medium Dry, Blackcurrant Medium Sweet

THE VEGAN WINE CLUB√ø§

Various — including 'Vin Eco' and 'Pure 2' ranges

VINCEREMOSø™

Red: Cepage Cabernet Guy Bossard, Chateau Barrail des Gravs St Emilion, Chateau Coursou Bordeaux, Chateau de Boisfranc Beaujolais Superieur, Chateau la Blanquerie Bordeaux Superieur, Chateau la Chapelle Maillard Bordeaux, Chateau Meric Graves, Chateau Musar, Domaine de Barjac VDP de Gard, Domaine de Clairac Primeur VDP de l'Herault, Domaine de Savignac Vin de Pays, Domaine St Michel Merlot Cabernet Sauvignon Syrah & Corbieres, Tenuta San Vito Chianti, Tenuta San Vito Vin Santo, Tenuta San Vito Vigna la Reina, Vignoble de la Jasse Cotes du Rhone, Vignoble de la Jasse Vin de Pays de Principaute d'Orange; *Rosé:* Domaine de Clairac Cabernet Sauvignon Rose, Jas D'Esclans Rose; *White:* Beaujolais Blanc Thierry Doat, Bianco Toscano Tenuta San Vito, Blanc de Blancs Guy Bossard, Blanc de Blancs Selection Menager, Can Vendrell Penedes, Champagne Carte D'Or & Cuvve Speciale Jose Ardinat, Champagne Jean Bliard, Chateau Canet Entre Deux Mers, Chateau Coursou Bordeaux Blanc, Chateau Gendre Marsalet Moelleux, Chateau La Croix Simon Entre Deux Mers, Chateauneuf du Pape Pierre Andre, Clairette de Die Brut & Tradition Achard Vincent, Costieres de Nimes Blac Jacques Frelin, Domaine de Clairac Joubic Blanc, Domaine de Petit Roubie VDP des Cotes de Thau, Domaine de Soleil Sauvignon Blanc — Chardonnay & Blanc de Blancs, Domaines Theulet Marsalet Monbazillac, Domaine St Michel Sauvignon Blanc — Chardonnay & Blanc de Blancs, Gewurztraminer Pierre Frick, Gros Plant Domaine de la Parentier, Gros Plant Guy Bossard, Millton Vineyard Chenin Blanc, Millton Vineyard Sauvignon Blanc, Millton Vineyard Semillon/Chardonnay, Muscadet de

Sevre et Maine Sur Lie Domaine de la Par-
entiere, Muscadet de Sevre et Maine Sur
Lie Hermine d'Or Guy Bossard, Muscadet
de Sevre et Maine Sur Lie Guy Bossard,
Muscat d'Alsace Pierre Frick, Muscat Sec
Clos St Martin VDP Catalan, Muscat de
Rivesaltes Clos St Martin, Petillant de
Raisin Domaine de la Tronque, Pinto Blanc
Pierre Frick, Rheinhessen Auslese Dietmar
Werner, Rheinhessen Kabinett Dietmar
Werner, Rheinhessen Muller Thurgau Diet-
mar Werner, Rheinhessen Spatlese
Dietmar Werner, Sancerre Christian et
Nicole Dauny, Sylvaner Pierre Frick,
Verdiglio Tenuta San Vito, Vin Mousseux
Thauad Guy Bossard

VINTAGE ROOTSø

Australia: Red: Cabernet Sauvignon Botobolar Vineyard 1991, St Gilbert Botobolar
Vineyard 1990, Shiraz Botobolar Vineyard
1990/91; *White:* Robinvale Chenin/Charo-
donnay Victoria 1993/4

Champagnes: Carte d'Or Serge Faust,
Carte Rouge George Laval, Cuvee de
Reserve Serge Faust, Fleury Carte Rouge,
Fleury Rosé, Fleury 1988 Brut, 1er Cru
Reserve Spéciale Brut George Laval;
Sparkling Wines: AOC Clairette de Die 'Tra-
dition' Archard Vincent, AOC Touraine
Rosé Huet, DOC Lessine Durello Fongaro,
Fleur de Muscat Foxonet

England White: Rivaner Sedlescombe
Vineyard 1993, Sedlescombe Late Harvest
Dry Sedlescombe Vineyard 1993

France Red: Beaujolais: AOC Beaujolais
Gerard Belaid 1992, AOC Morgon Gerard
Belaid 1992; *Bordeaux & Bergerac:* AOC
Bordeaux Superieur Chateau Coursou1

1992, AOC Cotes de Bourg Chateau Falfas
1990, AOC St Emilion Chateau Barrail des
Graves 1990; *Burgundy:* AOC Beaune 1er
Cru Les Reversees Rateau 1990, AOC
Bourg Cote Chalonn D'Heilly Huberdeau
1991, Cotes de Nuits Alain Verdet 1989;
Loire: VdP des Marches de Bretagne
Cabernet Bossard 1992/93; *Rhone:* AOC
Chateauneuf du Pape Pierre Andre 1990,
AOC Crozes Hermitage Domaine Combier
1991, AOC Cotes du Rhone Cuvee Cepage
Syrah 1990/91, AOC Cotes du Rhone
Cuvee St Apollinaire 1990/91, AOC Cote
du Rhone La Quintessence 1988, AOC
Gigondas Clos du Joncuas 1992, AOC Vac-
queyras Dom Clos de Caveau 1993; *South:*
AOC Corbieres Pech Latt 1992 & 1990
Vieilles Vignes, AOC Coteaux du Langue-
doc Dom de la Bousquette 1991, VdP de
Lastours Domaine de Brau 1992/93, VdP
du Gard Albaric 1993, VDQS Cabardes
Chateau de Brau 1993

France White: Alsace: AOC Gewürztramin-
er Andre Stentz 1992, AOC Tokay d'Alsace
Andre Stentz 1992; *Bordeaux:* AOC Blayais
Domaine du Grand Loup 1993, AOC Bor-
deaux Sec Ch Moulin de Romage 1993,
AOC Entre Deux Mers Ch Pouchaud Lar-
quey 1992/93, AOC Ste Foy Bordeaux
Chateau Trois Fonds 1992/3; *Burgundy:*
AOC Chablis Domaine Jean Goulley 1993,
AOC Chablis 1er Cru Montmains Jean
Goulley 1993, Cote de Beaune La Grande
Chatelaine 1991; *Loire:* AOC Coteaux du
Layon Domaine de Dreuille 1990, AOC
Muscadet de S&M sur Lie Parentiere 1993,
AOC Muscadet de S&M sur Lie Guy
Bossard 1993, AOC Sancerre Christian
Dauny 1993, AOC Vouvray Le Mont Sec
Huet 1992, VdP Bl de Blanc de Loire Selec-

tion Menager 1993; *Rhone:* AOC Chateauneuf du Pape Pierre Andre 1992, AOC Cotes du Rhone Viognier Dom St Apoll 1989/90; *South:* VdP de L'Aude Blanc de Brau 1993

Germany White: Scheurebe St Ursula Weinkellerei 1993

Italy Red: DOC Valpolicella Classico Ottomarzo 1993, DOCG Chianti Bacco Villa Angiolina 1991, DOCG Chianti Classico Villa Angiolina 1990/91, DOCG Chianti Villa Angiolina 1991; *Italy White:* Bianco di Poggio al Sorbo Villa Angiolina 1993, DOC Soave Superiore F Gino 1993, Narciso de Poeti Villa Angiolina 1993, VDT Chardonnay F Gino 1993

Rosé: AOC Cotes de Provence Domaine du Jas d'Esclans 1992, VdP Coteaux de Ceze Lou Pas d'Estrech 1993, VDP Lastours Domaine de Brau 1993

Spain: Red: DO Penedes Cab Sauvignon Col Leccio A I Noya, DO Penedes Tempranillo Col Leccio Albert i Noya, DO Valencia Dominio Los Pinos 1993; *White:* Dominio Los Pinos Valencia 1993, DO Penedes Can Vendrell Albet i Noya 1993, DO Penedes Macabeo Col Leccio 1993 Albet i Noya

USA: Red: Zinfandel Orleans Hill 1991; *White:* Sauvignon Blanc Orleans Hill 1991

WAITROSE

Good Ordinary Claret, Vin Rouge

WESTBAY DISTRIBUTORS

Marques de Monistol wines; *Mateus Wines:* Rosé, Signature (Red, White), White

Notes

- **beers** As a general rule traditional, cask-conditioned beers ('real ales') are usually clarified (cleared) with isinglass finings (The addition of the finings speeds up a process which would otherwise occur naturally). Keg, canned, beersphere and some bottled beers are usually filtered without the use of animal substances. Lagers are generally chill-filtered but a *few* may involve the use of isinglass. The only possibly animal-derived ingredient used in the production of keg beers is E471. Animal-derived finings continue to be used in all Guinness-, Scottish & Newcastle- and Bass-produced beers.
- **soft drinks** Be alert to the possible presence of animal-derived colourants, such as cochineal. *(See also APPLE JUICE & BETA-CAROTENE, page 13)*
- **spirits** The production of spirits does not appear to involve the use of animal substances (Vodka is now universally filtered using birchwood charcoal).
- **wines** Most wines on sale in off-licences and supermarkets have been fined using one of the following: Blood, bone marrow, chitin, egg albumen, fish oil, gelatine, isinglass, milk or milk casein. Non-animal alternatives include limestone, bentonite, kaolin and kieslguhr (clays), plant casein, silica gel, and vegetable plaques.

TOILETRIES & COSMETICS

BODY CENTRE (SCOTLAND) LTD

NATURAL QUALITY IN
BODY COSMETICS

DEVELOPED BY COMBINING NATURE'S FINEST
INGREDIENTS WITH THE BEST OF TODAY'S TECHNOLOGY.

BY EMBRACING NATURAL RESOURCES, WE HAVE CREATED A RANGE
THAT IS SIMPLE, GENTLE, NATURAL AND EFFECTIVE, WITH QUALITY,
PERFORMANCE AND VALUE BEING THE PRIME OBJECTIVES.

CHOOSE FROM OUR NATURAL VITAMIN E, ALOE VERA AND FRAGRANCE FREE
FACIAL CARE RANGES. HAIR CARE - BATH AND BODY CARE -
PERFUMES - AROMATHERAPY ESSENTIAL AND BLENDED OILS.
PLUS A RANGE FOR MEN.

NONE OF OUR PRODUCTS HAS EVER BEEN TESTED ON ANIMALS AND
ARE ALL FREE OF ANIMAL DERIVED MATERIALS.
SUITABLE FOR VEGANS.
BUAV LISTED.

WITH REGULAR USE, THE BODY CENTRE COLLECTION WILL KEEP YOU
LOOKING AND FEELING GOOD IN THE KNOWLEDGE THAT AS WELL AS CARING
FOR YOURSELF YOU ARE ALSO CARING FOR YOUR ENVIRONMENT.

For Mail Order Catalogue contact:
Body Centre (Scotland) Ltd.,
Units 15–18 Crosshill Centre, Main St., Crosshill,
Lochgelly, Fife KY5 8BJ
Telephone 01592 860489 - Fax 01592 860555

Or fill in details below and post to above address

Name _____

Address _____

_____

_____ Post code _____

72

BATH & SHOWER

AMYRIS√ø̸fcd76

Body Shampoo; *Foam Bath:* Base, Geranium & Lavender, Pineapple Coconut & Mango; *Shower & Bath Gel:* Apple & Sandalwood, Strawberry & Papaya

ANIMAL AID√ø̸§fcd76

Peach & Mango Foam Bath

BARRY M∆fcd82

Aromatherapy Bath Oil: Refreshing, Relaxing, Uplifting; *Aromatherapy Shower Gel:* Invigorating, Sensuous; *Body Shampoos:* Dewberry, Evening Primrose, Flirt Wash & Condition for Body & Hair, Perfect Peach, Strawberry, White Musk; *Foam Baths:* Dewberry, Evening Primrose, Flirt, Perfect Peach, Strawberry, White Musk; *Just For Men:* Body Shampoo, Foam Bath, Shower Gel; *Shower Gels:* Dewberry, Flirt, Perfect Peach, Raspberry, Strawberry, Tangerine, White Musk

BAY HOUSE AROMATICSø̸fcd76

Base Products: Bubble Bath, Dispersing Bath Oil, Shower Gel

BODY BEAUTIFULø̸

Almond & Coconut Bath Milk, Apricot Peaches & Cream Bath Oil, Rose Petal & Cream Bath Oil; *Bath Milk:* Melon & Apricot; *Foaming Bath:* Dewberry, Ginseng & Evening Primrose, Jasmine, Melon & Musk, Peach, Seaweed & Aloe Vera, Tropical Wilderness, White Musk; *Foam Baths:* Blackcurrant & Patchouli, Camomile & Peach, Juniper Berry & Ylang Ylang, Mint & Ocean Breeze, Orange Blossom, Pineapple & Mandarin, Raspberry & Cherry; *Men's:* Cologne & Peppermint Shower Gel, Sage & Pine Foaming Bath; *Shower Gel:* Dewberry, Geranium & Apple, Ginseng & Evening Primrose, Jasmine, Peach, White Musk

BODY CENTREø̸fcd84

Aromatherapy Bath Oils: Muscular, Refreshing, Relaxing; *Shower Gels:* Dewberry, Sage, Strawberry, Tropical, White Musk; *Bubble Baths:* Apple, Dewberry, Peach, Pineapple, White Musk

BODYLINEø̸fcd83

Aromatherapy Bath Soak, Evening Primrose Bath Essence, Sea Tempest Bath Fizzler, Silvan Fayre Bath Gel; *Aromatherapy Bath Fizzers:* Great Balls of Fire, Lets Get Fizzy Cool, Stress Buster, Think Plink; *Bath Oil:* Lavender Cream, Mandarin Orange, Rose & Almond; *Bubble Bath:* Banana & Brazil Nut, Chocs Away, Coconut, Coming Up Roses, Dewberry, Mango, Plan For All Seasons, Tea Tree, Turkish Dee, White Musk; *Foam Bath:* Apple & Gooseberry, Grapefruit & Lemon, Magnolia, Peach & Apricot, Raspberry & Strawberry; *Fruit Bath Fizzers:* Blueberry Pie, Bramley Apple, Fruit Choctail, Grapefruit Crush; *Shower Gel:* Aloe Vera, Apple & Gooseberry, Dewberry, Grapefruit, Grapefruit & Lemon, Magnolia Shower Gel, Mango & Kiwi Fruit, Peach & Apricot, Raspberry & Strawberry, Sea Foam Bath & Seaweed, Tranquillitea Shower Gel, Tutti Frutti; *Shower Power Body Shampoo:* Herbal, Strawberry Sundae

BODYTREATS√ø̸§fcd76

Bath Oils

TOILETRIES & COSMETICS

BONITA√ø§†fcd80

Floating Bath Oils: Bergamot & Peppermint, Lavender, Pine

BRONNLEY△

Bath Cubes, Crystals: Blue Poppy, Camellia, Daffodil, English Fern, Pink Bouquet, White Iris; *Bath Gelee:* Saponaria, Shambrilla; *Bath Milk:* Saponaria, Shambrilla; *Shower Gel:* Blue Poppy, Camilla, Daffodil, English Fern, Pink Bouquet, Saponaria, Shambrilla, White Iris

CAMILLA HEPPERø△

Fruity Bubble Bath, Lemon Verbena Body Shampoo/Shower Gel; *Bath Oil:* Herbal Body/Bath, Lemon Mint, Marigold; *Cocktail Shower Shaker:* 1,2,3; *Foam Bath:* Avocado, Caribbean, Orange Blossom; *Bath & Shower Gel:* Jasmin, Rose, Seaweed; *Body Shampoo:* Lavender, White Musk

CARABAY√ø

Seaweed Bath

CO-OPfcd85

Foam Bath: Avocado & Apple, Clover Moisturising, Cologne, Dewberry, Geranium Environment Care, Lemon Environment Care, Magnolia Moisturising, Peach & Apricot, Water Melon & Passion Fruit, Wild Herb; *Foaming Bath Oil:* Chestnut & Linden Balm, Mallow & Meadowsweet, Willow & Watermint Foaming; *Moisturising Creme Bath:* Honeysuckle, Jour, Matin, Nuit, White Lily, Wild Rose; *Shower Creme:* Avocado & Apple, Peach & Apricot, Watermelon & Passion Fruit; *Shower Gel:* Cologne, Corundum, Magnolia, Malachite, Wild Herb

COSMETIC HOUSEø

13 Rabbit Bubble Bath, Blue Skys Bubble Bath, Cosmetic Cafe Bath Oil, Crush Shower Gel, Fizzing Bath Salts, Fragrant Musketeer, Sibersave Bath Foam

CREIGHTONSø△fcd76

Apple Bath & Shower: Bath Gel, Bath Seeds, Shower Gel; *Apricot Care:* Bath Oil, Foaming Bath Gel; *Dewberry Bath & Shower:* Bath Gel, Bath Seeds, Shower Gel; *Foaming Bath Seeds:* Honeysuckle, Lavender, Wild Rose; *Ocean Harvest:* Creme Foam Bath; *Peach Bath & Shower:* Bath Gel, Bath Seeds, Shower Gel; *Strawberry Bath & Shower:* Bath Gel, Bath Seeds, Shower Gel

CULPEPERøfcd76

Herb Gold Pine Needle Milk, Lemon Verbena Essence, Mustard Bath, Seaweed Bath; *Bath Elixir:* Cold Weather, Elizabethan, Jasmine, Lavender, Rose Geranium, Sandalwood, Stephanotis, Sweet Violet; *Bath Salts:* Black Forest Pine, Cold Weather, Elizabethan, Jasmine, Lavender, Lemon Verbena, Rose Geranium, Sandalwood, Stephanotis, Sweet Violet

DOLMA√ø§†fcd76

Aromatic Body Shampoos: Antiseptic & Antiviral, Deep Relaxing, Invigorating, Relaxing, Relaxing & Refreshing, Stimulating

EAST OF EDEN√fcd85

Bath Soaks, Foaming Baths

ESSENTIALLY YOURS√ø△fcd76

Bath Concentrate, Foaming Bath: Crystel,

Reviver, Senses, Stress, Tenderness

FAITHø†fcd84

Foam Bath: Essential Blend, Seaweed

FARROW & HUMPHRIES√øfcd76

Bali: Bath & Shower Cream, Powdered Bath Milk, Sea Salts For The Bath; *British Empire:* Bath & Shower Gel; *Natural Extracts:* Bath & Shower Gel, Bath Seeds, Moisturising Bath Oil, Moisturising Cream Bath, Shower Gelée

FINDERS INTERNATIONALø

Dead Sea Magik Bath Salts

FLEUR AROMATHERAPY√ø™∆

Bath Oils: Invigorating/Toning, Relaxing/ Refreshing, Reviving/Uplifting, Soothing/ Sensual, Warming/Cleansing

GREEN THINGSø†∆fcd76

Bath & Shower Gel: Evening Primrose, Mandarin & Vitamin E; *Bath Oil:* Aromatic Foaming, Geranium & Orange Refreshing, Rosewood & Ylang Ylang Relaxing

G R LANEø

Tiki: Meadowsweet & Lime Blossom Foaming Bath Oil

HAMILTON'S OF CANTERBURY√ø∆

Body Conditioning Wash; *Bath Soak:* Anti Stress Calming & Relaxing, Aromatic Active Athletic, Body Firming, Stimulating Refreshing & Invigorating

HOLLAND & BARRETT

Nature's Garden Aromatherapy Refreshing Bath Oil; *Nature's Garden Aromatherapy Bath Foam, Bath Oils, Bath Salts:* Relaxing, Revitalising, Sensual; *Nature's Garden Bath Essence:* Orange/ Ginger, Passion/Babassu, Water Melon/ Kiwi; *Nature's Garden Creme Bath:* Bilboloba/Jojoba, Coconut/Mallow, Grapefruit/Yusu, Strawberry/Kukui; *Nature's Garden Shower Gel:* Banana, Lemon/ Lime, Mango/Papaya, Pink Grapefruit

HOLLYTREESø∆fcd76

Bubble Bath/Shower Gel

HONESTY√ø§fcd76

Essential: Clary Sage Sandalwood & Frankincense Bath Oil, Orange Geranium & Lavender Foam Bath; *Fruit:* Apple & Sandalwood Shower & Bath Gel, Pineapple Coconut & Mango Foam Bath, Strawberry & Papaya Shower & Bath Gel

HYMOSA√øfcd76

Bath Essence

JEROME RUSSELL√øfcd76

Herbal Bath & Shower Gel, Lemon & Ginseng Shower Gel, Lemongrass & Juniper Invigorating Foaming Bath Oil, Tea Tree Peppermint & Aloe Vera Shower & Bath Gel

KENT COSMETICS√ø

Shower Gelées

KHEPHRA√ø†§

Herbal Foam Baths

KITTYWAKE PERFUMES√ø†§

Bath Oils

KOBASHI√ø∆fcd76

Foam Bath: Citrus, Relaxing

TOILETRIES & COSMETICS

LITTLE GREEN SHOP√øfcd85

Foam Bath: Strawberry, Tropical; *Body Shampoo:* Apple & Orange, Peach & Strawberry

MARTHA HILLø∆fcd79

Essence of Rose Body & Hair Shampoo, Mountain Herb Shower Gel; *Bath Oil:* Coconut Cream, Lavender, Mountain Herb, Rosemary, Seaweed & Herb; *For Men:* Dual Shampoo & Shower Gel, Mountain Herb Shower Gel, Refresh Bath Oil, Relax Bath Oil

MICHELINE ARCIERø

Bath Oils: Anti-Stress, Aromatic, Elan Vital, Harmony, Kypros, Lavender, Rosemary, Sylvestre

MONTAGNE JEUNESSEø∆fcd76

Bath: Evening Primrose Oil, Jasmin Aromatherapy Oil, Orchid Oil, Orange Spice, Seaweed & Mineral, Wild Rose; *Shower:* Lotus Blossom Body, Orange Spice, Seaweed & Mineral, Ylang Ylang

NAPIERS√ø§fcd76

Bath Oil: Bright & Early, Sleepytime

NATURE'S BODYCARE√øfcd76

Bath Crystals: Elegant, Lulie, Pastel Musk, Sharelle; *Bath Oils:* Creamy Peach, Sofisticat; *Foam Baths:* Aloe, Oriental Musk, Wild Dewberry, Ylang Ylang

NATURE'S NATURALS√ø§fcd76

Aloe: Cleansing Bath, Moisture Bath

NEAL'S YARD REMEDIESø

Bath Oils: Aromatic Foaming, Base Dispersing, Exotic, Geranium & Orange, Seaweed & Arnica, Soothing, Stimulating, Wheatgerm; *Bath Salts:* Citrus, Geranium, Lavender; *Shower Gels:* Geranium & Orange, Rosemary & Elderflower

NORFOLK LAVENDERøfcd84

Bath Cubes, Bath Gels, Bath Seeds, Shower Gels: all

ORGANIC PRODUCT COøø∆fcd76

Aromatic Foaming Bath, Coconut Bath Milk, Rose Foaming Bath Oil, Strawberry Bath Essence; *Shower Gels:* Apple, Cherry, Evening Primrose

PURE PLANT√ø∆fcd76

Shower Creme

SHANTI√ø§

Aromatic Bath Oil

SUPERDRUGfcd87

Bath Salts: Cologne, Green Fjord, Peach Delight, Pink Blossom; *Tropical Fruits Creme Bath:* Banana & Brazil Nut, Cherry & Bilberry, Dewberry & Yuzu, Lime & Paw Paw, Mango & Guava, Passionfruit & Coconut; *Foam Bath:* Caribbean Shores, Country Garden, English Orchard, Mediterranean Grove; *Foaming Bath Oil:* Clover, Wild Rose; *Tropical Fruits Bath Blitzer:* Blackcurrant, Orange, Strawberry; *Tropical Fruits Bath Shake:* Peach Melba, Strawberry Delight; *Tropical Fruits Bath Cocktail:* Beachcomber, Caribbean Cocktail, Kir Royale, Pina Colada; *Tropical Fruits Shake'n'Soak:* Caribbean Cocktail, Citrus Surprise; *Tropical Fruits Shower Gel:* Banana & Brazil Nut, Dewberry & Yuzu, Lime & Paw Paw, Mango & Guava, Passionfruit & Coconut, Strawberry & Lychee; *Shower Creme:* Caribbean Shores, Country Garden, English Orchard, Mediterranean Grove, Wild Rose & Clover; *Shower Gel:* For Men, Mild & Gentle, Moisturising, Sports

TISSERAND√øfcd80

Bath Oils; *Bath Soaks:* Exotic, Relaxing, Revitalising, Sensual; *Shower Gels:* Exotic, Stimulating, Vitalising

TREFRIW WELLS SPA√øfcd84

Bath Soak

VERDEfcd76

Bath Cream: Rosewood Foaming, Sweet Orange & Geranium Foaming; *Bath Treatment Milk:* Calendula, Dreamtime, Hangover Relief, High Anxiety, Himalayan Sunrise, Indian Summer, Mobility, Relaxing, Toning, Tranquility, Vitality; *Shower Gel:* Celestial, Spring

WELEDAøfcd85

Bath Milk: Citrus, Lavender, Rosemary

YARDLEY

Lavender Body Scrub; *Bath Creme, Foam Bath, Shower Gel:* all

YOUR BODY√ø∆fcd84

Apricot Bath Oil, Aromatherapy Foam Bath, Fruity Shower Bath Gel, Sage Shower Bath Gel, Seaweed Foam Bath; *Aromatherapy Shower Bath Gels:* Lavender & Bergamot, Orange & Lemon, Rosemary & Cedarwood; *Dewberry:* Bubble Bath, Shower Bath Gel; *White Musk:* Bubble Bath, Shower Bath Gel

BRUSHES — PERSONAL USE

FLEUR AROMATHERAPY√ø™∆

Skin Brush

LARKHALL GREEN FARMø

Skin Brush

SHU UEMURAø

Range of nylon make-up brushes

CONDITIONERS & HAIR CARE

AMYRIS√øfcd76

Conditioner: Apple & Avocado, Base, Jojoba & Peach

ARBONNE√ø

Conditioner

AUSTRIAN MOOR√ø

Moor Life Hair Tonic

BARRY Mø∆fcd82

Aromatherapy Invigorating Scalp Massage Oil

BAY HOUSE AROMATICSøfcd76

Base Product: Hair Conditioner

BEAUTY WITHOUT CRUELTYø†fcd76

Henna Hair Conditioner

BERMARø

Hair Tonic

TOILETRIES & COSMETICS

BIOCEUTICALS√ø

Bonazi Lotion

BIORGANICS√øΔfcd76

Conditioners: Biogel, Biomin, Natural Body, Profile, Rebuild, Remoist, Right Now

BLACKMORESøfcd85

Apricot & Jojoba Hot Oil Treatment, Chamomile Conditioner, Protein Hair Spa

BODY BEAUTIFULø

Conditioners: Almond & Coconut, Dewberry, Jasmine, Mint & Ocean Breeze, Nettle & Geranium, Peach, Pineapple & Mandarin, Seaweed & Aloe Vera, Tropical Wilderness, White Musk; *Men's:* Cologne & Peppermint Conditioner

BODY CENTREøfcd84

Conditioners: Chamomile, Red Apple & Coconut

BODYLINEøfcd83

Conditioners: Aloe Vera, Banana & Brazil Nut, Coconut, Comfrey & Clover, Dewberry, Ginger & Beer Conditioner, Juniper Berry, Mens, White Musk; *Hair Treatment:* Banana & Brazil Nut, Mango & Kiwi

BOREAL!Søfcd76

Conditioners: all

CAMILLA HEPPERøΔ

Avocado Treatment Wax, Hair Loss Treatment Oil; *Conditioners:* Herbal Protein, Natural Orange, Raspberry, Rosemary Scalp, Seaweed

CO-OPfcd85

Henna & Arnica Intensive Treatment Wax; *Conditioners:* Frequent Wash, Gentle Environment Care, Permed Hair for Dry/Damaged, Styling System, Water Melon & Passion Fruit, Yarrow & Burdock Frequent Use

CREIGHTONSøΔfcd76

Conditioners: Lime Blossom & Birch, Orange Flower & Wheatgerm

CRIMPERS√øΔfcd76

Conditioner Dry/Damaged Hair, Intensive Conditioning Treatment

CULPEPERøfcd76

Herbal Hair: Conditioner, Lotion; *Herb Rinse For Hair:* Dark, Fair

DANIEL FIELD√ø

Body Builder Detangler Conditioner, Essential Plant Hair Conditioner, First Aid Conditioner, First Aid Pure Moisture Droplets, Mineral Hair Repair Mask, Plant Remoisturising Treatment Light Weight, Split End Care Conditioner, Split End Repair Droplets

DOLMA√ø§†fcd76

Aromatherapy Hair Treatment Oil, Nettle & Marigold Hair Lotion; *Hair Conditioners:* Cedarwood & Cypress, Lavender & Jojoba, Rosemary & Comfrey

FAITHø†fcd84

Conditioners: Aloe Vera, Jojoba, Rosemary, Seaweed

EBONY & IVORY RANGE OF HEALTH AND BEAUTY PRODUCTS

Conditioners, hair & body shampoos, lip balms, foam baths, facial sprays & scrubs, shower gels, deodorants, massage oils, cleansers, bath milks & oils, toners, creams & lotions, make-up removers, Men's, Baby's and Children's ranges, after sun, gift baskets . . .

For mail order catalogue telephone 0191 587 1581.

Body Beautiful Products Ltd, Unit 1A, Black Hall Colliery, Blackhall, Hartlepool, Cleveland TS27 4XX.

Not Tested on Animals

DOLMA
Vegan Perfumes, Toiletries and Aqueous Aromatics

Dolma offer an exclusive range of high quality original vegan perfumes and toiletries based on pure essential oils, herbal extracts, floral waters and vegetable oils. All products are carefully blended from safe, long established vegan ingredients and a fixed cut-off date of 1976 applies.

The range includes perfumes, aromatic shampoos for the body, hair, face and feet, lip salves, cleansers, toners, moisturisers, facial scrubs and masks, aromatherapy facial and massage oils, hair treatments and conditioners, shaving fluid, aftershave balm, pre-shave, hand cream and soaps etc.

Send SAE for free brochure and mail order price list or £11.50 for set of eight trial size perfumes to:

DOLMA, 19 ROYCE AVENUE, HUCKNALL, NOTTINGHAM NG15 6FU
Trade enquiries welcome. Agents required — excellent earning potential.

A member of the Cosmetics Industry Coalition For Animal Welfare

TOILETRIES & COSMETICS

FANTÔME√øfcd76

Meadow Herb Conditioner

FINDERS INTERNATIONALø

Dead Sea Magik Scalp Mud

HARTWOOD AROMATICSøfcd76

Lotus Hair Scalp & Tonic; *Lotus Oils:* Hair Deep Conditioning, Special Scalp Treatment, Special Very Dry & Damaged

HERBAL FORCE√ø†

Herbal Glo: Dandruff & Dry, Dry/Damaged, Grey/White Hair, Normal To Oily, Permed/Coloured Treated Hair, Sensitive Hair & Scalp, Thin/Fine Hair; *Herbal Glo Scalp Formula:* For Thinning Hair, For Thinning Hair For Women

HOLLAND & BARRETT

Nature's Garden Aromatherapy Stimulating Scalp Oil; *Nature's Garden Conditioner:* Apple/Aloe Vera, Banana/ Vitamin E

HONESTY√ø§fcd76

Fruit Conditioners: Apple & Avocado, Jojoba & Peach

HOUSE OF MISTRYø

Aloe Vera Jojoba Conditioner, Extract of Rosemary *w* Jojoba Oil Hair Tonic, Ginseng Herbal Conditioner

HYMOSA√øfcd76

Conditioner

JEROME RUSSELL√øfcd76

Conditioners: Banana, Camomile & Aloe Vera, Protein Enriched, Tea Tree Peppermint & Aloe Vera

KOBASHI√ø∆fcd76

Mellow Conditioners: Henna, Jojoba, Wheatgerm

G R LANEø

Tiki: Conditioner

L'ANZA√

Detangler, Hair Polish, Leave-In Conditioner, Leave-In Protector, Moisture Treatment, Power Treatment, Reconstructor, Revitaliser

LITTLE GREEN SHOP√øfcd85

Conditioner: Aloe Vera, Herbal, Sweet Orange

MAHARISHI AYUR-VEDø

Flaky Scalp Warm Oil Treatment; *Hair Conditioners:* Kapha, Pitta, Vata

MARTHA HILLø∆fcd79

Hair Treatment Cream, Seaweed & Herb Hair Tonic; *Conditioner:* Seaweed & Rosemary, Seaweed & Nettle, Seaweed & Sage; *For Men:* Herbal Hair Tonic

MICHELINE ARCIERø

Hair Oil

MONTAGNE JEUNESSEø∆fcd76

Chamomile & Jojoba, Henna & Kukui, Shea Nut, Vitamin E

NAPIERS√ø§fcd76

Tonic Shampoo; *Hair Lotion:* Eucalyptus, Rosemary; *Hair Oil:* Rosemary & Cedarwood

NATURE'S BODYCARE√øfcd76

Hot Air Protection; *Conditioners:* Coconut, Melissa

NEAL'S YARD REMEDIESø

Rosemary & Cedarwood Hair Treatment

NIRVANAøΔfcd76

Aloe Almond & Walnut, Camomile, Vanilla & Cocoa Butter Wax; *Shine Spray:* Camomile, Nettle & Jasmin

PAUL MITCHELL√

Awapuhi Moisture Mist, Hair Repair Treatment, Super Charged Conditioner, The Conditioner, The Detangler; *Creatives Herbal:* Finishing Rinse Conditioner, Gloss

PURE PLANT√øΔfcd76

Herbal Conditioner

SHANTI√ø§

Hair Tonic, Hair Oil

SUPERDRUGfcd87

Coconut Oil Conditioner, Pro-Vit Wash Plus Shampoo & Conditioner (Frequent Use), Wheatgerm and Peach Conditioner; *Family Conditioners:* Dry Hair, Extra Body, Frequent Use, Normal/Greasy Hair

TERESA MUNRO AROMATHERAPYøΔfcd76

Thursday Plantation Tea Tree Conditioner

TISSERAND√øfcd80

Scalp Oil Intensive Pre-Wash Treatment; *Conditioners:* Sandalwood & Myrrh, Yarrow & Rose

VERDEfcd76

Coconut & Rosemary Hair Repair, Phyto Hair Conditioner

WELEDAøfcd85

Rosemary Hair Lotion

WORLDS END TRADING CO√ø§fcd76

Henne Henna Products

YOUR BODY√øΔfcd84

Chamomile, Marigold, Red Apple, Rosemary, Seaweed

DEODORANTS & ANTI-PERSPIRANTS

AMYRIS√øfcd76

'American' Deodorant Stone, Rollette

ANIMAL AID√ø§fcd76

Anti-perspirant Deodorant

BARRY MøΔfcd82

Dewberry Roll on, White Musk Roll On, White Musk Stick; *Just For Men:* Deodorant Stick

BEAUTY WITHOUT CRUELTYø†fcd76

Roll-On, Anti-Perspirant Deodorant: Beau, Madonna Lilly, Yolanda

BLACKMORESøfcd85

Floral Fresh, Herbal Fresh

BODY BEAUTIFULø

Men's Cologne & Peppermint Deodorant; *Deodorant & Anti-Perspirant:* Dewberry,

TOILETRIES & COSMETICS

White Musk

BODY CENTREøfcd84

Roll On Anti-Perspirant Deodorant

BODYLINEøfcd83

Magnolia, Mens

CO-OPfcd85

Active System Roll On Anti-Perspirant Deodorant, Corundum Anti-Perspirant Deodorant, Corundum Roll On Deodorant, Soft Pink Roll On Deodorant; *Anti-Perspirant Deodorant:* Active System, Fragrance Free

CAMILLA HEPPERøΔ

Watercress Deodorant

CREIGHTONSøΔfcd76

Deodorant Roll-on, Ocean Harvest Deodorant

GREEN THINGSø†Δfcd76

Deodorant, Tea Tree & Juniper Deodorant For Men

HOLLAND & BARRETT

Roll On Deodorant: Aloe Vera, Fragrance Free

HOLLYTREESøΔfcd76

Deodorant

MARTHA HILLøΔfcd79

Herbal Deodorant; *For Men:* Herbal Deodorant

PURE PLANT√øΔfcd76

Roll on Antiperspirant/Deodorants: Ladies, Men, Peaches & Creme

QUEEN COSMETICSø

Top To Toe Deodorant Powder

SUPERDRUGfcd87

Aerosol Anti-Perspirant Deodorants, Roll-On Anti-Perspirant Deodorants: all

TERESA MUNRO AROMATHERAPYøΔfcd76

Thursday Plantation Tea Tree Deodorant

TREFRIW WELLS SPA√øfcd84

Body Spray

VERDEfcd76

Lemon Zest Body Deodorant

WELEDAøfcd85

Deodorant: Citrus, Herbal

YARDLEY

Deodorant Sprays, Roll On Anti-Perspirant Deodorant: all

YOUR BODY√øΔfcd84

Deodorant: Dewberry, For Men, For the Body, White Musk

ESSENTIAL & MASSAGE OILS

AMYRIS√øfcd76

Marigold Infusion, Rose Otto; *5% Blended Absolutes & Exotics, Absolutes, Carrier Oils, Essential Oils, Pre-Blended Lotions, Pre-Blended Massage Oils, Special Blend Oils:* all

BARRY MøΔfcd82

Aromatherapy Massage Oils: Facial, Relaxing, Sensual, Sports

BAY HOUSE AROMATICSøfcd76

White Lotion Base; *Blended Aromatherapy Oils, Blended Essential Oils For Your Zodiac Sign, Essential Oils, Vegetable Carrier Oils:* all

BIOCEUTICALS√ø

Base Oils

BODY BEAUTIFULø

Aromatherapy Oils: all; *Massage Oils:* Melon & Musk, White Musk

BODY CENTREøfcd84

Aromatherapy Facial Oils: Dry Skin, Normal Skin, Oily Skin, Sensitive Skin; *Essential Oils, Single Blend Aromatherapy Oils:* all

BODYLINEøfcd83

Aromatherapy Gift Set; *Absolutes, Carrier Oils, Essential Oils:* all; *Massage Oils:* Body, Invigorating, Relaxing

BODYTREATS√ø§fcd76

Oils: Body Massage, Organic Essential, Vegetable Carrier

BONITA√ø§†fcd80

Essential Oils

BOREALISøfcd76

Aromatherapy Oils: all

CAMILLA HEPPERøΔ

Essential Oils, Natural Oils: all

COSMETIC HOUSEø

Chocolate Aromatherapist Massage Oil, Therapy Massage Bar

CULPEPERøfcd76

Aromatherapy Massage Oils: Comforting, Neck & Shoulders, Normalising, Rejuvenating, Relaxing, Sexy, Uplifting; *Cosmetic Nut Oils, Essential Plant Oils:* all

DOLMA√ø§†fcd76

Oils: Aromatherapy Facial, Aromatic Massage

ESSENTIALLY CELTICøΔfcd76

Base Oils, Essential Oils, Massage Blends: all

ESSENTIAL OIL COø

Absolute Oils, Cold Pressed Carrier Oils, Pure Essential Oils: all

ESSENTIALLY YOURS√øΔfcd76

Oils: Base, Essential Body, Pure Essential (including Rare, Essential, Absolutes)

FAITHø†Δfcd84

Essential Body Oil

FANTÔME√øfcd76

Oils: Aromatherapy Carrier, Body Massage

FARROW & HUMPHRIES√øfcd76

Natural Extracts Body Oil

FLEUR AROMATHERAPY√ø™Δ

Aroma Rocks, Tinctures; *Oils:* Carrier,

TOILETRIES & COSMETICS

Essential, Massage

GREEN THINGSø†Δfcd76

Aromatic Body Massage Oils, Carrier Oils, Pure Essential Oils: all

HAMILTONS OF CANTERBURY√øΔ

Massage Lotions, Massage Oils

HARTWOOD AROMATICSøfcd76

Oils: Absolutes, Aromatherapy, Cold Pressed Vegetable, Essential, Vegetable

HERMITAGE OILSø

Essential Oils: all

HOLLAND & BARRETT

Pure Essential Oils: all; *Nature's Garden:* Wheatgerm & Jojoba Massage Oil; *Nature's Garden Aromatherapy Base Oils:* Body Massage, Face Massage, Sweet Almond, Wheatgerm; *Nature's Garden Aromatherapy Diluted Essential Oil:* Jasmine, Neroli, Rose Otto; *Nature's Garden Aromatherapy Massage Oil:* Refreshing, Relaxing, Sensuous

HOUSE OF MISTRYø

Oils: 100% Pure Tea Tree, Almond, Vitamin E, Evening Primrose, Neem, Wheat Germ

ID AROMATICSø

Base Oils, Essential Oils: all

KITTYWAKE PERFUMES√ø†§

Essential Oils for Aromatherapy

KOBASHI√øΔfcd76

Oils: Essential, Massage

LITTLE GREEN SHOP√øfcd85

Body Oils

MAHARISHI AYUR-VEDø

Aromatherapy Oils: all

MARTHA HILLøΔfcd79

Body Oils: Invigorating, Relaxing, Revitalising, Seaweed & Orange Body; *For Men:* Orange & Sandalwood Massage Oil

MICHELINE ARCIERø

Pure Essential Oils: all

MONTAGNE JEUNESSEøΔfcd76

Body Oils: Apricot, Evening Primrose, Lotus Blossom Massage

NAPIERS√ø§fcd76

Hot Oil Treatment; *Oils:* Essential, Massage

NATURE'S BODYCARE√øfcd76

Aromatherapy Oils

NEAL'S YARD REMEDIESø

Massage Oils: Aromatic, Base, Geranium, Sandalwood; *Oils:* Almond, Apricot Kernel, Avocado, Evening Primrose, Ginger & Juniper Warming, Grapeseed, Hazelnut, Jasmine Nourishing, Jojoba

NELSON & RUSSELLø

Carrier Oil, Rosewater; *All Aromatherapy Oils:* Aroma Mask, Essential, Organic, Premixed

NEW HORIZON AROMATICSøfcd76

Cold Pressed Oils, Pure Essential Oils: all

NORFOLK LAVENDERøfcd84

Aromatherapy Oils: all

ORGANIC PRODUCT COøΔfcd76

Massage Oils: Lavender & Geranium, Musk & Apple

TERESA MUNRO AROMATHERAPYøΔfcd76

Massage Cream; *Base Carrier Oils, Blended Oils, Essential Oil Distillates/Aromatic Waters, Essential Oils, Massage Oils:* all

TISSERAND√øfcd80

Lavender Gel, Massage Lotions; *Mini Packs:* Energise, Essential Sampler, Romance, Travel Kit; *Oils:* Blended Essential, Massage, Massage Bases, Organic Essential, Pure Essential

VERDEfcd76

All Oils: Blended, Essential Base, Pure Essential Blends, Verde Essential

WELL OILED√ø

Oils: Base, Essential Oils

YOUR BODY√øΔfcd84

Aromatherapy: Body Massage Oil, Gift Sets

EYE PRODUCTS

ARBONNE√ø

Bio Hydria Eye Cream, Gentle Eye Make Up Remover, Lash Colour, Pencil For Eyes, True Colour For Eyes

BARRY MøΔfcd82

Iced Cucumber Eye Gel

BEAUTY WITHOUT CRUELTYø†fcd76

Colour Options Magnetic System, Eye Cream, Eye Make-Up Removing Lotion, Soothing Eye Balm; *Eye Colour Crayons, Eye Definers, Khol Pencils, Loose Eye Shadow Powders, Mascaras, Pressed Powder Eye Shadows:* all

BLACKMORESøfcd85

Angelica Eye Nourish, Cornflower Eye Balm, Elderblossom Eye Make Up Remover

BODY BEAUTIFULø

Elderflower Eye Gel; *Eye Make Up Remover:* Cream, Oil

BODY CENTREøfcd84

Elderflower Eye Gel, Eye Make Up Remover Lotion

BODYLINEøfcd83

Eyebright Eye Gel, Eye Make Up Remover

CAMILLA HEPPERøΔ

Cucumber Eye Gel, Herbal Eye Cream; *Eye Make-Up Remover:* Lotion, Oil

CREIGHTONSøΔfcd76

Eyebright Gelee

DOLLOND & AITCHISON

Contact lens solutions: One 2 One Rapide System Cleaner, One 2 One Rapide Cleaning & Disinfecting Solution, One 2 One Rapide Rinsing & Neutralising Solution

DOLMA√ø§†fcd76

Eye Make Up: Remover, Removing Oil

FAITHø†Δfcd84

Aloe Vera Eye Gel

HOLLAND & BARRETT

Eye Make Up Remover, Nature's Garden Eye Gel Eye Bright

HOUSE OF MISTRYø

Eye Gel

JULIUS ROTHø

Eye Contour Therapy Gel

MARTHA HILLøΔfcd79

Elder Flower Eye Gel, Eye Make-Up Remover, Mascara, Under Eye Cream; *Cream Eye Shadow:* Blue, Bronze, Brown, Gold, Green, Silver; *Powder Eye Shadow:* Amber, Charcoal, Chocolate, Midnight, Olive, Rose

MONTAGNE JEUNESSEøΔfcd76

Eyebright Gel

NAPIERS√ø§fcd76

Eyebright & Vitamin E Eye Cream

NATURE'S BODYCARE√øfcd76

Eye Gels: Formula C2, Fragrance Free

ORGANIC PRODUCT COøΔfcd76

Elderflower Eye Gel, Eye Make-Up Removing Oil

QUEEN COSMETICSø

Eyelash Cream, Mascara; *Kohl Eye Pencils:* Black, Brown, Grey, Light Blue, Light Green, Violet

SAUFLON

Contact lens solutions: Aerosolv, One 2 One Buffered Saline Protein Remover Tablets, Soft Lens Daily Cleaner

STARGAZER√§fcd76

Eye Shadow, Mascara

ULTRA GLOWø

Mascara; *Liner Pencils:* all

VERDEfcd76

Vitamin E & Euphrasia Eye Make Up Remover

YARDLEY

Effective Eye Make Up Remover, Eye Definer Pencil; *Kohl Definer Pencil:* all; *Waterproof Mascara:* all

YOUR BODY√øΔfcd84

Elderflower Eye Gel, Eyebright Eye Make-Up Remover, Wheatgerm Oil Eye Cream

FOOT/LEG CARE

AESOP√ø§

Foot Deodorant Stone

AQUA NATURAL√øfcd76

Simply Smooth Natural Hair Removal System *(sugar wax)*

ARBONNE√ø

Herbal Foot Care

TOILETRIES & COSMETICS

AUSTRIAN MOOR√ø

Moor Life Foot Bath

BARRY Mø∆fcd82

Aromatherapy Foot Massage Oil, Hop & Mistletoe Foot Lotion, Peppermint Foot Gel

BAY HOUSE AROMATICSøfcd76

Peppermint Foot Lotion

BODY BEAUTIFULø

Arnica Knee & Elbow Cream, Lavender Herbal Foot Soak, Peppermint Foot Cream

BODY CENTREøfcd84

Peppermint Foot Lotion

BODYLINEøfcd83

Aromatherapy Foot Lotion, Peppermint & Menthol Foot Lotion, Peppermint Foot Spray

BONITA√ø§†fcd80

Foot Oil

CAMILLA HEPPERø∆

Aloe Vera Foot Lotion

CARABAY√ø

Seaweed Footbath

COSMETIC HOUSEø

Feet Of Clay Foot Mask

CREIGHTONSø∆fcd76

Peppermint Foot Lotion

CULPEPERøfcd76

Aromatherapy Foot Massage Oil, Foot &

Bath Salts

DOLMA√ø§†fcd76

Peppermint Foot Creme; *Aromatic Foot Shampoo:* Peppermint & Tea Tree, Lemongrass & Cypress

FAITHø†∆fcd84

Essential Foot Lotion

GREEN THINGSø†∆fcd76

Aromatic Foot Soak

HOLLAND & BARRETT

Nature's Garden Aromatherapy Refreshing Foot Lotion

JEROME RUSSELL√øfcd76

Tea Tree Peppermint & Aloe Vera Foot: Lotion, Soak, Spray

LITTLE GREEN SHOP√øfcd85

Lemon & Mint Foot Lotion

MARTHA HILLø∆fcd79

Comfrey & Elder Foot Treatment Cream, Foot Refresher, Seaweed & Peppermint, Seaweed Foot Balm, Seaweed Leg Gel

NAPIERS√ø§fcd76

Leg Balm

NATURE'S BODYCARE√øfcd76

Cream Gel For Tired Legs, Foot Cream, Herbal Foot Soak

ORGANIC PRODUCT COø∆fcd76

Herbal Foot Soak, Peppermint Foot Cream

SUPERDRUGfcd87

Tropical Fruits Foot Sprays: Lemon & Mint,

Lime & Papaya, Lime & Quince

TISSERAND√øfcd80

Foot Lotion

YOUR BODY√øΔfcd84

Peppermint Foot: Bath, Lotion, Powder, Spray

VERDEfcd76

Splash & Dash Foot Lotion

HAIR DYES

CAMILLA HEPPERøΔ

Natural Henna Hair Colours: Black, Chestnut Brown, Copper Gold, Natural Auburn

CULPEPERøfcd76

Henna Powders: Indigo Black, Neutral, Persian Red

DANIEL FIELD√ø

Semi-Permanent Plant Remoisturising Colours: Brazil Nut Dark Brown, Chestnut Red Brown, Cinnamon Gold, Hazelnut, Palm Nut Brown, Paprika Red, Saffron Gold, Walnut

JEROME RUSSELL√øfcd76

Cream Peroxide, Fun Colour Hair Sprays, Powder Bleach, Spray In Highlights, Spray On Hair Colour Thickener, Truzone Liquid Peroxide

LA RICHEø

Directions Semi-Permanent Conditioning Hair Dyes: all *(32 colours)*

NAPIERS√ø§fcd76

Henna Powder: Black, Natural, Red

NATURE'S BODYCARE√øfcd76

Natural Hair Colourants: Basic Red, Black Lustre, Brown, Natural

PAUL MITCHELL√

Creatives Color Infusing Shampoos: Chestnut, Ginger, Golden Blonde, Midnight Blue, Primary Red, True Red, Violet, Warm Brown

STARGAZER√§fcd76

Hair Dye

HAIRSPRAYS, GELS ETC

BIORGANICS√øΔfcd76

Stylelock Hairspray

BODY BEAUTIFULø

Cologne & Peppermint Blow Dry Lotion For Men; *Blow Dry:* Mint & Ocean Breeze, Nettle & Geranium

BODYLINEøfcd83

Tick Up Hairspray; *Hair Gels:* Curl Up, Mens

CAMILLA HEPPERøΔ

Jojoba Hair Gel

CO-OPfcd85

Styling System Mousse Mega; *Gels:* Hair Styling, Permed Hair Curling, Sheer Silk Sculpting, Styling System Spray Mega; *Hair Styling Mousse:* Maximum Hold, Natural Hold; *Pump action hairsprays:* all

TOILETRIES & COSMETICS

CRIMPERS√ø∆fcd76

Firm Hold Hairspray

DANIEL FIELD√ø

Anti Frizz Protective Hair Spray, Body Builder, Cactus Styling Gel Sap, Root Builder, Curl Hold It And Shine Spray, Styling Wax Concentrate

L'ANZA√

Bodifying Foam, Dramatic F/X, Finishing Freeze, Gel Mist, Hairspray, Mega Gel, Shine Gel, Special F/X, Spray Gel, Styling Foam, Styling Spritz

MACSILø

Just Jel: Firm Hold, Wet Look

MARTHA HILLø∆fcd79

Seaweed Styling Gel; *For Men:* Seaweed Hair Gel

NATURE'S BODYCARE√øfcd76

Hair Stylers: Coconut, Mandarin

NIRVANAø∆fcd76

Cinnamon Gold

PAUL MITCHELL√

Fast Drying Sculpting Spray, Foaming Pommade, Freeze & Shine Super Spray, Hair Sculpting Lotion, Sculpting Foam, Seal & Shine, Soft Sculpting Spray Gel, Soft Spray, Super Clean Extra Spray, Super Clean Sculpting Gel, Super Sculpt Styling Glaze, Volumniser Spray

SUPERDRUGfcd87

Hair Gel, Hair Thickener, Setting Lotion, Standard Hair Spray, Styling Mousse

YARDLEY†

Solid Brilliantine

HAND CARE

AMYRIS√øfcd76

Hand Cream *w* Comfrey

ARBONNE√ø

Hand Cream

BARRY Mø∆fcd82

Hawthorn Hand Creme; *Hand & Body Lotions:* Dewberry, Evening Primrose, Flirt, Perfect Peach, Strawberry, White Musk

BAY HOUSE AROMATICSøfcd76

Blended Hand & Body Lotions: Lemon & Rose, Orange Blossom & Marigold, Tea Tree & Lavender

BEAUTY WITHOUT CRUELTYø†fcd76

Hand & Body Lotion

BIO-D√ø™fcd83

'Working Hands' Skin Repair Cream

BLACKMORESø∆fcd83

Calendula Hand Creme

BODY BEAUTIFULø

Rose Petal & Glycerine Hand Lotion

BODY CENTREøfcd84

Shea Butter Hand Cream; *Hand & Body Lotion:* Aloe Vera, Jojoba, Marigold, Vitamin E, White Musk

BODYLINEøfcd83

Lemon Peel Hand Lotion; *Hand & Body Lotion:* California Dreaming, Cocoa Butter; *Hand Cream:* Coconut, Verbene & Glycerine

BOREALISøfcd76

Herbal Hand Cream *w* Cocoa Butter

BRONNLEY∆

Hand Cream: Blue Poppy, Camellia, Daffodil, English Fern, Pink Bouquet, White Iris; *Hand & Nail Cream:* Saponaria, Shambrilla

CAMILLA HEPPERø∆

Evening Primrose Hand Cream

CO-OPfcd85

Peach & Apricot Hand & Body Lotion

CREIGHTONSø∆fcd76

Cocoa Butter Hand & Body Lotion; *Apricot Care:* Hand & Body Lotion; *Comfrey Care:* Mayblossom & Comfrey Hand & Body Lotion; *Evening Primrose Skin Care:* Hand & Body Lotion

CULPEPERøfcd76

Handcream: Marigold, Travel Pack

DEB

Hand Cleansing Gels for Industrial Use: Deb Lime, Deb Natural, Swafega, Swafega Orange, Tufanega; *Hand Cleansing Wipes for Industrial Use:* Swarfega Red Box Workshop Wipes

DELTA

Hand Care: Care, Care Natural, Encore

DOLMA√ø§†fcd76

Aloe Vera Hand & Body Lotion, Lemongrass Hand Cream

EAST OF EDEN√fcd85

Hand & Body Creams, Hand Lotion

FANTÔME√øfcd76

Special Hand Treatment

FARROW & HUMPHRIES√øfcd76

Natural Extracts: Enriched Hand Cream, Hand & Body Lotion

FINDERS INTERNATIONALø

Dead Sea Magik Hand Cream

GREEN THINGSø†fcd76

Rosewood & Ylang Ylang Hand Cleansing Gel; *For Gardeners:* Tea Tree & Lemon Hand Cleansing Gel

HAMILTON'S OF CANTERBURY√ø∆

Safe Hands Environmental Protection Cream *(for gardeners, builders, mechanics, etc)*

HARTWOOD AROMATICSøfcd76

Lotus Hand Creams: Barrier, Dry, Luxurious

HOLLAND & BARRETT

Sun Flower Petal Hand Cream

HONESTY√ø§fcd76

Hand Cream *w* Comfrey, Lemon Sandalwood & Geranium Hand & Body Lotion, Peach & Almond Hand & Body Lotion

TOILETRIES & COSMETICS

KENT COSMETICS√ø

Hand & Nail Lotion

LITTLE GREEN SHOP√øfcd85

Cocoa Butter Hand & Body Lotion, Rich Hand Cream

MARTHA HILLøΔfcd79

Hand Creams: Gardeners, Herbal

MICHELINE ARCIERø

Hand & Nail Oil

MONTAGNE JEUNESSEøΔfcd76

Apricot & Almond, Coconut & Rose, Evening Primrose Oil

NATURE'S BODYCARE√øfcd76

Peach & Apricot Hand Cream; *Hand & Body Lotions:* Aloe, Avocado & Cucumber, Evening Primrose, Fragrance Free, Wild Dewberry

NATURE'S NATURALS√ø§fcd76

Aloe Hand & Body Lotion

NORFOLK LAVENDERøfcd84

Rose & Lavender Hand Cream

ORGANIC PRODUCT COøΔfcd76

Peach Hand Cream, Rose & Glycerine Hand Lotion

PAUL MITCHELL√

Dejoria Hand & Body Lotion

QUEEN COSMETICSø

Hand Lotion

SUPERDRUGfcd87

Hand and Body Lotions: Aloe Vera Cream, Aloe Vera Lotion, Cocoa Butter Cream, Cocoa Butter Lotion, Original Dry Skin Lotion, Peach, Wild Rose & Clover

TERESA MUNRO AROMATHERAPYøΔfcd76

Thursday Plantation Tea Tree Hand/Body Lotion

TISSERAND√øfcd80

Hand & Nail Cream

VERDEfcd76

Italian Lemon Hand Cream

YOUR BODY√øΔfcd84

Aromatherapy Hand & Body Lotion, Marigold Hand Lotion

LIP PRODUCTS

AMYRIS√øfcd76

Unscented Lip Balm

ARBONNE√ø

Pencil For Lips, Sheer Shine, True Colour For Lips

BEAUTY WITHOUT CRUELTYø†fcd76

Protective Lip Balm; *Lip Crayons, Lipliners, Lipsticks:* all

BODY BEAUTIFULø

Lip Balms: Apricot & Peach, Coconut, Banana, Passion Fruit & Cherry, Peach, Pineapple & Mandarin, Rich Plum, Straw-

TOILETRIES & COSMETICS

berry & Cream, Wild Dewberry

BODY CENTREøfcd84

Lip Balms: Morello Cherry, Passion Fruit, Strawberry

CAMILLA HEPPERø△

Lip Smoothies: Banana, Mint, Passion Fruit, Strawberry

DOLMA√ø§†fcd76

Lipsalves: Fennel, Mandarin, Spearmint

HONESTY√ø§fcd76

Unscented Lip Balms

JULIUS ROTHø

Vitamin Lip Balm

MARTHA HILLø△fcd79

Lipgloss; *Lipstick Pots & Cases:* Cerise, Pink, Wine

MONTAGNE JEUNESSEø△fcd76

Orange Lip Gloss Balm

NATURE'S BODYCARE√øfcd76

Lip Balm: Apple, Coconut, Mint, Strawberry

ORGANIC PRODUCT COø△fcd76

Lip Balm: Apple, Cherry, Mint

STARGAZER√§fcd76

Lip Liner, Lipstick

VERDEfcd76

Calendula & Vitamin E Lip Balm

YARDLEY

Lip Definer Pencil

YOUR BODY√△øfcd84

Lip Balms: Apricot, Banana, Kiwi Fruit, Morello Cherry, Orange, Strawberry

NAIL PRODUCTS

BEAUTY WITHOUT CRUELTYø†fcd76

Nail Colours: all

BRONNLEY△

Hand & Nail Cream: Saponaria, Shambrilla

DOLMA√ø§†fcd76

Nail & Cuticle Oil

HARTWOOD AROMATICSøfcd76

Lotus Nail Creams: Cuticle Softener, Nail Strengthener, Nourishing Nail

MARTHA HILLø△fcd79

Cuticle Cream

MONTAGNE JEUNESSEø△fcd76

Vitamin Nail Repair

STARGAZER√§fcd76

Nail Colour

PRIME TIME√ø†△fcd88

Nail Strengthener

YARDLEY†

Nail Enamel: all

PERFUMES ETC

BARRY Mø△fcd82

Fragrance Spray: Dewberry, Flirt, Perfect

Peach, White Musk; *Just For Men:* Body Splash On; *Perfume Oils:* Dewberry, Flirt, Perfect Peach, White Musk

BEAUTY WITHOUT CRUELTYø†fcd76

Perfumes: Yolanda, Suma, Calista, Gemini 1, Gemini 3, Kyphi; *Colognes:* Suma, Yolanda

BODY BEAUTIFULø

Body Scent: Dewberry; *Body Spray:* Dewberry, Peach, White Musk; *Perfumes:* Dewberry, White Musk

BODY CENTREøfcd84

Body Spray: Dewberry, White Musk; *Perfumed Oil:* Dewberry, White Musk; *Spray Atomiser Perfumes:* all

BODYLINEøfcd83

A Feast of Fine Fragrances Perfume Oils: Amour, Apple Blossom, Bambi, Cleopatra, Coconut, Dewberry, Freesia, Herb, Honeysuckle, Jardine, Lavender, Lemon, Lilac, Magnolia, Mango, Peach, Rose, Sandalwood, Spring, Strawberry, Vanilla, White Musk; *Body Spray:* Dewberry, Mens, Sea Mist, White Musk; *Men's:* Body Splash; *Perfume:* Dewberry, White Musk; *Perfume Atomisers:* Amazone, Arpino, Beau, Dewberry, Giovarni, Illusion, Kiri, Narcotique, Sonata, Tempo, White Musk

BRONNLEY∆

Body Spray: Blue Poppy, Camellia, Daffodil, English Fern, Pink Bouquet, Saponaria, Shambrilla, White Iris; *Eau de Toilette:* Blue Poppy, Camellia, Daffodil, English Fern, Pink Bouquet, Saponaria, Shambrilla, White Iris; *Splash Cologne:* Blue Poppy, Camellia, Daffodil, English Fern, Pink Bouquet, White Iris

CAMILLA HEPPERø∆

Perfume Oils: Honeysuckle, Hyacinth, Jasmin, Lavender, Lemon Verbena, Lily of the Valley, Orange Blossom, Pot-Pourri, Rose, Sandalwood, White Musk

CO-OPfcd85

Body Spray: Corundum, Malachite, Soir; *Fragrance Body Spray:* Jour, Matin, Nuit Fine

CULPEPERøfcd76

Toilet Water: Elderflower, Eau De Cologne, Elizabethan, English Lavender, Jasmine, Rose, Sandalwood, Stephanotis, Sweet Violet, Sweet Violet Spray, Witch Hazel

DOLMA√ø§†fcd76

Amethyst Mist, Cushie B, Opus In Pastels, Prelude, Raga, Rondo, Sarabande, Sonata

FANTÔME√øfcd76

Eau De Parfum Femelle

FLEUR AROMATHERAPY√ø™∆

Classic Perfume Blends in Jojoba: Jasmine, Neroli, Rose; *Perfume Kits:* 1, 2

GREEN THINGSø†∆fcd76

Juniper Splash Cologne

HARTWOOD AROMATICSøfcd76

Cosmic Atomiser Perfumes: Cloud 9, Jasmine, Joy, Neroli, Rose, Sandalwood, Tranquility

KENT COSMETICS√ø

Eau de Parfum

TOILETRIES & COSMETICS

KITTYWAKE PERFUMES√ø†§

Handmade Perfumes

MARTHA HILLøΔfcd79

For Men: David Hill Cologne; *Fragrances:* 1,2,3,4, Perfume Sample Pack

MICHELINE ARCIERø

Perfumes: Arabimou, Feuilles De Rose

NATURE'S BODYCARE√øfcd76

Concerto, Etude, Prelude, Rhapsody, Sonata, Symphony

NORFOLK LAVENDERøfcd84

Colognes: all

SUPERDRUGfcd87

Body Sprays: Apple & Melon, Citron & Peach, Dewberry & Yuzu, Lime & Paw Paw, Raspberry & Watermelon

THE PERFUMERS GUILD√ø§Δfcd76

Country House Collection, Classics Collection for Gentlemen, Classics Collection for Ladies, Traditional Collection

VERDEfcd76

Anjou Body Splash for Men, Eau de Verde Cologne, Maya Body Fragrance, Numi Body Fragrance

YARDLEY†

Lavender Perfume, Lavender Water; *Body Sprays, Cologne Sprays:* all; *Eau:* Energie, Fraiche, Sensuelle; *Eaux de Toilette, Female Perfume, Mens Colognes, Perfum De Toilette:* all

YOUR BODY√øΔfcd84

Dewberry: Body Spray, Perfume Oil; *Perfume Oils:* Apple Blossom, Canterbury Rose, Country Garden, Dewberry, English Lavender, Lotus, Sandlewood, Seville Orange, Strawberry, Tea Rose,White Musk, Wild Honeysuckle; *White Musk:* Body Spray, Perfume Oil

SHAMPOOS

AMYRIS√øfcd76

Apple & Rosemary Conditioning, Aromatherapy Invigorating Hair & Scalp, Base, Body, Chamomile & Orange, Nettle Sage & Lavender, Peach & Coconut, Raspberry

ARBONNE√ø

Normal To Dry, Normal To Oily

ANIMAL AID√ø§fcd76

Herbal Shampoo

AUSTRIAN MOOR√ø

Moor Life Shampoo

BARRY MøΔfcd82

Coconut Ice, Dewberry Wash & Condition, Sage & Dandelion, Strawberry, White Musk; *Just For Men:* Ginseng Shampoo

BERMARø

Shampoo

BIOCEUTICALS√ø

Bonazi

BIORGANICS√øΔfcd76

Isobath, Isonate

BLACKMORESøfcd85

Marshmallow, Wild Nettle

BODY BEAUTIFULø

Almond & Coconut, Cactus & Freesia, Grapefruit & Lemon Balm, Hair & Body, Jasmine, Marigold & Peppermint, Men's Cologne & Peppermint Hair & Body Shampoo, Nettle & Geranium, Peach, Pineapple & Mandarin, Rosemary & Greenblossom, Seaweed & Aloe Vera, Tropical Wilderness, White Musk

BODY CENTREøfcd84

Chamomile, Coconut Oil Conditioning, Dewberry Conditioning, Mens Conditioning, Red Apple & Coconut, Rosemary, White Musk Conditioning

BODYLINEøfcd83

Aloe Vera, Apple & Gooseberry, Banana & Brazil Nut, Camomile & Jojoba, Coco Cabana, Coconut, Deep Ocean Mud, Dewberry, Grapefruit & Lemon, Herb Cocktail Rejuvenating, Lichen Anti Dandruff, Magnolia, Mango & Kiwi, Mens Shampoo & Shower Gel, Nettle & Limeflowers, Northern Exposure, Peach & Apricot, Peppermint & Ocean Salt, Raspberry & Strawberry, Rosemary & Hawthorne, Tea Tree, White Musk, White Henna Cream, Wild Cherry & Thyme, Willow & Birch Conditioning

BOREALISøfcd76

Shampoos: all

BRONNLEY△

Animal Friends

CAMILLA HEPPERø△

Camomile, Coconut Oil, Herbal, Jojoba Oil, Lavender & Sesame Oil, Men's Conditioning, Natural Orange, Rosemary, Seaweed, Ti-Tree & Thyme, Watercress

CAURNIE SOAP CO√ø△fcd76

Avocado, Pure

COLORA√fcd76

Henna

CO-OPfcd85

Anti Dandruff for Greasy, Anti Dandruff for Normal/Dry, Avocado & Apple, Camomile & Coltsfoot Enriched, Clover, Enriched, Enriched Environment Care, Frequent Wash, Gentle Environment Care, Honeysuckle, Medicated, Mild, Peach & Apricot, Rosehip & Hawthorn Gentle, Water Melon & Passion Fruit, Wild Herb

COSMETIC HOUSEø

Antiphilitron

CULPEPERøfcd76

Herb For Dark, Herb For Fair; *Liquid:* Chamomile For Fair, Henna For Auburn, Rosemary For Dark; *Luxury:* Dry Hair, Normal Hair; *Powders:* Chamomile, Rosemary

CREIGHTONSø△fcd76

Capucine, Chamomile & Wheatgerm, Lime Blossom & Rosemary, Orange Flower & Birch, Watercross & Almond, Yarrow & Wild Nettle; *Conditioning:* Apple Bath & Shower, Apricot Care, Comfrey Care, Dewberry, Peach, Strawberry; *Hair & Body:* Ocean Harvest

TOILETRIES & COSMETICS

CRIMPERS√ø∆fcd76

Dry/Damaged Hair, Frequent Wash

DANIEL FIELD√ø

Body Builder Therapy, Dandruff Scalp Therapy, First Aid Therapy, Frequent Wash Scalp Therapy, Medicated, Mineral Shampoo & Shine, Revitalising, Split End Therapy, Spring Water Therapy

DOLMA√ø§†fcd76

Nettle & Pectin Hair Shampoos: Bitter Orang & Tangerine, Cedarwood & Rosewood, Jojoba & Sandalwood, Lavender & Sage, Rosemary, Tea Tree & Thyme

EAST OF EDEN√fcd85

Shampoos

FAITHø†∆fcd84

Aloe Vera, Jojoba, Rosemary, Seaweed

FANTÔME√øfcd76

Meadow Herb

FARROW & HUMPHRIES√øfcd76

Natural Extracts: Gentle Shampoo Gelée

FINDERS INTERNATIONALø

Dead Sea Magik Shampoo

GREEN THINGSø†∆fcd76

Chamomile & Mullein, Mallow & Coconut Oil, Juniper & Orange Body & Hair Shampoo For Men, Rosemary & Sage, Seaweed & Nettle, Tea Tree & Cedarwood

G R LANEø

Tiki: Camomile, Marigold, Nettle, Rosemary

HOLLAND & BARRETT

Nature's Garden: Apple, Banana

HAMILTON'S OF CANTERBURY√ø∆

Hair & Body Wash: Anti Stress Calming & Relaxing, Aromatic Active Athletic, Stimulating Refreshing & Invigorating

HERBAL FORCE√ø†

Herbal Glo: Dandruff & Dry, Dry/Damaged, Grey/White Hair, Normal To Oily, Permed/Coloured Treated Hair, Sensitive Hair & Scalp, Thin/Fine Hair

HOLLYTREESø∆fcd76

Conditioning, Hair & Body

HONESTY√ø§fcd76

Essential: Nettle Sage & Lavender; *Fruit:* Apple & Rosemary Conditioning, Chamomile & Orange, Peach & Coconut, Raspberry

HOUSE OF MISTRYø

Shampoo: Aloe Vera Jojoba, Ginseng Herbal, Tea Tree Oil Herbal; *Shampoo & Conditioners:* Rosemary 2 in 1, Tea Tree Oil

HYMOSA√øfcd76

Shampoos

JEROME RUSSELL√øfcd76

Camomile & Aloe Vera, Coconut Oil Protein, Jojoba Oil Conditioning, Tea Tree Peppermint & Aloe Vera

KOBASHI√ø∆fcd76

Mellow Shampoos: Henna, Jojoba, Wheatgerm

L'ANZA√

Deep Cleansing, Moisturizing, Protein Plus, Remedy, Shampoo Plus

LITTLE GREEN SHOP√øfcd85

Apple, Herbal, Orange Blossom, Peach Blossom

MAHARISHI AYUR-VEDø

Flaky Scalp Herbal Shampoo

MARTHA HILLøΔfcd79

Coconut Conditioning Shampoo, Seaweed & Nettle, Seaweed & Rosemary, Seaweed & Sage; *For Men:* Herbal Conditioning, Protein, Seaweed & Herb

MONTAGNE JEUNESSEøΔfcd76

Chamomile & Jojoba, Grapefruit & Aloe, Henna & Kukui, Seaweed & Mineral, Vitamin E

NATURE'S BODYCARE√øfcd76

Camomile, Coconut, Nettle; *With Him In Mind:* Cologne Hair & Body Shampoo, Sandalwood Hair & Body

NIRVANAøΔfcd76

Camomile, Lavender, Lemon & Lime, Nettle & Jasmin, Orange Barley, Rosemary, Wild Mint

NORFOLK LAVENDERøfcd84

Shampoo

ORGANIC PRODUCT COøΔfcd76

Botanical Deep Action Wash, Botanical Hair Wash & Finish, Herbal Hair & Body Wash

PAUL MITCHELL√

Creative Herbal: Moisture & Shine; *Shampoo:* 1,2,3, Awapuhi, Baby Don't Cry, Tea Tree

PURE PLANT√øΔfcd76

Comfrey & Sage, Grapefruit & Almond, Lime & Hops, Marshmallow & Raspberry, Orange Spice & Ginger, Orchid 2-in-1 Shampoo & Conditioner

SHANTI√ø§

Herbal

SUPERDRUGfcd87

Anti-tangle Conditioning, Frequent Use, Mild & Gentle Frequent Use, Natural Extract Henna; *Family Shampoos:* Extra Body, Frequent Use, Dry Hair, Normal/Greasy Hair

TERESA MUNRO AROMATHERAPYøΔfcd76

Thursday Plantation Tea Tree Shampoos: Dry, Normal/Oil

TISSERAND√øfcd80

3 in 1, Lemon & Tea Tree, Melissa & Grapefruit, Peru Balsam & Oakmoss, Sandalwood & Palmarosa

TREFRIW WELLS SPA√øfcd84

Shampoo, Toning Hair & Body Shampoo For Men

VERDEfcd76

Phyto Hair

WELEDAøfcd85

Calendula, Rosemary

TOILETRIES & COSMETICS

YARDLEY

Original

YOUR BODY√øfcd84

Chamomile, Marigold, Red Apple, Rosemary, Seaweed, Ti Tree Oil; *Conditioning Shampoos:* Aromatherapy, Coconut; *For Men:* Jojoba, Medicated

SHAVING PRODUCTS

AMYRIS√øfcd76

Unscented Aftershave Balm

ARBONNE√ø

Pour Homme: Smooth Shave Cream, Soothing Treatment Lotion, Pre Shave Cleansing Scrub

BARRY Mø∆fcd82

Just For Men: Brush On Shaving Creme

BEAUTY WITHOUT CRUELTYø†fcd76

Aurelius Aftershave For Men

BODY BEAUTIFULø

Men's Cucumber Aftershave

BODY CENTREøfcd84

Mens Body Spray, Mens Shaving Cream, Sugaring Leg Wax; *Mens Spray Atomiser Aftershaves:* Citrus/Floral, Fresh/Green, Oriental, Warm Musk

BODYLINEøfcd83

Mens: Aftershave Balm, Shaving Cream; *Mens Aftershave:* Giovarni, Illusion, Larwood, Renaido

BOREALISøfcd76

Soapless Shaving Lotion

CAMILLA HEPPERø∆

After-Shave Balm, Birch Shaving Cream, Panthar Aftershave, Teaza Splash Cologne; *Perfume Oils:* Coe-Na-Mara *(for men)*

CO-OPfcd85

Shaving Foam: Corundum, Gabbro, Malachite

COSMETIC HOUSEø

Razorantium Shaving Cream, Trichophobia Sugaring

CULPEPERøfcd76

Shaving Soaps: Eau De Cologne, Lavender, Sandalwood

DOLMA√ø§†fcd76

Wet Shaving Fluid (Unisex); *For Men:* Alcohol Free Pre-Electric Shave/Skin Toner, De-Luxe Aftershave Balm, Sandalwood & Orange Skin Protector

FANTÔME√øfcd76

Cologne Pour Homme Les Jours D'Or

FARROW & HUMPHRIES√øfcd76

British Empire: After Shave Lotion

GREEN THINGSø†∆fcd76

Juniper & Sandalwood Aftershave Toner, Juniper & Tea Tree Shaving Gel

HONESTY√ø§fcd76

Unscented Aftershave Balm

KITTYWAKE PERFUMES√ø†§

Handmade Aftershaves

LITTLE GREEN SHOP√øfcd85

Prohibition Aftershave

MAHARISHI AYUR-VEDø

Herbal Shaving Cream

MARTHA HILLøΔfcd79

For Men: After Shave Gel, Herbal Cleansing & Shaving Cream

NATURE'S BODYCARE√øfcd76

For Silky Legs: Ladies After Shave Salve, Sugareen; *With Him In Mind:* Cologne Balm, Pre Wet Shave Cream, Sandalwood Balm

NEAL'S YARD REMEDIESø

Aromatic Aftershave

ORGANIC PRODUCT COøΔfcd76

Men's Herbal: Aftershave Balm, Shaving Cream

TISSERAND√øfcd80

After Wax Oil

TREFRIW WELLS SPA√øfcd84

Aftershave Balm

VERDEfcd76

Essential Man: Aftershave Gel, Aftershave Lotion

YARDLEY†

Aftershave Lotions: all

YOUR BODY√øfcd76

Coconut Shaving Cream; *After Shave Balms:* Aman, Azarro, Nevin

SKIN CARE

AMYRIS√øfcd76

Papaya Facial Wash; *Cleansing Lotion:* Base, Chamomile, Grapefruit & Geranium, Lavender & Orange; *Moisturising Cream:* Base, Elemi Lavender & Clary Sage, Jojoba, Orange Lavender & Elemi, Unscented w Added Vitamin E, Ylang Ylang Geranium & Lemon; *Hand & Body Lotion:* Lemon Sandalwood & Geranium, Peach & Almond; *Moisturising Lotion:* Base, Cocoa Butter; *Toners:* Chamomile Facial, Comfrey & Ginseng, Marigold & Yarrow

ARBONNE√ø

Cleansing Gel, Cleansing Lotion, Cleansing Cream, Body Lotion, Facial Lotion, Facial Scrub, Freshener, Rejuvenating Cream, Skin Conditioning Oil, Toner; *Bio-Contour:* Body Scrub, Body Shaper; *Bio-Hydria:* Alpha Complex Hydrating Masque, Alpha Complex Moisture For Day, Gentle Exfoliant, Night Energizing Cream; *Bio Matte:* Oil Free Cleanser, Oil Free Personalizer, Oil Free Moisture For Day, Oil Free Moisture For Night; *Masque:* Extra Strength, Mild; *Moisture Cream:* Normal To Dry, Normal To Oily; *Night Cream:* Normal To Dry, Normal To Oily

AUSTRIAN MOOR√ø

Moor Life: Body Lotion, Cleansing/Toning Lotion, Day/Cream Moisturiser, Face

Cream, Face Mask

BARRY MǿΔfcd82

Evening Primrose Facial Oil, Ultra Rich Dry Skin Reviver; *Exfoliators:* Dewberry Body Scrub, Dewberry Face Scrub, Sarsparilla Sluffer Face Scrub; *Facial Cleansers:* Dewberry, Evening Primrose; *Facial Toners:* Dewberry, Evening Primrose; *Facial Washes:* Dewberry Washing Gel; *Just For Men:* Facial Moisturising Gel

BAY HOUSE AROMATICSǿfcd76

Orange Flower Water, Rose Water; *Base Creams:* Comfrey, Marigold, Sweet Almond; *Blended Skin Creams:* Almond & Palmarosa Moisturising, Lemon & Rose Revitalising Face, Marigold & Vitamin E Night; *Lotion Base:* Cleansing, White

BEAUTY WITHOUT CRUELTYǿ†fcd76

Avocado Moisturiser, Cream Face Mask, Flowers of Lilac Cleansing Cream, Rose Petal Skin Freshener, Scrub Cream, Sunflower & Wheat Cream

BLACKMORESǿfcd85

White Ivy Body Scrub; *Cleansing:* Almond Cleansing Creme, Cucumber Cleanser, Herbal Clay Face Masque, Marshmallow Comp Soap, Papaya Foaming Cleanser, Thyme Lotion; *Toning:* Aloe Toner, Witch Hazel Toner; *Moisturising:* Apricot Day Creme w Sunscreen, Evening Primrose Body Lotion w Vitamin E, Marshmallow Moisturiser; *Nourishing:* Apricot E Oil, Avocado Night Creme plus Vitamin E, Gentian Balancing Night Creme, Vitamin E Creme; *Replenitive:* Camellia Protective Day Creme, Macadamia Hydrating Masque, White Lily Creme; *Treatments:* Anti-Bacter-

ial Face Wash, Anti-Bacterial Pimple Gel, Oil Free Moisturiser

BODY BEAUTIFULǿ

Elderflower Wash Cream, Jojoba Neck Gel, Juniper Berry & Rosemary Facial Sauna, Oriental Wash Grains; *Body Lotion:* Dewberry, Ginseng & Evening Primrose, White Musk; *Cleanser:* Exotic Orchid Cleansing Milk, Jasmine, Melon Cleansing Lotion, Mild & Gentle Fragrance Free, Peach, Rosemary & Lotus, Seaweed & Aloe Vera; *Day Creams:* Carrot Oil Cream for Dry Skin, Comfrey & Cucumber, Exotic Orchard, Ginseng & Evening Primrose, Melon, Mild & Gentle Fragrance Free, Vitamin E; *Face & Body Lotion:* Jasmine, Lavender & Rosemary Face Lotion, Peach; *Face Mask:* Exotic Orchid, Lavender & Rosemary, Melon & Apricot, Seaweed & Aloe Vera; *Facial Scrub:* Jasmine & Oat, Oat & Passion Fruit, Peach & Oat ; *Face Spray:* Jasmine, Peach; *Moisturising Lotion:* Marshmallow & Avocado, Seaweed & Aloe Vera; *Night Creams:* Melon, Mild & Gentle Fragrance Free, Seaweed & Aloe Vera; *Toner:* Exotic Orchid, Grapefruit & Strawberry, Jasmine, Melon, Mild & Gentle Fragrance Free, Peach, Sage & Elderflower, Seaweed & Aloe Vera

BODY CENTREǿfcd84

Body Lotion: Dewberry, White Musk; *Cleanser:* Aloe Vera, Lemon Facial Scrub, Lime Blossom, Marshmallow, Mens Facial Scrub, Pineapple Facial Wash, Vitamin E; *Cream:* Aloe Vera Moisturising Day, Aloe Vera Repair Complex Night, Evening Primrose Night, Linden Flower Moisturiser, Mens Protein Moisturiser, Orchid Oil Day, Vitamin E Moisturiser, Vitamin E Regenerative Night; *Facial Mask:* Almond Oil, Pineapple; *Toner:* Aloe Vera Skin, Vitamin E, Witch Hazel

BODYLINEøfcd83

Aloe Vera Gel, Apricot Neck Cream, Aqua Cleanser, Banana & Brazil Nut Facial Wash Cream, Carrot Oil Cleansing Lotion, Coconut Body Milk, Cucumber Cleansing Milk, Elderflower Water, Fragrance Free Cleanser, Fragrance Free Moisturiser, Great Grandmothers Facial Wash, Lemon & Oatmeal Facial Scrub, Oatmeal Facial Lather, Tea Tree Cleansing Gel, Vitamin E Day Cream, Vitamin E Night Cream, Watermelon Facial Spray; *Body Lotion:* Apple & Gooseberry, Fresh As A Daisy, Grapefruit & Lemon, Magnolia, Peach & Apricot, Raspberry & Strawberry, Sheer Water, White Musk; *Face Pack:* Banana, Cucumber, Lemon, Mud, Strawberry; *Mens:* Moisturiser, Wash & Scrub; *Moisture Cream:* Glycerine & Rosewater, Jojoba & Rose, Marigold & Carrot, Pure & Kind; *Moisture Lotion:* Aloe Vera, Tea Tree, Vitamin E Enriched; *Toners:* Elizabethan Skin, Fragrance Free, Orange Flower Water Facial, Tea Tree

BODYTREATS√ø§fcd76

Facial Oils, Organic Flower Waters

BONITA√ø§†fcd80

Cucumber Cleansing Lotion; *Floral Waters:* Orangeflower, Rose; *Toners:* Orange Blossom, Rosewater

BOREALISøfcd76

Cocoa Butter Cleanser, Comfrey & Calendula Cream; *Lotions:* Cocoa Butter & Lavender, Cocoa Butter & Rosewater, Lavender & Seaweed; *Night Cream:* Avocado & Yarrow, Wild Rose

CAMILLA HEPPERøΔ

Cleanser: Azufre, T-Zone Foaming; *Cleansing Milk:* Lemon Balm, Meadowsweet; *Cream:* Avocado Moisture, Azufre, Camilla's Cleansing, Evening Primrose Night, Facial Wash, Herbal, Regenerative, T-Zone Moisturising Control, Wheatgerm & Marigold Moisture; *Facial Treatments:* Exfoliating Tropical Skin Polisher, Herbal Clay Mask, Nint & Olive Stone Scrub, Oatmeal & Almond Oil Mask, Rich Skin Food; *Lotions:* Jojoba Oil Moisture, Orange Blossom & Cocoa Butter Body, Rose Body, White Musk Body; *Mens:* Face Protection, Face Wash, Mint & Olive Stone Scrub; *Toners:* Azufre Lotion, Elderflower Skin, Orange Flower Water, Rose Flower Water, T-Zone Balancing Freshener, Yarrow Skin

CO-OPfcd85

Active System Anti-Bacterial Face Wash, Lily & Elderflower Cleansing Lotion, Orange Blossom & Freesia Body Conditioning Milk, Peach & Walnut Shell Facial Scrub, Pineapple & Oatmeal Gentle Exfo Facial Wash, Primrose & Watercress Moisturiser Lotion, Rosewater & Glycerine Toner, Sheer Silk Enriched Moisture Cream; *Peach & Apricot:* Cleanser, Facial Mask, Facial Wash, Moisturiser, Toner

COSMETIC HOUSEø

Staff of Life Face Mask, Starcraft Cleanser, Sympathy For The Skin Body Lotion; *Toners:* Tagette Water, Tea Tree Water; *Moisturisers:* Skin Drink, Vitality Float

TOILETRIES & COSMETICS

CREIGHTONSø∆fcd76

Apricot Care: Cleansing Lotion, Facial Gel, Facial Oil, Moisturising Lotion; *Comfrey Care:* Comfrey & Vitamin E Moisture Lotion; *Evening Primrose Skin Care:* Cleansing Lotion, Facial Wash, Moisturising Day Lotion, Toning Lotion

CULPEPERøfcd76

Cleansing Creams & Skin Foods: Elderflower, Orange, Red Elm; *Lotions:* Balm, Miel De Mignonette, Miel Of White Violets, Milk of Lilies, Three Flower Toning Cleanser

DEB

Protective Skin Creams for Industrial Work: Deb Care, Proteks Dry, Proteks Wet

DOLMA√ø§†fcd76

Cleansers: Almond & Orange Facial Scrub, Aromatic Face Shampoo, Cleansing Cream, Cucumber Facial Mask, Lavender & Chamomile Cleansing Lotion, Oil Free, Rosemary & Seaweed Facial Mask; *Facial Oils:* De-Luxe, Sensitive Skin; *Toners:* Astringent, Freshening, Gentle, Purifying; *Moisturising Creams:* Avocado & Ylang Ylang, Geranium & Evening Primrose Night, Marigold & Lemongrass, Wheatgerm & Lavender

EAST OF EDEN√fcd85

Face & Body Scrubs, Moisturisers

FAITHø†∆fcd84

Almond Scrub, Aloe Vera Moisturising Cream, Essential Facial Wash, Jojoba Moisturising Lotion, Rose & Wheatgerm Moisturising Cream, Rosewater Toning Lotion, Seaweed Cleansing Lotion

FANTÔME√øfcd76

Face Cleanse, Face Tone, Moisture Creams

FARROW & HUMPHRIES√øfcd76

Bali: Body Soother; *Natural Extracts:* After Bath Body Creamer, Skin Conditioning Lotion

FINDERS INTERNATIONALø

Dead Sea Magik: Body Lotion, Exfoliant, Moisturiser, Mud Mask, Skin Softener, Super Night Cream

GREEN THINGSø†∆fcd76

Cleansing: Coconut Oil Cleansing Lotion, Marigold & Elderflower Cleanser, Marigold Facial Cleansing Gel, Tea Tree Face & Body Wash; *Toning:* Calendula Lotion, Geranium & Rosewater Toner, Orange Flower Water Toner, Tea Tree Toner

G R LANEø

Tiki: Marigold Cream, Vitamin E High Potency Oil; *Tiki Cleansers:* Camomile, Cucumber & Lime Blossom, Witch Hazel; *Tiki Moisturisers:* Camomile, Cucumber & Lime Blossom, Vitamin E, Witch Hazel; *Tiki Toners:* Camomile, Cucumber & Lime Blossom, Witch Hazel

KENT COSMETICS√ø

Moisturising Body Lotions; *Moisture Response:* Moisture Creams

HAMILTON'S OF CANTERBURY√ø∆

Hydrotherapy Treatment: Body Shaping Lotion & Moisturiser, Complete Face & Body Refining Cream

HARTWOOD AROMATICSøfcd76

Lotus Body Care Creams, Oils, Lotions: Dry & Mature Skin, Luxurious Rose, Normal & Combination, Oily & Problem Skin, Sensitive Skin; *Lotus Facial Creams, Oils, Lotions:* Dry & Mature Skin, Luxurious Rose, Night Nourishment, Normal & Combination, Oily & Problem Skin, Sensitive Skin

HOLLAND & BARRETT

Cleansing Lotion, Facial Scrub, Facial Wash, Orchid Toning Lotion, Passion Flower Moisture Lotion, Vitamin E Night Cream; *Nature's Garden:* Cucumber/Gentian Toner, Geranium/Thyme Cleanser, Guava/Melon Body Lotion; *Nature's Garden Aromatherapy:* Dry Skin Massage Cream

HONESTY√ø§fcd76

Essential: Comfrey & Ginseng Toner, Elemi Lavender & Clary Sage Moisturising Cream, Frankincense Lavender & Orange Facial Oil, Grapefruit & Cleansing Lotion, Lavender & Orange Cleansing Lotion, Marigold & Yarrow Toner, Orange Lavender & Elemi Nourishing Cream, Sandalwood Ylang Ylang & Orange Body Oil, Ylang Ylang Geranium & Lemon Moisturising Cream; *Fruit:* Papaya Facial Wash; *Unscented:* Cleansing Lotion *w* Chamomile, Facial Toner *w* Chamomile, Moisturising Lotion *w* Cocoa Butter

HOUSE OF MISTRYø

Aloe Vera Cocoa Butter Moisturising Cream, Arnica Cream, Arnica Lotion, Calendula Cream, Calendula Lotion, Ginseng Cleanser & Toner, Ginseng Herbal Scrub, Ginseng Night Cream, Ginseng Moisturising Cream *w* Vitamin E, Ginseng Natural Skin Toner, Neem Cream, Vitamin E Cream

HYMOSA√øfcd76

Cleansing Milk, Hand & Body Lotion, Moisturising Lotion, Skin Freshener, Vitamin E Creme

JEROME RUSSELL√øfcd76

Body Lotions: Cocoa Butter, Tea Tree Peppermint & Aloe Vera; *Cleansers:* Passion Fruit Cleansing Gel; *Moisturisers:* Aloe Vera, Vitamin E; *Toners:* Elderflower Skin Tonic

JEYESfcd83

Germaloids Tissues, Quickles Face Cleaner Pads

JULIUS ROTHø

Clarification Facial Scrub, Clarification Gel, Clary & Calendula Cleansing Cream, Clary & Calendula Toning Gel, Flower Balm, Flower Gelée, Formula B, Jasmin Body Lotion, Orchid Blossom Cream Cleanser, Orchid Blossom Exfoliating Cream, Orchid Blossom Refiner, Revitalising Lotion; *Cleansing Lotions:* Angelica, Clarification Deep, Papaya, Pomegranate, Poppy Petal, Revitalising; *Elixir:* Black Poppy, White Grape; *Moisturising Cream:* Clarification, Clary & Calendula, Intense, Oakmoss, Poppy Petal, Revitalising; *Night Therapy:* Clary & Calendula, Mulberry, Oakmoss, Revitalising, Veronica; *Toning Lotions:* Chamomile Flowers, Elderflowers, Jasmine Flowers, Orangeflower

KOBASHI√ø∆fcd76

Cleanser, Moisturiser, Rose Facial Lotion, Toner

TOILETRIES & COSMETICS

LAMBERT HEALTHCARE

NaPCa Skin Moisturiser, Vitamin E Cream 5000µ *w* Aloe Vera

LITTLE GREEN SHOP√øfcd85

Cream: Avocado & Wheatgerm Nourishing, Camomile & Orange Flower Cleanser, Moisturising, Mariold & Elderflower; *Lotion:* Camomile & Orange Toning, Cocoa Butter Moisturising, Marigold & Elderflower, Peach Oil

MAHARISHI AYUR-VEDø

Body Lotion: Kapha, Pitta, Vata; *Herbal:* Cleansing Cream, Cleansing Gel, Skin Toner, *Herbal Day Moisturiser:* Kapha, Pitta, Vata; *Herbal Night Moisturiser:* Kapha, Pitta, Vata; *Herbal Face Mask:* Kapha, Pitta, Vata; *Herbal Facial Scrub:* Kapha, Pitta, Vata; *Herbal Youthful Skin:* Restoring Cream, Restoring Mask

MARTHA HILLøΔfcd79

Body Lotion, Evening Primrose Massage Cream, Mint Mud Mask, Moisture Mist, Seaweed Face Pack, Seaweed Peeling Mask, Spray On Skin Refresher, Super Travel Pack; *Evening Primrose:* Cleanser, Gel Toner, Moisturiser, Multi-Purpose Cream; *For Men:* Daytime Moisturiser & Skin Shield, Multi Purpose Cream; *Chamomile:* Cleansing Gel, Enriched Moisture Cream, Hydro Cream, Moisture Milk, Skin Tonic; *Standard Skin Care:* Day Cream, Herbal Cleansing Milk, Night Cream, Toning Gel

MICHELINE ARCIERø

Body Oils: Geranium Lavender, Health, Joy, Vitality; *Jojoba:* Face Cream, Face Tonic; *Jojoba Body Oils:* Jasmin, Radiance, Rose; *Jojoba Face Oils:* Aurora, Bois De Rose, Camomile, Dawn, Radiance, Rose, Starlight, Sunrise; *Jojoba Individual Face Oils:* Face Oil For Gentlemen, Formula 1, Formula 2

MONTAGNE JEUNESSEøΔfcd76

Purest Plant Facial Wash, Vitamin E EMUR; *Body:* Peach Souffle, Vitamin Moisturiser, Ylang Ylang; *Masks:* Avocado & Pineapple, Seaweed & Mineral Mud; *Skin EPO:* Cleansing Lotion, Day Cream, Night Cream, Skin Toner

NAPIERS√ø§fcd76

Fragrant Flower Facial Steam, Nutribiotic Face Wash, Rosewater, Toner; *Cream:* Calendula, Camomile, Camomile & Peppermint; *Lotion:* Calendula & Myrrh, Napiers No 2

NATURE'S BESTø†fcd85

Creams: Annely All-Purpose, Evening Primrose Day, NaPCa Skin Moisturiser, Vitamin E/Aloe Vera

NATURE'S BODYCARE√øfcd76

Creams: All Purpose Skin, Evening Primrose Deep Moisturiser, Foundation Base Day, Fragrance Free Day & Night, Skin Treatment, Ultra Violet Filter, Vitamin E; *Facial Cleansers:* Almond Oil, Elderflower Cream Wash, Fennel & Cucumber Cleansing Gel, Neck Gel, Oatmeal Facial Scrub, Orchid Cleansing Milk, Passion Fruit Facial Exfoliator; *Facial Mask:* Apple Blossom, Marshmallow; *Toning Lotions:* Astringent, Orange Flower Water, Rosemary Herbal

NATURE'S NATURALS√ø§fcd76

Aloe: Balancing Lotion, Beauty Gel, Body Refining Scrub, Clarifying Scrub, Moisture Dew Cream, Nutrive Cream, Purifying Lotion, Revitalizing Cleanser, Sensigen Cream, Soothing Toner, Youth Essence Cream

NEAL'S YARD REMEDIESø

Chamomile Cleanser, Citrus Facial Oil, Clay Toning Mask, Exotic Skin Conditioning Oil, Flower Freshener, Rose Facial Oil, Skin Conditioning Oil, Stimulating Skin Conditioning Oil; *Water:* Chamomile Flower, French Chamomile, French Cornflower, French Lavender, French Orange Blossom, French Rosewater, Lavender, Orange Flower, Rose

NORFOLK LAVENDERøfcd84

Hand & Body Lotion

ORGANIC PRODUCT COø∆fcd76

Aloe Vera Cleansing Cream, Aloe Vera/Evening Primrose Body Lotion, Angry Skin Soother, Arnica Skin Softening Cream, Avocado Moisturing Lotion, Fragrance Free Cleansing Lotion, Herbal Skin Repair Cream For Men, Herbal Wash Cream, Lotus Cleansing Gel, Orchid Cleansing Milk, Skin Repairing Moisturiser; *Creams:* Aloe Vera Night, Carrot Oil, Cucumber Moisturising, Melon Day, Melon Moisturising, Vitamin E; *Face Masks:* Apple, Ginseng Gel, Jojoba; *Facial Scrub:* Oatmeal & Apricot, Passion Fruit; Rosemary Spot Lotion, Teatree & Lavender Treatment Cream; *Toner:* Aloe Vera, Elderflower, Rose Water, Strawberry

PRIME TIME√ø†∆fcd88

Astringent Tonic, Cleansing Lotion, Light Moisturiser, Moisturising Cream, Refreshing Toner

PURE PLANT√ø∆fcd76

Aloe Vera: Deep Cleansing Lotion, Deep Moisturising Lotion, Nourishing Creme, Toner; *Peaches & Creme:* Cleanser *(facial wash)* Tube, Facial Scrub w Almond Shell, Moisture Cream for the Day Tube, Nourishing Creme w Vit E Jar, Toner

QUEEN COSMETICSø

Astringent Lotion, Face & Body Lotion, Medicated Cleansing Lotion, Moisturiser, Muscle Oil, Non-Alcoholic Toning Lotion, Rich Cream Cleanser, Skin Freshener; Face *Masques:* Dry/Normal, Normal/Oily

SUPERDRUGfcd87

Skin Tuition II: Cleanser, Deep Moisturising Lotion, Facial Scrub, Foaming Facial Wash, Toner; *Camomile:* Cleansing Lotion, Facial Scrub, Facial Wash, Moisturising Lotion, Skin Freshener; *Fragrance Free:* Cleansing Lotion, Facial Scrub, Facial Wash, Moisturising Lotion, Skin Freshener; *Vitamin E:* Facial Scrub, Moisturiser Vitamin E Body Scrub, Oil, Toner

STARGAZER√§fcd76

Cleanser, Moisturiser, Night Cream, Toner

TISSERAND√øfcd80

Moist Tissues: Lavender & Blue Mountain Sage, Tea-Tree & Kanuka

TREFRIW WELLS SPA√øfcd84

Body & Hand Lotion, Luxury Facial Wash,

Moisturiser, Night Cream, Skin Toner, Cleanser

ULTRA GLOWø

Caring Complex

VERDEfcd76

Aloe Vera & Rose Petal Mist, Essential Repair Cream, Rejuvenating Exquisite Vitamin E Skin Oil, Rose Petal & Clay Face Mask, Seaweed & Green Clay Face & Body Detox Mask, Sweet Sensuality Body Performance Oil; *Cream:* Carrot & Frankincense Moisturising, Chamomile & Marshmallow Moisturiser, Egyptian Chamomile Moisturising, Orange Blossom & Rose Repair; *Essential Man:* Anjou Body Cream, Sandalwood Moisturising Cream, Unfragranced Lubricant; *Facial Oil:* Rose & Neroli; *Gel:* Aloe Vera & Rose Eye, Grape-fruit & Elderflower Moisturising, Palma Rosa Cleansing; *Moisturising Fragrance:* Bergamot & Lavender, Sandalwood & Rose, Sweet Orange & Geranium, Tranquility; *Mousse:* Egyptian Cleansing, Lavender Cleansing, Maya Exotic, Numi Exquisite; *Toning Lotion:* Chamomile & Rose, Elderflower & Bergamot, Orange Blossom & Rose

WELEDAøfcd85

Almond: Face Pack, Moisturising, Oil, Skin Care Triple Pack; *Iris:* Gel, Skin Care Triple Pack

WORLDS END TRADING CO√ø§fcd76

Vicco Turmeric Cream

YARDLEY

Enriched Day Cream, Gentle Cleansing

No more medicine.....
I feel bad enough already.

MT.

Cream, Nourishing Night Cream, Refreshing Skin Tonic, Replenishing Daily Moisturiser

YOUR BODY√øΔfcd84

Aromatic Facial Wash Gel, Jojoba & Soya Face Protector, Lime Blossom Cleansing Cream, Rosewater Skin Freshener, Seaweed Cleansing Lotion; *Cleansing Milk:* Cucumber, Herbal, Orchid Oil; *Creams:* Aloe Vera Moisture, Avocado Moisture, Evening Primrose Night, Ginseng Moisture, Linden Flower Moisturiser, Vitamin E; *Facial Mask:* Almond Oil, Pineapple; *Facial Wash:* Aromatherapy, Pineapple; *Facial Scrub:* Lemon, Olive, Orange & Almond; *Lotion:* Cocoa Butter Body, Dewberry Body, Jojoba, Marshmallow Cleansing, Orchid & Jasmin Body, White Musk Body; *Toner:* Elderflower, Witch Hazel; *Tonic:* Cucumber, Sage & Yarrow Skin, White Grape Skin

SKIN MAKE UP

ARBONNE√ø

Concealing Wand, Cream Concealer, Translucent Finishing Powder, Translucent Pressed Powder; *True Colour:* For Cheeks, Soft Finish Makeup SPF 8

BEAUTY WITHOUT CRUELTYø†fcd76

Cover Up Stick, Loose Face Powder; *Compressed Face Powder, Liquid Make-Up, Make-Up Bases:* all

BODYLINEøfcd83

Facial Powder: Dry Skin Rescue, Floral Fancy, Packet Full of Posy's, Power of Flowers, Reel A Peel

JEROME RUSSELL√øfcd76

Temporary Tattoos

MARTHA HILLøΔfcd79

Cream Rouge, Powder Blusher Compact; *Cover Up Concealer:* Dark, Light; *Loose Powder Pots:* Dark, Light; *Sun Barrier Foundation:* Dark, Ivory, Light Medium; *Tinted Moisturiser:* Dark, Light Rose Beige, Soft Beige; *Powder Compact & Blusher Refills:* Amber Blusher, Dark Powder, Deep Rose Blusher, Light Powder; *Powder Compact:* Dark, Light

QUEEN COSMETICSø

Face Powders: Apricot, Beige, Deep Peach, Natural, Ochre Rose, Peach, Rachel 1, Rachel 2, Rachel Natural, Rachel Soleil, Sunburn, White; *Tinted Foundation Creams:* Honey Beige, Misty Beige, Warm Amber, Warm Peach

STARGAZER√§fcd76

Blusher, Foundation, Loose Powder, Pressed Powder,

ULTRA GLOWø

Caring Aloe Vera Bronzing Gel, Caring Tinted Moist, Liquid Tint, Original Loose Bronzing Powder, Translucent Powder (Loose/Pressed)

YARDLEY

Easy Bronze: Body Gel, Face Cream, Face Powder, Gel Stick; *Powder Cream Foundation:* all

TOILETRIES & COSMETICS

SOAPS

AMYRIS√øfcd76

Seaweed; *Citrus:* Grapefruit, Mandarin & Ginger, Minted Lime; *Complexion:* Cocoa Palm, Oat Bran; *Fragrant:* Apple & Elderflower, Lavender; *Gentleman's Soap:* Macassar; *Marine Soap:* Old Navy Scrubber; *Spice:* Cinnamon & Sandalwood, Nutmeg & Vanilla, Saffron & Almond

AUSTRIAN MOOR√ø

Moor Life Soap/Cleansing Bar

BARRY Mø∆fcd82

Liquid: Dewberry, Evening Primrose, Perfect Peach; *Just For Men:* Lather Bar

BEAUTY WITHOUT CRUELTYø†fcd76

Coconut & Palm Oil, Yolanda Beauty Soap

BLACKMORESø∆fcd83

Marshmallow Comp, Purifying Body

BODY BEAUTIFULø

Aromatherapy, Fruit, Herbal

BODYLINEøfcd83

Coconut Milk, Cucum Bar, Dewberry, Honeydew Melon, Magnolia, Peach, Sandalwood Shower, Strawberry, White Musk; *Handmade Aromatherapy Oil:* Australian Tea Tree, Calamine & Geranium, Sea Mud & Patchouli, Sea Salt & Lavender, Seaweed & Peppermint; *Novelty:* Orange, Pink, Purple, Yellow

BRONNLEY∆

Animal Friends, Saponaria, Shambrilla

CAMILLA HEPPERø∆

Avocado Oil, Coconut Oil, Grapefruit, Orange Blossom, Vitamin E

CAURNIE SOAP CO√ø∆fcd76

Pure Soap Block; *Handmade:* Dill, Fennel, Poppyseed, Rosemary, Scotch Barley; *Wholesoap:* Almond, Cucumber, Lavender, Mandarin

CO-OPfcd85

Environment Care Pure Vegetable, Oatmeal Vegetable, Peach & Apricot Liquid, Water Melon & Passion Fruit Liquid

COSMETIC HOUSEø

Assorted soaps

CREIGHTONSø∆fcd76

Apricot, Evening Primrose, Apple, Peach, Strawberry; *Fruit Fragrance Pure Vegetable:* Avocado, Blackcurrant, Tangerine; *Vegetable Translucent:* Apple, Apricot, Blue Iris, Dewberry, Magnolia, Strawberry, Wild Rose; *Speciality:* Aloe Vera, Fragrance Free w Vitamin E, Oatmeal, Jojoba

DEB

Anti-Bacterial Soaps for Industrial Use: Green, Flora Free; *Soap Systems for Industrial Use:* Maxipor, Hypor; *Washroom Lotion Soaps for Industrial Use:* Heiress, Peach, Pure, Sceptre, Verve

DOLMA√ø§†fcd76

Peppermint Liquid Soap, Vitamin E; *Wholesoaps:* Almond, Lavender, Mandarin, Original, Rose

EAST OF EDEN√fcd85

Variety

TOILETRIES & COSMETICS

darin, Original, Rose

EAST OF EDEN√fcd85

Variety

FAITHø†∆fcd84

Pure Vegetable: Lavender, Orange, Pine, Rosemary, Seaweed

FARROW & HUMPHRIES√øfcd76

Assortment

FINDERS INTERNATIONALø

Dead Sea Magik: Black Mud Soap, Cleansing Bar

FLEUR AROMATHERAPY√ø™∆

Olive Oil Natural Soap

GREEN THINGSø†∆fcd76

Vegetable: Evening Primrose, Geranium & Orange

G R LANEø

Tiki: Vitamin E

HOLLAND & BARRETT

Nature's Garden Aromatherapy: Refreshing, Relaxing; *Nature's Garden Translucent:* Dewberry/Mallow, Lime/Tangerine, Strawberry/Raspberry

HOUSE OF MISTRYø

Calendula Ginseng Aloe Vera Paba Lotion, Calendula Powder, Natural Organic w Vitamin E, Peppermint & Juniper For Men, Tea Tree Liquid

HYMOSA√øfcd76

Beauty

KAYS√

Pure Vegetable range

KOBASHI√ø∆fcd76

Mellow Pure Liquid: Almond, Lavender, Peppermint, Rose Petal

LITTLE GREEN SHOP√øfcd85

Parlemour Liquid Handsoap

MARTHA HILLø∆fcd79

Lavender, Lemon, Lime, Mountain Herb, Orange, Rose, Rosemary; *For Men:* Peppermint & Juniper

MAXIM PHARMACEUTICAL√™§

Amber Beauty Soap w Moisturising Cream and Sandalwood Fragrance

MONTAGNE JEUNESSEø∆fcd76

Cucumber, Evening Primrose Oil, Orchid Oil, Passion Fruit, Peach Soap On a Rope, Seaweed & Mineral, Vitamin E; *New Radical:* Evening Primrose Oil, Passion Fruit, Prickly Pear Cactus, Rainforest Harvest, Seaweed & Mineral, Soap of Tranquility, Vanilla Bean

NEAL'S YARD REMEDIESø

Aloe Vera & Oatmeal, Geranium & Orange, Geranium & Sweet Almond Oil, Lavender & Olive Oil, Lavender & Tea Tree, Lime & Green Clay, Sandalwood & Coriander, Seaweed

NORFOLK LAVENDERøfcd84

Lavender, Men of England, Rose w Lavender

OXFAMø

Vegetable

PACIFIC ISLE

Pacific Isle, Pacific Isle Jasmin

SUMA™

All

SUPERDRUGfcd87

Glycerine, Vegetable

TERESA MUNRO AROMATHERAPYø∆fcd76

Thursday Plantation Tea Tree

TISSERAND√øfcd80

Lavender & Evening Primrose, Sandalwood & Wheatgerm, Tea-Tree & Avocado, Ylang Ylang & Peach Kernal

TREFRIW WELLS SPA√øfcd84

Luxury Hand, Toning Body

VERDEfcd76

Tea Tree Liquid

WELEDAøfcd85

Rosemary

WORLDS END TRADING CO√ø§fcd76

Chandrika Ayurvedic, Mysore Sandalwood

YARDLEY

Lavender Liquid

SUN CARE

AMYRIS√øfcd76

Aftersan Lotion, Tanning Butter; *Suntan Lotion:* High, Low, Medium

ARBONNE√ø

After Sun Lotion, Lip Protector SPF 15; *Take Cover SPF 15:* Face, Hand & Body

BEAUTY WITHOUT CRUELTYø†fcd76

After Sun Moisturiser, Sun Deflectant Cream; *Sun Tan Lotions:* Factor 2, Factor 6, Factor 8

BODY BEAUTIFULø

Coconut After Sun, Totally Tropical Sun Screen Lip Balm; *Suntan Lotion:* Coconut, Factor 4, Factor 8, Factor 12

CAMILLA HEPPERø∆

Tropical: After-Sun Soother, Coconut Suntan Oil, Suntan Lotion Factor 10, Suntan Oil Factor 8, Tanning Butter Factor 6

CULPEPERøfcd76

Aromatherapy: Sunburn Lotion, Sunburn Oil, Sun Visor

FLEUR AROMATHERAPY√ø™∆

Essential Travel Pack, Exotic Travel Pack

HARTWOOD AROMATICSøfcd76

Lotus After Bath Splash, Bath Drops, Cream, Lotion, Oils: After Sun

HONESTY√ø§fcd76

Fruit: Jojoba Moisturising Cream *w* UVB

TOILETRIES & COSMETICS

Filter; *Suntan Lotions:* Aftersun, Low Protection SPF4, High Protection SPF10, Holiday Pack, Medium Protection SPF6, Tanning Butter

HYMOSA√øfcd76

After Sun Cream, Barrier Cream

KENT COSMETICS√ø

Deep Bronze: Factor 2, 4, 8, 12

MARTHA HILLø△fcd79

After Sun Gel, After Sun Milk, Sun Block Cream Factor 10, Sun Block Gel Factor 10, Sun Protection Lotion Factor 10, Zinc Sun Block (Total Protection); *For Men:* All Weather Skin Shield Factor 10

MICHELINE ARCIERø

Aromatica Helios Sun Cream, Helios Sun Oil

NATURE'S BODYCARE√øfcd76

After Sun, Skin Repair; *Factor:* 4 *(coconut)*, 8 *(insect repellent)*, 12 *(insect repellent)*; *Sun Care:* Lip Protector

NEAL'S YARD REMEDIESø

Chamomile & Aloe Vera After Sun Lotion, Lavender Sun Block; *Lemongrass:* Sun Lotion, Sun Oil

PRIME TIME√ø†△fcd88

Self Tanning Lotion

QUEEN COSMETICSø

Suntan Lotion

TALCUM POWDERS

ANIMAL AID√ø§fcd76

Fragrant Talc

BARRY Mø△fcd82

Dewberry, Evening Primrose, Flirt, White Musk; *Just For Men:* Sports

BEAUTY WITHOUT CRUELTYø†fcd76

Yolanda Dusting Powder

BODYLINEøfcd83

Dusting Powder: Apple & Gooseberry, Dewberry, Magnolia, Peach & Apricot, Raspberry & Strawberry, White Musk

BODY CENTREøfcd84

Talc: Dewberry, White Musk

BONITA√ø§†fcd80

Lavender, Pine, Unperfumed Hypoallergenic

BRONNLEY△

Animal Friends, Blue Poppy, Camellia, Daffodil, English Fern, Pink Bouquet, White Iris

CAMILLA HEPPERø△

Avocado, Orange Blossom, White Musk

CO-OPfcd85

Cool Green, Corundum, Peach & Apricot, Sparkling

CREIGHTONSø△fcd76

Apricot Care, Ocean Harvest

CULPEPERøfcd76

Elizabethan, Jasmine, Lavender, Lemon Verbena, Rose Geranium, Sandalwood, Stephanotis, Sweet Violet

DOLMA√ø§†fcd76

Lavender, Pine

KENT COSMETICS√ø

Apple Blossom Perfumed

HYMOSA√øfcd76

Talcum Powder

MARTHA HILLøΔfcd79

Talcum Powder; *For Men:* Body Talc

NEAL'S YARD REMEDIESø

Geranium & Orange

NORFOLK LAVENDERøfcd84

English Lavender, Men Of England, Rose *w* English Lavender

PURE PLANT√øΔfcd76

Talc

QUEEN COSMETICSø

Talcum Powder

SUPERDRUGfcd87

Caribbean Shores, Country Garden, English Orchard, Mediterranean Grove; *Tropical Fruits:* Apricot and Vanilla, Dewberry

YARDLEY

All Talcs

YOUR BODY√øΔfcd84

Dewberry, White Musk; *Aromatherapy:* Lavender & Bergamont, Orange & Lemon, Rosemary & Cedarwood

TOOTHPASTES & ORAL HYGIENE

ARROWMEDø

Sarakan Mouth Fresh Rinse

AUSTRIAN MOOR√ø

Moor Life: Mouth Wash, Toothpaste

BIOFORCE

Echinacea Toothpaste

BLACKMORESøfcd85

Toothpastes: Natural Mint (Original), Natural Spearmint

CAMILLA HEPPERøΔ

Natural Spearmint Mouthwash

CARTER-WALLACE

Pearl Drops

CO-OPfcd85

Antiseptic Mouthwash: Freshmint, Mildmint; *Mouth Wash:* Extra Strength, Pre Brush; *Tablets:* Extra Strength Denture, Denture; *Toothpaste:* Anti Plaque, Flouride Free, Fresh Mint Fluoride, Mild Mint Fluoride, Sensitive Teeth; *Powder:* Denture Cleansing, Pearlete Denture

HOLLYTREESøΔfcd76

Breathfresher, Toothpowder; *Mouthwashes:* Calendula, Fennel, Sage; *Natural Toothpastes†:* Fennel, Orange, Lemon,

Strawberry

HOUSE OF MISTRYø

Neem Aloe Pennel Toothpaste

JOHNSON & JOHNSON

Reach Dental Floss & Tape: all

KINGFISHER√fcd85

Toothpastes: Baking Soda Mint, Children's Strawberry, Fennel, Fennel (Flouride-Free), Natural, Mint *w* Lemon, Mint *w* Lemon (Flouride Free)

MAHARISHI AYUR-VEDø

Herbal Tooth: Paste, Powder

MAXIM PHARMACEUTICAL√™§

Amber Sugar Free Toothpaste

NATURE'S BODYCARE√øfcd76

Toothpastes: Fennel, Mint

PRIME TIME√ø†∆fcd88

Tooth Whitener

SUPERDRUGfcd87

Mint: Fresh, Mild

VERDEfcd76

Lavender & Myrrh Mouthwash

WELEDAøfcd85

Toothpaste: Calendula, Herbal, Krameria, Plant Gel, Salt

WORLDS END TRADING CO√ø§fcd76

Vicco Herbal Toothpaste

Notes

• **contact lenses** Classed as a medicine under the Medicines Act, all contact lens solutions and associated products have been safety-tested (which invariably entails animal testing at some point). Such products are listed in the *Animal-Free Shopper only* if the company under whose name they are sold meets the Shopper's 'animal testing' criterion *(see **ANIMAL-FREE CRITERIA**, page 164).*
• **Nature's Bodycare** Some products are marked in Braille

REMEDIES & SUPPLEMENTS

REMEDIES & SUPPLEMENTS

AINSWORTHø

Range of homoeopathic remedies *(liquid and pilule forms only)*

ALOE VERA THERAPY CENTREøΔ

Forever Living Products: Aloe Activator, Aloe Vera Gel, Aloe Vera Gelly, Aloe Vera Juice, Nature-Min

AMS

Ergomax Tablets, Maxim Pure Energy Fuel

AQUA SOURCEø

Blue Green Algae

ARROWMEDø

Lusitania Aloe Vera: Gel, Juice, Moisturising Cream, Spray

AUSTRIAN MOOR√ø

Moor Life: Bath, Body Cream, Body Massage Oil

BAY HOUSE AROMATICSøfcd76

Aloe Vera Juice; *Creams:* Chamomile & Yarrow Eczema, Lavender & Comfrey Healing, Tea Tree Antiseptic Skin; *Essential Oil Lotions & Potions:* Acne & Oily Skin, Anti-Stress, After Exercise/Tired Joints, After Sun, Antiseptic, Athlete's Foot, Catarrh/Sinusitis, Cellulitis, Dandruff, Dry & Cracked Skin, Eczema, Hair Tonic, Mature Skin, Menopause, Mental Tonic/Pick Me Up, Muscle Cramp/Spasms, PMT, Psoriasis, Rheumatic Pain/Childbirth, Stretchmarks, Threadveins

BACH FLOWER REMEDIESø

Rescue Remedy *(liquid only); Flower Remedies:* all

BIOCEUTICALS√ø

Biovitamin E Oil, Biolina Spirulina (Tablets, Powder), Evening Primrose Oil, Korean Ginseng Extract, Panax Guarana Elixir, Psyllium Husk; *Bio:* Aloe Vera Juice, Lecithin Granules, Linseed Oil

BIO-STRATH

Liquid: Artichoke, Chamomile, Liquorice, Thyme, Valerian, Willow; *Tablets:* Yeast

BLACKMORESøfcd85

Apple Fibre Chewable Complex, Bio Calciu, Bio Zinc, Lyp-Sine Tablets; *Digestive Products:* Acidophilus & Pectin Tablets, Acidophilus Bifidus, Colon Care, Digestive Aid Bitters, Digestive Aid Tablets; *Herbals:* Alfalfa Tablets, Cactus & Hawthorn Complex, Cape Aloes & Cascara Complex, Celery, Cornsilk, Dandelion, Garlix, Ginseng Tablets, Dong Quai, Echinacea, Echinacea Ace & Zinc, Euphorbia, Ginger Tablets, Gingko Extract, Gingko Plus, Herbal Fluid Balance, Horseradish & Garlic, Hypericum, Liquorice, Kelp Tablets, Milk Thistle, Odourless Garlic Tablets, Raspberry Leaf, Rose Hip Tablets, Sarsparilla, Skullcap & Valerian Complex, Slippery Elm, Super Horseradish & Garlic, Valerian, Witch Hazel; *Vitamins:* B_1, B_2, B_3, B_5, B_6, B_{12}, Balanced B Tablets, B Complex, B Complex & Brewers Yeast, Buffered C Complex, Bio ACE, Bio C, B Plus C, Citrus C w Acerola, Executive Formula B, Lemon Bioflavonoids, Multi Vitamins & Minerals, Vitamin A Tablets, Vitamin C Protein Coated, Vitamin E Tablets

BODY BEAUTIFULø

Anti-Wrinkle Cream w Wheatgerm, Facial

Blemish *w* Marshmallow & Tea Tree, Horse Chestnut & Yarrow Leg & Vein Cream, Rosemary & Juniper Anti-Cellulite Massage Oil, Vitamin E Oil for Stretch Marks; *Aromatherapy Bath:* Geranium & Lavender for PMT, Geranium for Tension, Marjoram for Arthritis & Sports Injuries, Rosemary & Juniper Anti-Cellulite, Ylang Ylang an Aphrodisiac; *Cade (for psoriasis, dandruff, dry scalps):* Conditioner, Cream, Shampoo

BODYLINEøfcd83

Aromatherapy Muscle Rub, Vitamin A Anti Wrinkle Cream, Oriental Balm; *Mother & Baby:* Nipple Gel, Stretch Mark Cream

BOREALISøfcd76

Anti Wrinkle Cream

BRITTANIA HEALTH

Vita Brit Gelatin Free Capsules: Beta Carotene, Evening Primrose Oil, Garlic, Vitamin E, Wheatgerm Oil

CAMILLA HEPPERøΔ

Marsa-Med Cleansing Bar *(soap-free for oily/spotty skin); Aromatherapy Oils:* Muscular Massage Oil, Relaxing Bath Oil, Soothing Bath Oil *(for period pain),* Tension Oil; *Ointments:* Comfrey, Garlic, Leg & Vein, Marigold

CARABAY√ø

Carrageen Moss; *Kelp:* Powder, Tablets

CEDAR HEALTH

Tablets: Minalka, Porosis D

CHLORELLA HEALTHø

Chlorella Tablets

CO-OP

Antiseptic, Bronchial Mixture, Health Salts, Hot Lemon Cold & Flu Relief, Vitamin C

CULPEPERøfcd76

Aromatherapy Massage Oils: After Sport, Before Sport, Cellulite, Clear Thinking, Stiffness; *Herbal Creams & Ointments:* Comfrey, Haemorrhoidal, Healing Body Balm; *Herbal Pills & Tablets:* Balmony, Feverfew, Ginger Root, Passiflora *(aids sleep),* Pilewort, Seaweed, Valerian; *Herbal Tonics & Remedies:* Cough Relief, Elderflower & Peppermint, Head Cold & Throat, Herbal Mixture, Herbal, Influenza Mixture

DAVINA HEALTH & FITNESSø

Bio Fuel Energy Drink (Lime & Lemon), Get Set Energy Drink (Lime & Lemon), Vegetarian Zinc 50 Tablets, Vitamin C; *Soya Protein:* Chocolate, Hazelnut, Plain

EFAMOL

Evening Primrose Oil *(dropper bottle)*

ESSENTIALLY YOURS√Δøfcd76

Pure Essential Oils: Antiseptic Cream, B1, Breatheasy Concentrate, Celluway, Crystel, Dermatect, R1, Reviver, Stress Away, T1, Tenderness; *Multi Blend Aromatherapy Oils:* Anti-Cellulite, Muscular, Relaxing, Stimulating

FLEUR AROMATHERAPY√ø™Δ

First Aid Kit; *Bath Oils:* Cellulite, Muscle & Joint; *Massage Oils:* Cellulite, Muscle & Joint

FRESENIUS

Provide Liquid Protein Supplement & Mal-

todextrin *Drink:* Apple, Blackcurrant, Lemon & Lime, Tropical Fruit

G & G FOOD SUPPLIESø

Cal-M Calcium Magnesium Drink

GOLDSHIELD

Cytacon *(B_{12})* Liquid

GRANGER'S

Sting Pad

GRANOVITAø

Vita Slim: Banana, Chocolate, Peach, Strawberry, Vanilla

G R LANESø

B_6, Biobalm, B-Plex, Brewers Yeast Tablets, Charabs, Herbalene, Herbelix Specific, Lecigran, Lustys Kelp Tablets, Spirulina, Top C, Vegevit B_{12}, Vitamin C, Wheatgerm Oil, Zinc; *Olbas:* Oil, Pastilles; *Thompsons Slippery Elm Food:* Malted, Unmalted

HAMILTONS OF CANTERBURY√ø∆

Far Eastern Formula: Muscle Balm, Pain Relieving Soak, Soothing Muscle Cream

HARTWOOD AROMATICSøfcd76

Lotus Foot Cream: Corns & Bunions, Foot Infections; *Lotus Foot Cream, Lotions:* Anti-Blister, Anti-Fungal, Luxurious, Peppermint; *Lotus Nail Cream, Drops:* Nail Infections; *Lotus Facial Care Cream, Lotions, Oils:* Thread Veins, Wrinkles; *Starlight for The Mind Auric Perfumes, Inhalers, Oils for Burners:* Artistic & Creativity, Clear Thoughts *(memory refresher)*, Concentration & Memory, High Tech *(anti VDU)*, Total Confidence

HEALTH INNOVATIONSø

BM Hair Stimulant

HERBAL FORCE√ø†

Fruit Plus, Herbal Glo Wrinkle Cream

HOLLAND & BARRETT

Nature's Garden Aromatherapy: Anti-Cellulite Massage Oil, Muscle Relax Bath Oil, Muscle Tone Massage Oil, Pre-Menstrual Bath Soak, Soothing Antiseptic Cream

HOUSE OF MISTRYø

Aloe Vera Juice, Ginseng *w* Vitamin E Tablets, Korean Ginseng Tablets 600mg, Libamin Tablets, Libamin Powder, Livertone, L Lysine Tablets, Manganese, Mega/Multivitamins, Multimins, Natural Papaya Enzyme Tablets, Selenium, Torpedo, Vegetarian Sustained Release Mega B Complex, Vitamin B_6 *w* Zinc & RNA, Vitamin C 500mg, Vitamin C 1000mg *w* Bio Flavanoids, Zinc; *Potentised:* Guarana Lozenges, Zinc Lozenges *w* Vitamin C

JEROME RUSSELL√øfcd76

Bitter Sweet Tablets

JESSUP MARKETING√ø

Body Protect Antioxidant; HRI Tablets: Calm Life, Catarrh, Clear Complexion, Natural Beta Carotene, Night, Water Balance

J L BRAGG√

Medicinal Charcoal: Biscuits, Tablets

LAMBERT HEALTHCARE

Alfalfa 450mg, Ascorbic Acid (Vitamin C), Ascorbyl Palmitate (Vitamin C), Boron 3, Calcium Ascorbate (Vitamin C), Calcium

Pantothenate 500mg (Vitamin B$_5$), Chelated Multi-Minerals, Duo Zinc (Liquid), Ester C Powder (Vitamin C), Ginkgo Biloba, Kelp, Kelp Tablets, Jay Vee Tablets, Lecithin Granules, Magnesium Ascorbate (Vitamin C), Mineralzinc, Octacosanol 5000µ, Pangamic Acid 100mg, Pineapple Bromelain 40mg/Papain Enzymes, Quarazinc, Quaridon, Rutin (50mg), Spirulina 500mg, Supazinc, Trace Mineral Complex, Vitamin B$_6$ 50mg, Vitamin/Mineral Complex, Zinc

LARKHALL GREEN FARMø

(Cantassium, Green Farm, Natural Flow, Nature's Plus, Trufree)

Acidophilus 500, Adult Ideal Quota, Alfalfa, Amino Acid Complex, Aminomega 2000, Amino MS, Amino PG, Anti Smoking, Antoxymega, Appegest, B$_1$ Thiamin 100mg, B$_{12}$ 50µ, B$_{12}$ 250µ, B$_{12}$ 1000µ, B$_{13}$ Calcium 500, B$_{13}$ Chromium, B$_{13}$ Iron 50, B$_{13}$ Zinc 100, B Complex, Beateasy, Best Agnus Castus, Bioflavonoids 500mg, Bio Flora 1, Biotin & Folic Acid, Boldo Herbal Aid for Slimmers, Boron & Calcium, Calcium Special Delivery, Calcimega 500, Cantamac, Cantamega 2000, Cantassium Discs, Cantassium Vitamin E Tablets, Cantopal 500mg, Caprylic Acid Plus, Cardeymin, Carrot Acidophilus, Changing Times, Chlorella, Choline 250mg, Choline & Inositol, Chromium GTF 200, Coenzyme Q10 (Crystalline), Coenzyme Q10 (Tablet), Coldclere, Colonite Tablets, Didamega,

REMEDIES & SUPPLEMENTS

DLPA 375, DMG B_{15}, Dolomite 500mg, Dolomite with A & D, Echinacea, Especially Yours, Executive Life Complex, Eyebridge Extra, Female, Feverfew, Folic Acid 100μ, Folic Acid 500mg, Folic Acid 800μ, Folic Acid Microtabs, Full B Complex w 250mg Vitamin C, Garlic ACE, Garlic & Lecithin, Garlimega 2000, Garlite, Glucomannan 500, Green Essence, Green Lightning, Green Magma, Guarana 500, Ginkgo 2000, Ginkgo Combo, Hair Nutrition, Hedclere, Histidine, Immun Actin, ImmunForte, Imunomega, Inositol 250mg, Iron, Isosport Drink Powder, Kalm B, L Arginine, L Carnitine, L Cysteine, L Glutamine, L Taurine, L Tyrosine, Lecithin 95 Granules, Libomega, Lysine, Magnesium, Magnesium B_{13}, Mamade, Manganese, Manganese B_{13}, Mega B Complex, Mega C 1500mg, Mega Mins, Mega Multi, Methionine, Micro Garlic, MicroMulti, Nail Nutritional, Natural Dried Ocean Kelp, Niacinamide 100mg, Nicotinamide 500mg, Nicotinic Acid 500mg, Nutra Aerobics Phase 3, Nutritional Integrators (Female, Male), Ocutrien Eye Nutrition, Olive Oil Cream, Organic Selenium 50μ, Oxygenic, Pantothenic Acid 500mg, Psyllium Husks loose, Potassium, Potassium B_{13}, Potent C, Quercetin Plus, Quiet Days, Quiet Nite, Quiet Tyme, Red Panax Ginseng 500mg, Regular 10 Powder, RNA w DNA, Rheumatic Pain, Rutin 500mg, Se-Power Selenium Plus, Silica, Selenium Supplement 50μ, Slimswift Day Trim, Slimswift Nite Trim, Smoke Screen, Spring Clean, Stillnite, Strong Whole B Complex, Strong Whole Multiminerals, Super Kelp, Super Selenium Complex, Super Vitamin C 1000mg, Super Vitamin C Complex, Sylk Lubricant, The Multivitamin, Toneup, Tong Kwai, Travel Sickness, Triple Ginseng, Trufree Switch Off, Trufree Vitamins & Minerals, Ultra Prenatal Complex, Pau D'Arco, Vibran C Complex, Vitamin A 10,000μ, Vitamin A 25,000μ, Vitamin A & Beta Carotene, Vitamin A & Beta Carotene 5000μ, Vitamins & Minerals w Evening Primrose, Vitamin C & E, Vitamin C 500mg, Vitamin C 1000mg, Vitamin C Chewable, Vitamin C Pure Powder, Vitamin C Ultrafind Powder, Vitamin C 500mg w Rosehips & Acerola, Vitamin C 1000mg w Rosehips & Acerola, Vitamin FF Cream, Water Naturtabs, Whole Amino Acid Compound, Whole Vitamin C With Bioflavonoids, Zinc 10mg, Zinc 10mg w Minerals, Zinc w B_6, Zinc + B_6; *Cantassium, Natural Flow:* Nicotinic Acid 100mg, Pyridoxine 100mg; *Cantassium, Nature's Plus:* B_2 Riboflavin 100mg, Bromelain, Calcium Ascorbate; PABA 500mg; *Foresight:* Iron, Magnesium Plus, Manganese Plus, Multi Minerals, Vitamin C & Garlic, Vitamins, Zinc Plus; *Natural Flow, Nature's Plus:* Zinc 50mg; *One A Day:* Clear Skin Formula, Cold Winter Formula, Hair Formula, Osteo Formula, Pregnancy Formula, Premenstrual Formula, Slimmers Formula, Vitality Formula

LIFEPLAN

Actilife, Brewers, Calcium Pantothenate, Caltabs, Ceezinc, Chewable Calcium, Cholasitrol, CoQ10 10μ, CoQ10μ, DLPA, Dolomite 500μ, Dolomite 800μ, Echinaca Root, Extravits, Formula 8 + Iron, Formula 8 without Iron, Fortyplan, Fortywinx, Hairkare, Happy Garlic, Kelp & Alfalfa Plus, Magnezie, Maxifiber, Maximune, Mentar, Omnitrace, Peacetime, Relaxon, RNA/DNA, Rutin, Selenium, Selenium Bonus, Skin-Kare, SOD, Thincide 8, Vitraday, Vitrafem, Wise Hayflower, 100mcg; *Vitamins:* B$_6$ 50µ, B$_6$ 100µ, B$_6$ TR, B Complex + C, B Complex Mega, B Complex PR, B Complex TR, Buffered C 500µ, C PR, Chewable C, Multi-Vitamins & Iron, Super Flavorola C, Time Release C

MAHARISHI AYUR-VEDø

Almond Energy Drink Mix, Blissful Rest, Calciocare, Golden Transition 1, Golden Transition 2, Healthy Hair Dietary Supplement, Herbal Iron Rich, Herbal Youthful Skin Dietary Supplement, Mind Plus Syrup, Mind Plus Tablets, Radiant Skin, Smooth Cycle, Vital Man, Vital Woman; *Herbal:* Aci-Balance, Cleanse, Di-gest, Soothe 1, Soothe 2, Throat East Tablets, Throat Soothe Liquid; *Hepeta Care:* Syrup, Tablets

MARIGOLD

Engevita Nutritional Yeast Flakes

MARKIM & ASSOCIATES√ø

Nature's Balance: 100% Pure Premium Grade Chlorella Powder, Pure Premium Grade Chlorella

MARS

Tunes: Blackcurrant, Cherry

MICHELINE ARCIERø

Dermarome Water Solution *(spots, burns, bruises, scars, tired legs); Aromatic Preparations:* Coldarome *(colds, flu),* Dermarome *(first aid),* Sleeparome *(insomnia); Aromatherapy Kits:* Anti-Infection, Exotic & Uplifting, Pick Me Up, Pregnancy, Unwinder; *Body Oils:* Healarome *(scars, bruises, sprains, burns, aches, pains); Pregnancy Oils:* Lavender *(aches, pains, fluid retention),* New Breath *(fortifying tonic),* New Life Body Oil (Nourishing, Stretch Marks); *Slimaroma Products:* Body Oil, Face Oil

NAPIERS√ø§fcd76

Aloe Vera, Boldo, Composition Essence, Fullers Earth, Herbal Drink, Herbal Tonic, Lobelia Cough Syrup, Napiers Anti-Hist Formula, Napiers Cough Syrup, Sleepeze Formula, Slippery Elm Powder; *Cream:* Chickweed, Comfrey, Seven Herb; *Massage Oil:* Arthritis, Cellulite, Circulation, Muscle Ache, Psoriasis, Ranunculus, Warming; *Oil:* Eczema, Stretch Mark, Tea Tree; *Ointment:* Arnica & Comfrey, Calendula, Poke Root, P/Q, Red; *Tablets:* Alterative, Cayenne, Echinacea, Garlic, Napiers 969, Natural Herb, Parsley Piert Co, Passiflora, Relax, Slippery Elm

NATURAL MEDICINA 2000√ø§

Golden Yacca Food Supplement: Plus, Sport Plus

NATURE'S AIDø

Brewers Yeast, Dolomite, Vitamin C

NATURE'S BESTø†fcd85

Acerola Plus, Alfalfa, Biotin, Calcium Ascorbate, Calcium Pantothenate, Caprylic Acid, Chelated Zinc, Dolomite, Fibre Mix, Ginkgo Biloba, Kelp Tablets, Lecithin Granules, Mega Potency Korean Ginseng, Megavit, Octacosanol, Pangamic Acid, Selenium, Spirulina, Trace Mineral Complex, Vitamin B$_6$

NATURE'S NATURALS√ø§fcd76

Aloe Vera Juice (100% Pure Premium Grade)

NATURE'S OWN

Acidophilus + Powder, Bromelain, Kelp & Bladderwrack, Spirulina, Pangamic Acid, Rutin, Siberian Ginseng, Vitamin C Powder; *Bound Nutritional Supplements:* Choline, Inositol, PABA; *Bound Vitamin Supplement range (tablets):* Anti-Oxidant Nutrients, Betacarotene, Niacin, Thiamin, Riboflavin, Pantothenic Acid, Vitamin B_6, Vitamin B Complex + Vitamin C & Magnesium, Vitamin C Ascorbic Acid, Vitamin E; *Minerals (tablets):* Calcium & Magnesium Carbonates, Calcium Orotate, Chromium Orotate, Copper Orotate, Dolomite, Magnesium Orotate, Multi-Mineral, Potassium Orotate, Zinc Orotate; *Vitamins (tablets):* Betacarotene, Niacin, Pantothenic Acid, Riboflavin, Thiamin, Vitamin B_6, Vitamin B Complex Plus, Vitamin C, Vitamin C + Bioflavonoids

NEAL'S YARD REMEDIESø

Cellulite Oil

NELSONSø

Wide range of homeopathic remedies (liquid form only), Pyrethrum Spray *(insect bites, stings)*, Creams: Calendula *(multipurpose)*, Evening Primrose *(dry, tired skin)*, Graphites *(dermatitis)*, Haemorrhoid, Hypercal *(cuts, sores)*, Rus Tox *(rheumatic pain)*, Tea Tree *(antiseptic)*

PHARMA NORDø

Bio-Fiber, Bio-Selenium + Zinc

POTTERS

Adiantine, Balm of Gilead, Comfrey Oil, Composition Essence Peerless, Diuretabs, EPC Essence, Elixir Damiana & Saw Palmetto, Herbal Shampoo, Indian Brandee, Jamaican Sarsaparilla Liquid, Kasbah Remedy, Lifedrops, Lightning Cough Remedy, Medicated Extract of Rosemary, Nine Rubbing Oils, Veg Cough Remover; *Mixtures:* Appetise, Catarrh, Chest, Horehound & Aniseed Cough, Indigestion, Nodoff, Watershed; *Ointments:* Comfrey, Dermacreme, Eczema, Herbheal; *Tablets:* Acidosis, Boldo, Buckwheat, Chlorophyll, Echinacea, Feverfew, GB, Herbprin, Lion Cleansing Herb, Tabritis, Tabritis Super, Watershed, Wellwoman

PRIME TIME√ø†∆fcd88

Anti-Oxidant Formula, Energy Booster, Pressure Relief Formula; *Vitabites:* Daily Complex for Teenagers, for Women, for Men, 50+; *The Essential Diet:* Opti-Meal, Slimmers Extra

PROBIOTICS™

Protexin Natural Care: Powder, Tablets

PURE PLANT√ø∆fcd76

Spotoway Antiseptic Cream *(tube)*, Spotoway Antiseptic Lotion

QUESTø

Cell Life, Chewable Vitamin C, Electro C, Enzyme Digest, Enzyme Plus, Folic Acid *w* B Complex Vitamins, Kyolic High Potency 102, Kyolic Liquid, Mega B50, Mega B100 Timed Release, Multi B Complex, Super Mega B & C, Synergistic Boron, Synergistic Magnesium + Calcium Phosphorus & B_6, Synergistic Selenium + Vitamins C & E, Synergistic Zinc + Copper & Vitamin A, Ultra Carbo, Vitamin B_6, Vitamin C, Vitamin C & Bioflavonoids, Vitamin C Timed Release

REMEDIES & SUPPLEMENTS

RICOLA

Lozenges: Lemon Mint, Menthol Eucalyptus, Original Herb; *Sugar Free Pearls:* Lemon Mint, Menthol Eucalyptus, Orange Mint, Original Herb; *Sugar Free Lozenges:* Lemon Mint, Orange Mint, Original Herb

R M SCOTT

JL Bragg's Medicinal Charcoal Biscuits

ROMANDA HEALTHCAREø

Food Supplement Powders: B-Calm Formula, Hair Formula, New C-Complex Drink, Powerhouse

SHANTI√ø§

Sinus/Head & Nose Pain Relief; *Lotions:* Antiseptic Acne, Burn, Hair Lice; *Oils:* Anti-Cellulite, Coldsore, Eczema/Psoriasis, Sciatica Relief, Tinnitus Control, Varicose Vein Pain Relief

SUNSTREAMø

Sunstream Wild Blue Green Algae: Powder, Tablets

SUPERDRUGfcd87

Antibacterial Facial Gel, Facial Wash, Medicated Cleansing Lotion

TERESA MUNRO AROMATHERAPYø∆fcd76

Massage Oils: Cellulite, Jet Lag, Muscle & Joint, Pre-Sports; *Thursday Plantation Tea Tree Products:* Antiseptic Cream, Lotion

TISSERAND√øfcd80

Antiseptic Products: Natural Antiseptic Cream, Tea Tree Lotion

VERDEfcd76

Anti-Ageing Phytocream, Arnica Tincture; *Essential Mother & Child:* Extra Rich Stretch Mark Oil, Labour Day Oil, Magic Myrtle Blend, Post Birth Bath Blend, Pre-Birth Bath Blend, Tea Tree Gel *(sore nipples & post partum); Gel:* Arnica, Burdock & Sage Anti-Acne, Clarity Headache, Mobility, Tea Tree

WEIDER HEALTH & FITNESS

Carbo-Energizer *(supplement for weight training/bodybuilding)*

WELEDAøfcd85

Range of homoeopath remedies *(liquid form only)*

XYNERGY

Aloe 99 Gel, Biogenic Aloe Vera Juice, Spirolight Bar; *New Generation Spirulina:* Tablets, Powder; *Pure Planet Power Carob-Mint Spirulina:* Tablets, Powder

YOUR BODY√ø∆fcd84

Medicated Cream

Notes

• **alternatives** Herbalists, homoeopaths, acupuncturists etc; self-health books; and remedies available from health/whole-food shops and chemists, may provide an alternative to animal-tested synthetic drugs. Be alert to the likelihood of lactose in homoeopathic tablets — as well as the possible inclusion of animal-derived minerals.

• **capsules** Most are still made of gelatine.

• **prevention** Regular exercise; rest and relaxation; avoidance of caffeine, tobacco, alcohol etc; bodily awareness; and a predominantly wholefood animal-free diet, may help prevent the onset of many minor complaints and reduce the risk of developing certain long-term illnesses.

BABY INFANT & CHILD CARE

BABY, INFANT & CHILD CARE

FOOD & DRINK

BABY ORGANIX

Dry Cereal: Baby Rice *w* Apples, Oat Cereal *w* Apples & Strawberries

BEECH NUT

Baby's First: Applesauce, Bananas *w* Tapioca, Bartlet Pears, Carrot, Peaches, Peas, Squash, Sweet Potatoes; *Stage 1:* Applesauce, Bananas *w* Tapioca, Bartlet Pears

BICKIEPEGS√

Teething Biscuits

BLACKMORESøfcd85

Chewable Multi Vitamins & Minerals, Chewable Vitamin C

COW & GATE

Pure Baby Rice

HEINZ

Farleys Soya Formula; *From 3 months:* Apple & Apricot Cereal, Banana Delight [can], Country Vegetables & Rice [can], Farmhouse Vegetable Special [jar], Fruity Tomato Sauce, Pour Over Sauce, Pure Fruit Apple & Apricot [can], Pure Fruit Apple & Banana [can, jar], Pure Fruit Just Apple [can], Pure Fruit Mixed Fruit [can, jar], Pure Fruit Summer Fruit [can], Tropical Fruit Cereal, Vegetable Bake *w* Coriander [can]; *From 7 months:* Country Bean Casserole [jar], Country Vegetables *w* Mushrooms [can], Harvest Vegetable Rissole [jar], Vegetable Bake *w* Coriander [can], Vegetable Risotto [can]; *Fruity Juice Dessert from 3 months [jar]:* Apple & Banana, Apple & Mandarin, Apple & Mango, Apple & Orange, Fruit Salad, Pear & Cherry, Pineapple

MILUPA

Fennel Infant Drink *(sugar-free); Junior Herbal Drinks (7 months+):* Camomile, Hibiscus & Rosehip, Hibiscus Apple & Raspberry; *Organic Cereals:* Country Harvest Breakfast, Pure Baby Rice, Wheaty Breakfast Cereal

WAITROSE

Baby Apple & Blackcurrant

FOOTWEAR

ALCHURINGA√ø§

Boots, shoes & sandals for children

DIADORA

Super Star Screw Junior Football Boot

GREEN SHOESø

Dart Shoe; *Boots:* Ankle, Buckle, Ivy; *Sandals:* Bar, Bridge, T-Bar, Tap

L A GEAR

Range of infant trainers, sizes UK2H–7H

REMEDIES & SUPPLEMENTS

FLEUR AROMATHERAPY√øΔ™fcd 76

Range of remedies for babies and young children

HAMILTON'S OF CANTERBURY√øΔ

Factor 15 Total Sun Protection; *Mother & Baby Evening Primrose Baby:* Bath & Shampoo, Bottom, Lotion

HARTWOOD AROMATICSøfcd76

Aromatherapy products for babies and children

HOUSE OF MISTRYø

Junior Vitamin Tablet

LARKHALL GREEN FARMø

Children's Chewable Multi, Junamac Junior Orange C; *Tandem:* Ideal Quota, IQ Junior Chewable

LIFEPLAN

Junior Multi-Vitamins, School Life, Top Marks

NAPIERS√ø§fcd76

Children's Blend Cough Syrup

VERDEfcd76

Essential Mother & Child: Camomile Baby Body Balm, Myrtle & Eucalyptus Children's Chest Rub

TOILETRIES ETC

BODY BEAUTIFULø

Baby's: Body Lotion, Conditioner, Factor 15 Suntan Lotion, Foaming Bath, Hair & Body Shampoo, Talcum Powder; *Children's:* Bubble Bath, Foam Bath, Shampoo

BODYLINEøfcd83

Mother & Baby: Barrier Cream, Bubble Bath, Dusting Powder, Lotion, Oil, Shampoo

BODYWISE√øfcd76

Natracare: Baby Bath, Baby Lotion, Baby Shampoo, Nappy Cream

CO-OPfcd85

Toothpaste; *Bubble Bath:* Green, Orange; *Babywise:* Baby Bath, Baby Oil, Baby Powder, Baby Shampoo, Baby Wipes, Extra Thick Baby Wipes, Fragrance Free Extra Thick Baby Wipes, Sterilising Tablets, Thick Baby Wipes Travel Pack, White Petroleum Jelly

HARTWOOD AROMATICSøfcd76

Blue Bird Childrens Care (2–12 yrs) Creams, Lotions, Oils: Dry Skin Soother Unfragranced; *Blue Bird Childrens Care (2–12 yrs) Creams, Lotions, Oils, Perfumes:* Lavender, Rose; *Blue Bird Childrens Care (2–12 yrs) Creams, Lotions, Perfumes:* Confidence, Harmony, Peach; *White Dove Baby Creams, Lotions, Oils:* Dry Skin Soother Unfragranced, Lavender, Rose; *White Dove Creams:* Nappy Rash, Teething

JEYESfcd83

Baby Wet Ones

KINGFISHER√fcd85

Children's Strawberry Toothpaste

KOBASHI√øfcd76

Baby Care Lotion

MAHARISHI AYUR-VEDø

Hepeta Care: Junior

BABY, INFANT & CHILD CARE

MICHELINE ARCIERø

(2–14 yrs): Face & Body Oil, Sila Jiva Bath Oil, Svetlina

NAPIERS√ø§fcd76

Children's Blend Bath Oil

NEAL'S YARD REMEDIESø

Baby Barrier

POWER HEALTHø

Baby Naturals: Bubble Bath, Cream, Lotion, Oil, Powder, Scalp Oil, Shampoo, Wipes

SUPERDRUGfcd87

Baby: Bath, Fragranced Lotion, Fragrance-Free Lotion, Oil, Shampoo

VERDEfcd76

Essential Mother & Child — Baby: Calendula Bath, Gentle Shampoo, Soothing Massage Oil

WAITROSE

Baby Talc

WELEDAøfcd85

Calendula: Baby Powder, Oil

YOUR BODY√øΔfcd84

Baby Shampoo

Natracare

100& non-chlorine bleached feminine hygiene products to include All-Cotton Tampons, Press-on Pads and Plastic-free panty shields Rayon is widely used in the manufacture of tampons, but Natracare tampons are made from just pure cotton..Reliable, gentle and convenient to use.

High quality, Cruelty-Free Babycare toiletries suitable for sensitive skins. No fragrances or colourings used. All products are VEGAN. Includes 250ml bottles of Bath, Shampoo, Lotion and 95ml jar of nappy cream.

Mail order service available. Call us on 01454 615500 Credit cards or cheques accepted

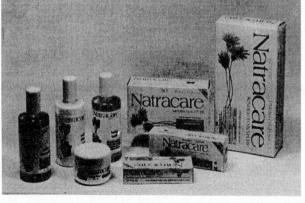

FOOTWEAR & CLOTHING

FOOTWEAR & CLOTHING

BELTS, WALLETS & BAGS ETC

AESOP√ø§

Bags: Business Attache, Business Portfolio, Briefcase, Linen Shoulder, Portfolio Hand, Recycled Rubber Min-Shoulder, Recycled Rubber Shoulder, Rubber Skin Shoulder *(2)*; *Belts:* Coach Style, Fine 'Suede', Flat Finished, Garrison Style, Military, Silver Tipped *(2)*, Rough 'Suede', Skinny (Women's); *Wallets:* Bill Fold *(2)*, Cork Bill Fold, Cork Trifold, French Purse, Recycled Rubber Card Holder, Recycled Rubber Wallet, Rubber Skin Trifold, The Organizer, Window Trifold

BUAVø

Nylon Wallet

COISAS PORTUGUESASø

Cork Bags: Drawstring Shoulder, Envelope Shape Shoulder, Round Hand, Triangular Flap, Rucksack; *Cork Purses:* Brass Framed, Chest, Clutch, Clutch *w* Brass Clip, Rigid Sided; *Cork Wallets:* Gentleman's, Ladies

ETHICAL WARES√ø™§

Belts

HEARTLAND PRODUCTS√ø

Belts: Non-Leather, Reversible, Webb; *Bags:* Attache Case, Backpack, Heritage Deluxe Overnighter Briefcase; *Wallets:* Billfold *(small wallet)*

LACS√ø§

Non-leather filofaxes; *Nylon:* Attache Case, Wallet

NAVS√ø§

Selection of non-leather wallets

UNION HEMP√ø

Pouch, Wallet; *Bags:* Bud, Courier/Record, Drawstring, Passport, Rucksack; *Belts:* Natural, Tie-Dye; *Cannabis Hemp Boot Laces:* Loose Natural, Loose 'Rasta' Dyed

VEGETARIAN SHOESø

Belts: Jean, Suit, X

VEGETARIAN SOCIETYø

Belts, Credit Card Holder, wallets

VEGGIE JACKS√ø

Bags, belts, purses, wallets

CLOTHING

AESOP√ø§

Socks: Ecologic Crew, Hiking, Men's, Women's Slouch

ETHICAL WARES√ø™§

'Fleece' Jackets: Bobcat, Coti, Jaguar, Pull-On; *Socks:* Forester, Euro Non-Woollen Walking

HEARTLAND PRODUCTS√ø

High Performance Blister-Free Cool Max Socks

SECOND SKIN

T-shirts *(individually hand printed, ethically sourced unbleached cotton, lead-free non-animal tested water-based inks, recycled materials in all packaging/promotion)*

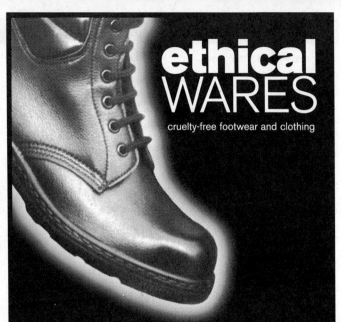

FOOTWEAR & CLOTHING

THOUSAND MILE SPORTSWEARø

Original 1000 Mile Sock

UNION HEMP√ø

Black Jeans, Blow Pinafore Dress, Cannabis Jams, Slate Top, Trousers, Waistcoat; *Billup Shirts:* Full Button, Half Button, Stand Collar; *Jackets:* Black Jean, Sleeveless, Stoned; *Shirts:* Gange, Reefer; *Skirts:* Grass, Moroccan

VEGETARIAN SHOESø

Jackets: Biker Style, Bomber, James Dean, Jean

VEGETARIAN SOCIETYø

Biker Jacket

VEGGIE JACKS√ø

Jackets *(including wax cotton)*, natural & recycled clothing

WOOLIBACKSø

Clothing made of natural linen, unbleached raw cotton, unchemically treated hemp

FOOTWEAR — GENERAL

AESOP√ø§

Men's Boots: Desert, Military Style, Pull Up Winter; *Men's Shoes:* Casual Oxford, Eco Sneak High, Eco Sneak Low, Gaia Oxford, Hopsack, Military Style Oxford, Wingtip; *Women's Boots:* Above The Knee High, Below The Knee High, Military Style, Spring/Fall, Western, Winter Ankle; *Women's Shoes:* Casual Oxford, Casual Walker, Eco Sneak High, Eco Sneak Low, Envirolite's T-Strap, Gaia Oxford, Military Style Oxford, Penny Loafer, Service Shoe, Super Comfort Pump Flat, Super Comfort Pump High Mid, Super Comfort Pump Low Mid, Tie, Western, Wing Tip; *Sandals:* Birkenstock Arizona, Massage, Men's Vagabond, Rope, The Smoothie, Women's Vagabond, Women's Envirolite, Women's Nimby

ALCHURINGA√ø§

Boots, shoes, sandals for men and women

BURTON McCALLø

Viking: Country Sport, Dry Boot, Pontoon, Puddler

ETHICAL WARES√ø™§

Earthwalker Sandal, Purist Sneaker; *Boots:* Buckle, Linen Derby, Safety

GATES RUBBER

Century Safety rubber boots

GREEN SHOESø

Boots: Buckle, Brutus Calf, Brutus Knee High, Dartmoor *(8/10 eyelets — with/without toecap)*, Field, Ghillie; *Sandals:* Bar, Bridge, Bridge T-Bar, Clasp, Ghillie, Holne, Postbridge, Tap, Wide Bar; *Shoes:* Dartmoor *(with/without toecap)*, Oxford

HEARTLAND PRODUCTS√ø

Men's: Birkenstock Sandals, Black Denim High Top Boot, Black Dress Shoes, Black High Top, Boat Shoe, Canvas Sneakers, DMs Boot, DMs High Boot, DMs Shoe, Dress Boot, Dress Shoe, Hemp Shoes, Low Khaki, Khaki, Nunn Bush Canvas Dress, Oxford, Ranger, Ranger Israeli Boots,

FOOTWEAR & CLOTHING

Rope Sandal, Safety Shoe, Sandal, Scout, Scout Israeli Boots, Sierra Sneaker, Tracker, Western Boot; *Women's:* Birkenstock Sandals, Black Denim High Top Boot, Black Dress Shoes, Booty, Canvas Twill, Clogs, Corduroy Sneaker, Denim High Top Boot, Dress Casuals, Dress Flat Shoe, Dress Oxfords, Dress Pump Shoe, DMs Boot, DMs Shoe, High Khaki, High Top, Israeli Style Patriot, Israeli Style Scout, Fashion Boot, Final Touch Slip-On Dress Casuals, Low Khaki, Macarame Shoes, Mary Jane, Moccasin, Penny Loafer, Ranger, Rope Sandal, Saddle Shoe, Sam & Libby, Sandal, Scout, Tracker, Western Boot, Western Ropers Boots, Western Shoe, White Service Shoe

MADE TO LASTø

20 styles — including Buckle Shoe, Derby Boot, Open Toe Sandal, Oxford Shoe, T-Bar Shoe

MARKS & SPENCER

All synthetic footwear

MERRELL

Sandals: Anastazi, Baja, Belize, Molokai, Mombassa, Rubber Sole

RTR SAFETY COø

FS4 Safety Workboot

UNION HEMP√ø

Hemp Para Boot

VEGETARIAN SHOESø

Birkenstock, Creeper, Deck, Chunky Gibson, Chunky Monk, Court, Plain Gibson, Strappy Sandal, Timbercat; *Boots:* Biker, Boat, Bush, Hi Commando, Hi Plain, Jod-phur, Logger, Para, Safety, Toe Cap, World; *DM:* Boot, Brogues, Chelsea, Desert, Shoe, Ranger, Ten Eye Boot; *Men's:* Brogues, Loafers, Oxfords; *Women's:* Buckle Jodphurs, Loafers, Trim Loafers

FOOTWEAR — SPORTS

AESOP√ø§

Men's Shoes: Athletic, Fitness Trainer, Performance Court, Performance Running, Performance Walker, Ridge Runner, Trail Rover, Tretorn Nylite, Vegan Hiking Boot; *Women's Shoes:* Fitness Trainer, Performance Aerobic, Performance Court, Performance Running, Performance Walker, Sporty Canvas Hiker, Ridge Runner, Trail Rover, Tretorn Nylite, Vegan Hiking Boot

CADER IDRISø

Walking boots

DIADORA

Football Boots: Premier Screw, Super Star Screw

ETHICAL WARES√ø™§

Training shoes; *Leisure Boots:* Trekking; *Walking Boots:* Ranger, Weald, Woodland

HEARTLAND PRODUCTS√ø

Men's: Basketball Shoe, Etonic Trainer, Hiking Shoe, Miami Don Basketball Shoes, Non Safety Hikers, Running Shoe, Sport Cleats *(golf, football, baseball, soccer)*, Stability Trainer, Tretorn Canvas Court; *Women's:* Etonic Trainer, Fitness Walker,

FOOTWEAR & CLOTHING

Hiking Shoe, Mid High Aerobic, Sneakers, Sport Cleats *(golf, football, baseball, soccer)*, Stability Trainer, Tretorn Canvas Court, Wide Walking Shoe

SAUCONY

Aya, Blaze, Classic Trainer, Courageous III, Express, Fastpack, Procyon, Raven, Shadow 6000, Vang, V-Grid 9000, Wincyon RXT; *Grid:* America, Courageous, Sensation, Shadow, Tech; *Jazz:* 4000, 5000,

VEGETARIAN SHOESø

DM Hiker, Veggie Trekkers

VEGGIE JACKS√ø

Hiking boots

HEADWEAR

PETA(EUROPE)√ø§

Berets: Black, Grey

SPORTS ACCESSORIES

HEARTLAND PRODUCTS√ø

Non-Leather Baseball/Softball Fielders Glove

WATERPROOFERS, POLISHES & CLEANERS

CARR & DAY & MARTIN

Wipe 'N' Shine Shoe Wipes; *Shoe Polishes:* all

ETHICAL WARES√ø™§

Nikwax waterproofing products

GRANGER'S

Footwear: G-Sport, Weltseal; *Snow sports:* Ski-Clean, Ski-Gard, Ski-Pruf, Ski-Tex, Wash 'N' Pruf; *Fabrics & clothing:* Fabsil Gold, Superpruf,

Notes

• **footwear** Quality animal-free footwear is generally available only by mail order from specialist companies. Cheap (invariably non-leather) styles are stocked by many high street shoe retailers. It has become common practice to use synthetic adhesives.

• **running and training shoes** Models change frequently and are invariably manufactured in the Far East. Many sports footwear companies stock models with non-leather/suede uppers but commonly are unable to guarantee, or are unwilling to ascertain, that the adhesives used are non-animal.

Be wary of the term 'synthetic leather'; it may well describe a non-leather material but it *may* also indicate leather which has been treated differently to 'normal' leather! 'Nubuck' is leather; 'Durabuck' is non-leather, animal-free and tends to be more expensive.

• **motorcyclist clothing** For details of gloves, boots and suits contact the Vegan Bikers Association *(see **CONTACTS**, page 182).*

ALF SUPPORTERS GROUP

T-shirt (xl only)......£7.00 (£1p&p)
Mug.......................£4.50 (£1p&p)
SAE for full merchandise list
ALF SG (CFS2), BCM 1160, London, WC1N 3XX.
The ALF SG is a legal organisation - it doesn't encourage or fund illegal acts.

HOME & OFFICE

ADHESIVES

COW PROOFINGS

Original Cow Gum Rubber Solution

DUNLOP

All solvent-based adhesives

HUMBROL

All adhesives

SELLOTAPE√

All products

AIR FRESHENERS

AMYRIS√øfcd76

Pure Essential Oils for the Vaporiser: all

BAY HOUSE AROMATICSøfcd76

Egyptian Liquid Incense: Hathor, Khensu, Nun, Onouris, Tawaret, Thoth; *Fragrance Oils:* Air Freshening Blend, Arabian Nights, Relaxing Blend, Warm n' Spicy; *Incense Sticks:* Airs Botanical, Airs Californian, Bombay, Bombay Premium, Extasy, Magical Mist, Nitiraj Organic

CO-OPfcd85

Air Fresheners: Alpine Meadow, Everyday, Lavender Breeze, Wild Rose, Woodland Berries; *Air Fresheners for Large Spaces:* Adagio, Aria, Mazurka, Minuet; *Air Fresheners for Small Spaces:* Adagio, Aria, Mazurka; *Odour Neutraliser:* Gel, Spray; *Pot Pourri Refresher Sprays:* Forest, Seaspray, Summer Fruits; *Solid Air Freshener for Large Spaces:* Adagio, Aria, Mazurka, Minuet

ESSENTIALLY YOURS√Δøfcd76

Environmental Perfuming: Awareness, Peace; *Pure Essential Oils Room Fragrances:* Crystel, Reviver, Senses, Stress Away, Tenderness

FLEUR AROMATHERAPY√ø™Δ

Vaporisers: Aroma Stone, Fragrance Burner, Night Lights, Vaporising Ring

HARTWOOD AROMATICSøfcd76

Aquarian Air Sprays: Citrus, Floral, Special, Spicy

LITTLE GREEN SHOP√øfcd85

Sprays: All Purpose Deodoriser, Perfumed Air Freshener

MICHELINE ARCIERø

Burning Essences: all

NORFOLK LAVENDERøfcd84

Room Spray

TERESA MUNRO AROMATHERAPYøΔfcd76

Fragrant Oils, Terracotta Fragrant Apples: all

THE PERFUMERS GUILD√ø§fcd76

Super Concentrated Room Freshening Essence

VEGAN CANDLES√ø§

Incense, Oils

VERDEfcd76

Essential Room Fragrances: Blue Mountain, Cedar Sunset, Fragrant Warrior, Spring Morning, Tranquillity

WORLDS END TRADING CO

Mysore Incense Cones, Spanish Saffron; *Incense Sticker:* Himalayan Breeze, Lakshmi Temple, Siromani

BLEACHES

CO-OPfcd85

Citrus Fresh Fragranced Thick, Everyday, Fresh Fragranced Thick, Standard, Thick

DELTA

Delta Catering: Bleach; *Delta Health And Hygiene:* Bleach

JEYES83

Brobat†, Izal†, Jeyes Cleaning†, Parozone, Parazone Block

SUPERDRUGfcd87

Thick

CANDLES

AMYRIS√øfcd76

Essential Oil: Amour, Cedarwood, Cinnamon, Clove, Concentration, Eucalyptus, Floral, Geranium, Harmony, Ho Leaf, Lavender, Orange, Patchouli, Pine, Relaxing, Respiratory, Rosemary, Sandalwood, Sharp Citrus, Soft Citrus, Stimulating, Vertivert, Woodland, Ylang Ylang; *Essential Oil Blend:* Lavender & Citronella, Orange Cinnamon & Clove, Patchouli & Citronella

BOLSIUS√

Tapered, Scented, Floating: all

SHEARER CANDLES

Candles, Nitelights & Tapers: all — **except** Beeswax range

VEGAN CANDLES√ø§

Nightlights; dipped, scented and aromatherapy candles

CARPET PRODUCTS

ASTONISHø

Carpet Shampoo

CARR & DAY & MARTIN

Carpet Shampoo

CO-OPfcd85

Carpet Freshener: Adagio, Minuet

DELTA

Delta Floor Care: Carpet 2000

LITTLE GREEN SHOP√øfcd85

Statofix Carpet Shampoo

VAX

Carpet Cleaner, Wool Carpet Cleaner; *Carpet Shampoos:* Brush-On, Sponge; *Stain Solutions:* Deep Action Gel, Hi Foam Mousse, Hi Foam Spray, Spill Absorbing Crystals

CIGARETTE PAPERS

RIZLA

Rolling Papers: all

HOME & OFFICE

CLEANERS — GENERAL

ARK√øfcd89

All Purpose Cleaner, Window Cleaner

ASTONISHø

Anti-Bacterial Cleanser, Cream Cleaner, Paste Cleaner, Spray & Wipe Cleaner, Synthetic Chamois

BIO-D√ø™fcd83

Glass & Mirror Cleaner, Multi-Surface Cleanser, 'Squeaky' Hand Cleaner

CARR & DAY & MARTIN

Wipe 'N' Shine Wipes: Glass, Spectacle

CO-OPfcd85

Cleaners: Anti-Bacterial Household, Aquamarine Bathroom, Aquamarine Cream, Aquamarine Spray & Foam Kitchen/Bathroom, Everyday Lemon Multipurpose Liquid, Fresh Pine Cream, Pine Fresh Heavy Duty, Ultra Concentrated Liquid, Window *w* Vinegar

ECOVER

Cleaners: Cream, Multi Surface

HOMECARE PRODUCTS√øfcd80

4 Hob Solid Electric Hotplate Polish, Bar Keepers Friend, Bath Brite, Ceramic & Halogen Hob Conditioning Cloth, Ceramic Hob Scraper, Copper Glo, Hob Brite, Homecare Plus, Shiny Sinks

HONESTY√ø§∆fcd76

All Purpose Cleansing Concentrate, Cream Cleaner

JANCO√ø§fcd76

Liquid Concentrate, Super Clean S100

JEYESfcd83†

Kleenoff Products

LABORATORY FACILITIES√

Ataka: Bath Stain Remover, Kettle Descaler

LITTLE GREEN SHOP√øfcd85

Descaler, Glass Cleaner Spray, Rapid S Cream Cleaner, Ovenfix Super Concentrated, All Purpose Household Cleaner

SUPERDRUGfcd87

Lemon Cream Cleanser, Spray Window Cleaner

CLEANERS — INDUSTRIAL

DEB

Hard Surface Cleaners & Degreasers for Industrial Use: Ambisan, Janitol Original, Janitol Plus, Janitol Rapide, Janitol Sanitiser, Marinol; *Machinery & Parts Degreasers for Industrial Use:* Jizer, Jizer Bio; *Maintenance Products for Industrial Use:* Contect Duck Oil; *Speciality Cleaners for Industrial Use:* Altrans, Deb Wash & Wax

DELTA

(Delta:) Anti-Graffiti: Activator, Euregard Coating, Euregard Primer, Graffsol Gel, Polysol; *Building:* Etch, Floc, Free, Oil Patch Remover, Scale, Tech Anti-Slip Coating, Tech Dust Seal, Tech Fast Lane, Tech Fast Set, Tech Gun Cleaner, Tech Gun Shot, Tech New Roof, Tech Pave

Neuf, Tech Stay Dry, Tech Tough Set; *Catering:* Attack, Chlor, Clean, Encore, Power, Samurai, Sparkle, Delta Wash, Wipe 'N' Clean, Zyme; *Health & Hygiene:* Bright, Chlor, Encore, Fresh, Jet, Pine, Power, Spring, Spring Clean, Triple Flush; *Janitorial:* Breeze, Etch, Floc, Force, Gleam, Grove, Pine, Power, Scale, Shine, Spring, Spring Clean; *Plant & Equipment Maintenance:* Etch, Free, Force, Grove, Lectrosafe, Lube, Oil Patch Remover, Power, Protex, Samurai, Solve, Slip, Tech Anti-Slip Coating, Tech Dust Seal, Tech Epoxycote, Tech Fast Lane, Tech Fast Set, Tech Gun Cleaner, Tech Gun Shot, Tech New Roof, Tech Pave Neuf, Tech Stay Dry, Tech Tough Set; *Washroom Maintenance:* Bright, Fresh, Fresh, Jet, Spring Clean, Triple Flush; *Waste Management:* Breeze, Floc, Force, Lube, Protex, Samurai, Zyme

CORRECTION PRODUCTS

TIPP-EX√

All correction products

DISHWASHER PRODUCTS

BIO-D√ø™fcd83

Dishwasher: Liquid, Rinse Aid

CO-OPfcd85

Concentrated Liquid, Powder, Rinse Aid, Ultra Concentrated Powder

LITTLE GREEN SHOP√øfcd85

Super Shine Dishwasher Rinse

DISINFECTANTS

ASTONISHø

Germ Clear Disinfectant

CAURNIE SOAP CO√ø∆fcd76

DES Disinfectant

CO-OPfcd85

Antiseptic, Everyday Pine Disinfectant; *Thick Disinfectant:* Fresh Pine, Pot Pourri

DEB

Detergents & Disinfectants for Industrial Use: Fastapine, Florafresh, Tot, Treetop

HONESTY√ø§∆fcd76

Disinfectant

JEYESfcd83

Disinfectants: Jeyes Ibcol, Ibcol Concentrated, Izal Pine

LITTLE GREEN SHOP√øfcd85

Pine Oil Disinfectant

SUPERDRUGfcd87

Antiseptic Disinfectant

DIY GENERAL

ARTEX

Ready Mixed Products: PVA, Sealer, Spraytex, Stabilex

DUNLOP

All solvent-based sealants

HOME & OFFICE

GRANGER'S

Repair Kits: Airbed, Boat, Mudwall & Groundsheet, Nylon, Nylotack, Patchkit, Vinyl, Vinyltack

DYES

DYLON√

Fabric Paints, Dyes

FABRIC CONDITIONERS

BIO-D√ø™fcd83

Fabric Conditioner

CO-OPfcd85

Vegetable Fabric Softener

ECOVER

Concentrated Fabric Conditioner

JEYESfcd83†

Sosoft Fabric Conditioner

RECKITT & COLMANfcd87

Down To Earth: Concentrated Fabric Conditioner

FLOOR PRODUCTS

ECOVER

Concentrated Floor Cleaner

CARR & DAY & MARTIN

Trojan Liquid Floor Wax

DELTA

Delta Floor Care: Gel, Royal Shield, Sheen, Strip, Tech Anti-Slip Coating, Tech Dust Seal, Tech Fast Lane, Tech Fast Set, Tech Pave Neuf, Tech Tough Set

VAX

Hard Floor: Cleaner, Defoamer

FURNITURE & OTHER POLISHES

BIO-D√ø™fcd83

General Purpose Polish

CARR & DAY & MARTIN

Wax Polish *(for floors, furniture, wood etc)*

CO-OPfcd85

All furniture polishes — **except** aerosols

LIBERON WAXES

Black Bison Wax

HOMECARE PRODUCTS√øfcd80

Copper Glo

LITTLE GREEN SHOP√øfcd85

Furniture Spray Polish

SUPERDRUGfcd87

Clean and Shine Polish

HAND CLEANERS (HEAVY DUTY)

ECOVER

Heavy Duty Hand Cleaner

LITTLE GREEN SHOP√øfcd85

Manox Red Heavy Duty Handcleaner

PAINT BRUSHES — DIY

HARRIS

Ranges: Aqua Brush, No Loss

PAINTS, VARNISHES & WOOD PRODUCTS — DIY

ARTEX

Ready Mixed Products: Artex XL, Force 8 Masonry Paint, Hyclad Exterior Texture Finish, Hyclad Plus Exterior Texture Finish

AURO ORGANIC PAINT SUPPLIESø

Boiled Linseed Oil, Borax Natural Wood Preservativ, Chalk Paint *(off white)*, Clear Varnish (Full Gloss, Interior), Colour Concentrate for Wall Paint, Coloured Top Coat (Gloss), Herbal Linseed Oil, Metal Primer & Undercoat, Radiator Paint *(white)*, Resin Oil Glaze, Resin Oil Primer, White Undercoat; *White Top Coats:* Eggshell, Gloss; *Woodfillers:* External, Internal

CROWN BERGER

All paints

FADS

All paints

HUMBROL

Paints & Industrial Finishes: all

SANDTEX

All paints

TOILET PRODUCTS

BIO-D√ø™fcd83

Toilet Cleaner

CO-OPfcd85

Lavatory Cleaners: Aquamarine, Fresh Pine, Pot Pourri; *Toilet Flush (in cistern):* Blue, Green; *Toilet Freshener (in bowl):* Aquamarine, Fresh Pine, Pot Pourri

JEYESfcd83

Sanilav Liquid Toilet Cleaner†, Bloo 2000†, Bloo, Bloo Green, Sanilav Rim Blocks†, Izal Toilet Cleaner, Izal Medicated Toilet Paper†, Hackle Moist†

LITTLE GREEN SHOP√øfcd85

Toilex Toilet Cleaner

RECKITT & COLMANfcd87

Down To Earth: Toilet Cleaner

SUPERDRUGfcd87

Toilet Flush; *Toilet Cleaners:* all

WASHING POWDERS ETC

ACDO√øfcd76

Acdo: Machine & Handwash, Superwash Concentrate; *Glo White:* White-Super Whitener, Wonderbar, Net Curtain Whitener, Rescue-Colour Run Remover, Stain Remover, Stain Travel Wash, Ultra Boost

ARK√øfcd89

Compact Washing Powder, Laundry Liquid

ASTONISHø

Starch

BIO-D√ø™fcd83

Laundry Liquid, Washing Powder

CO-OPfcd85

Biological Auto Wash Liquid, Biological Automatic Washing Powder, Biological Ultra Concentrated Automatic Powder, Bio Ultra Concentrated Auto Wash Liquid, Non Biological Auto Wash Liquid, Non Biological Automatic Washing Powder, Everyday Automatic Washing Powder, Non Biological High Foam Washing Powder, Non Biological Ultra Concentrated Automatic, Non Bio Ultra Concentrated Auto Wash Liquid; *Bio Colour Care:* Ultra Concentrated Auto Washing Powder; *Environment Care:* Ultra Concentrated Auto Washing Powder

ECOVER

Concentrated Auto Wash Liquid, Concentrated Washing Powder, Laundry Bleach, Liquid Clothes Wash, Stain Remover, Wool Wash

LITTLE GREEN SHOP√øfcd85

Super Soft Clothes Wash Liquid

RECKITT & COLMANfcd87

Down To Earth: Concentrated Washing Powder Refill, Washing Liquid

SUPERDRUGfcd87

Liquid Wash, Washing Powder

WASHING UP PRODUCTS

ARK√øfcd89

Washing Up Liquid

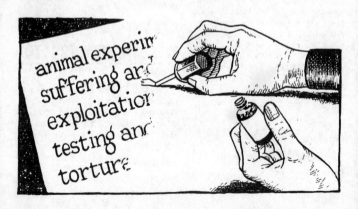

animal experim
suffering ar
exploitatio
testing an
torture

BIO-D√ø™fcd83

Washing-Up Liquid

CAURNIE SOAP CO√øΔfcd76

Wash Up Liquid

CO-OPfcd85

Washing Up Liquid: Concentrated Green, Concentrated Lemon, Green, Everyday, Lemon

LITTLE GREEN SHOP√øfcd85

Prodish Washing Up Liquid

RECKITT & COLMANfcd87

Down to Earth: Washing Up Liquid

SUPERDRUGfcd87

Lemon Concentrated Washing-up Liquid

Notes

• **animal testing** Products labelled 'new' or 'improved' may have involved yet more animal testing.
• **Artex** The powder mixes contain gelatine.
• **incense sticks** May contain gelatine or other animal substance as a binder.
• **matches** The heads contain gelatine which is used as a binder.
• **postage stamps** The gum on British stamps is animal-free. It consists of polyvinyl alcohol and dextrin. The vinyl alcohol is petroleum-based and the dextrin is derived from starch.
• **rubber gloves** All gloves made by the London Rubber Company (makers of the Marigold range) involve the use of milk casein as a processing aid in the latex.
• **water filters** The charcoal is vegetable-based.

ANIMAL CARE

ANIMAL CARE

FOODS & FOOD SUPPLEMENTS

AUSTRIAN MOOR√ø

Moor Life: Harvest Feed Supplement for Livestock, Wild Forage Horse Feed Supplement

CARABAY√ø

Seaweed Meal for Animals; *Seahorse:* Seaweed Meal for Agricultural Animals

DENES

Healthy Life Style — Health: Biscuit, Bite, Log, Treats

HAPPIDOGø†

Happidog Health Food (Vegan formulation)

HARBINGERS OF A NEW AGE√ø§

Vegedog *(supplement — which when added to recipes supplied provide complete meals for dogs & puppies)*

KATZ GO VEGAN√ø§

Vegecat, Vegekit *(supplements — which when added to recipes supplied provide complete meals for cats/kittens)*

LARKHALL GREEN FARMø

L-Tryptophan *(veterinary use only)*

LITTLE SALKED MILL√ø

Dog Meal, Hen Wheat

MARKIM & ASSOCIATES√ø

Nature's Balance 100% Pure Premium Grade Chlorella Veterinary Supplement

NATURAL DOG FOOD CO√ø

Natural Dog Food Cereal

RUSHALL FARMSø

Dog Biscuits

SEPTICO√øfcd76

Seaweed Feed Supplement *(for all domestic animals)*

WOOFERS

The Amaizeing Chew For Dogs

HEALTH & CARE PRODUCTS

AUSTRIAN MOOR√ø

Moor Life Pet Care: Cream, Shampoo

LEO LABORATORIES

Antiodor: Breath Spray, Liquid Spray *(for carpets, furniture, etc),* Stain Remover

NATURAL DOG FOOD CO√ø

Green Food Supplement, Herbal Tonic, Herbie Wellbeing, Pure Garlic Powder, Pure Seaweed Powder, Raspberry Leaf Powder, Rhino, Slippery Elm Gruel

NATURE'S NATURALS√ø§fcd76

100% Pure Premium Grade Aloe Vera Juice *(for arthritis, digestive problems, healing wounds & infections)*

HUMANE TRAPS

JANUSø

Live capture traps for cats, crows, dogs, foxes, magpies, mice, mink, rabbits, rats

LANCE NICHOLSON∅

Live capture squirrel traps

WHOLISTIC RESEARCH∅

The Whole Live Mouse Trap: Maxi Trip-Trap, Mini Trip-Trap

Notes

• **Happidog** Retailers generally stock the D_3-containing cans and/or D_3-containing dry mix packs. As a general rule, the D_2 animal-free dry packs are available by mail order only.

• **Larkhall Green Farm** Advises that all its supplements are suitable for animals. Nutritional advice available.

• **Pets** The inclusion of an 'Animal Care' section should not be construed as indicating support for the pet industry or ownership of pet (companion) animals. Pets exist solely for human gain — in the case of the pet trade: financial; in the case of pet owners: pleasure — and their freedom is necessarily restricted. In the quest for the 'perfect' pet, breeds of dog, cat, bird and fish have, through genetic manipulation, been created with 'aesthetically-pleasing' deformities. Many animal-free shoppers find pet ownership incompatible with their animal rights philosophy and those who find themselves caring for animals often do so because tens of thousands of domestic animals are unwanted and would otherwise be destroyed.

GARDEN & LEISURE

GARDEN & LEISURE

ARTISTS' MATERIALS

CRAYOLA

Chalks, Coloured Pencils, Fibre Tipped Pens, Wax Crayons, Washable Crayons: all

DALER ROWNEY†

Artist Oil Colours — **except** Ivory Black, Blue Black; Cryla and Cryla Flow — **except** Ivory Black; Dalon & Cryla Brushes Series 240, 270 and 280; Georgian Oil Colours — **except** Ivory Black, Prussian Green, Coeruleum; painting surfaces & equipment — **except** Saunders Waterford Paper, Canvas Panels, Rabbit Skin Size; *Designers Gouache, F W Artist Inks, Pearlescent Liquid Acrylic Colours, Rowney Block Printing Colours, Rowney Screen & Fabric Printing Colours, System 3 Acrylics:* all

EBERHARD FABER

FIMO Soft *(fluorescent modelling material)*

WINSOR & NEWTON†

Artists Acrylic Colours — **except** Ivory Black; Cotman Brushes

CAMERAS — ELECTRONIC

[Use floppy disks instead of film — see Notes]

CANON

Canon Ion RC 560

CLEANERS — OUTDOORS

LITTLE GREEN SHOP√øfcd85

Roloxid 10 Moss & Algae Treatment; *Cleaners:* Barbeque, Patio

SEPTICO√øfcd76

Septic Tank Conditioner

CONTRACEPTIVES

MAPA GmbH

H T Specials *(condoms suitable for gay and/or anal sex — extra strong and elastic)*

SIME HEALTH

Jiffi De Luxe Condoms Classic: Natural (translucent); *Jiffi De Luxe Condoms Cocktail:* Caribbean Coconut, Chocolate Cocktail, Peach Punch, Pina Colada; *Jiffi De Luxe Condoms Flavours:* Banana, Cherry, Coffee, Lemon, Lychee, Orange, Peppermint, Strawberry; *Jiffi De Luxe Condoms Rainbow:* Black, Blue, Green, Ivory, Orange, Pink, Purple, Yellow

GARDENING & COMPOST PRODUCTS

AUSTRIAN MOOR√ø

Flora-Moor Plant Food

CARABAY√ø

Seahorse Seaweed Fertiliser: General, Lawn, Liquid

CHASE ORGANICSø

Cocoa Shell Mulch; *Chase:* Calcified Seaweed, Organic Garden Potash, QR Organic Compost Activator, Rock Phosphate, Seaweed Meal, SM3 Seaweed Extract, SM6 Seaweed Extract; *Dickinson's:* Garden Compost; *Nature's Own:* Moorland Gold, Organic Comfrey Fertiliser

I A M SYSTEMS

Danu: Organic Growing Medium *(multipurpose compost),* Soil Conditioner & Fertiliser

FISONS

Composts, inorganic fertilisers (eg Growmore), liquid fertilisers (eg Liquinure, Tomorite): all; *Houseplant Care range:* all — **except** Insect Spray for Houseplants

MAXICROP

Complete Garden Feed, Lawn Fertiliser, Moss Killer & Lawn Tonic, Organic Calcified Seaweed, Organic Concentrate, Organic Original Plant Growth Stimulant, Organic Seaweed Meal, Plus Sequestered Iron, Professional (Triple), Tomato Fertiliser

PBI

Baby Bio

PHOSTROGEN

Acid Plant Food & Tonic, All Purpose Soluble Plant Food, Easyfeeder Hose End Dilutor, House Plant Food, House Plant Food Concentrate, Jobe's Plant Food Spikes, Lawn Feeding Regime, Plant Food Tablets, Rose Food & Tonic, Soluble Tomato Food, Water Signals

SEPTICO√øfcd76

Compost Maker

VEGANIC GARDEN SUPPLIERSø

QR Herbal Compost Activator

INSECT REPELLENTS

ARROWMEDø

Natrapel Insect Repellent

BOREALISøfcd76

Granny's Insect Repellant

GRANGER'S

Insect Repellent, Insect Repellent Wipes

GREEN THINGSø†∆fcd76

Citronella Insect Repellant

KOBASHI√ø∆fcd76

Insect Repellent

MOTOR VEHICLE PRODUCTS

DELTA

Delta Transport: De-Icer, Lectrosafe, Lube, Oil Patch Remover, Protex, Screen Wash, Slip, Smart, Solve

LITTLE GREEN SHOP√øfcd85

Car Polish, Car Shampoo, Glass Cleaner Spray

TURTLE WAX√

Beat Rust, Black Chrome, Bumper Shine, Carisma Trim Polish, Clean Machine, Cockpit Shine, Color Back Restorer, Color Magic,

GARDEN & LEISURE

Engine Clean, Glass Clean, Glass Polish, High Gloss Car Wash, High Gloss Car Wax, Hot Wax Car Wash, Minute Clean, Minute Wax, Polishing Compound, Renew Upholstery Cleaner, Rubbing Compound, Rust Eater, Rust Master, Screen Clean, Screen Wash, Silver Chrome, Trim Clean, Turtle Wax Metallic, Turtle Wax Original, Turtle Wax Plus Teflon, Wheel Clean, Zipwax Car Wash; *Foam 'n Shine:* Bumper Polish, Car Wax, Tyre Shine, Wheel Clean; *Wash & Shine Car Wash Fragrances:* all

MUSICAL EQUIPMENT

ANDY MANSONø

Hand made guitars and other fretted instruments to order

WATERPROOFERS — GENERAL

GRANGER'S

For Tents: Fabsil, Mesowax, Seamsealants, Zipease

Notes

• **contraceptives** The manufacture of most condoms (including Durex and Mates) involves the use of milk casein as a processing aid in the latex — and, in the case of Mates, the inclusion of non-fat dry milk powder. The only contraceptive pill free of animal ingredients (but not animal testing) is Gold Cross Pharmaceutical's Femulen — a progestogen-only pill.

• **film** All photographic film contains gelatine.

ᴄᴀɪɢʜ ⁿᴬ ᴍᴀʀᴀ

(HOUSE BY THE SEA) Veducation Centre

the original scottish vegetarian guest house

described by bbc veg good food mag as an "oasis" and by in britain magazine as "one of those places you dream about". gourmet, idyllic lochside seclusion on legendary loch broom.

highland veducation services.

contacts for vegetarian society, vegan society, viva and caterveg, information, courses and fax service available for scottish caterers and visitors to the highlands.

flor iomhaigh - (perfect image)

mail order/marketing service for original gifts, t.shirts, guides and recipe books. also vegan food, veggie haggis, seaweed etc.

tel/fax jackie or tony - 01854 655282 (24 hours)

Tigh na Mara Vegetarian Guest House.

ANIMAL-FREE CRITERIA

To qualify for inclusion in the *Animal-Free Shopper*
products must, as far as is possible and practical,
be *entirely* free of animal involvement.

NO ANIMAL INGREDIENTS

**The manufacture and/or development of the product, and where
applicable its ingredients, must not involve, or have involved, the
use of any animal product, by-product or derivative**

SUCH AS:

• **animal-derived additives** — *(see ADDITIVES, page 166)* • **animal
fibres** — angora, astrakhan, cashmere, mohair, wool • **animal
milks** • **animal milk derivatives** — casein, caseinates, lactates, lactic
acid, lactose • **bee products** — bee pollen, bee venom, beeswax,
honey, propolis, royal jelly • **dairy products and by-products** —
butter, cheese, whey, yoghurt • **items obtained directly from the
slaughter of animals** — fish (including anchovies), game and their
derivatives (eg meat/fish extracts and stocks), poultry, meat •
marine animal products — ambergris, capiz, caviar(e), chitin, coral,
fish scales, fishmeal, isinglass, marine oils and extracts (eg fish oils,
shark oil (squalene or squalane), seal oil, whale oil), natural
sponge, pearl, roe, seal meat, shellfish, sperm oil, spermaceti wax,
whale meat • **miscellaneous** — amniotic fluids, animal and fish
glues, carmine/carminic acid, catgut, chamois, cochineal, crushed
snails or insects, fixatives (eg musk, civet, castoreum) hormones (eg
oestrogen, progesterone, testosterone) ivory, lanolin(e), oil of
mink, parchment, placenta, silk, shellac, snake venom, some vitamins (eg D$_3$), urea, vellum, and any carriers, processing aids or
release agents containing/comprising substances of animal origin
• **slaughter by-products** — animal fats (eg dripping, lard, suet, tallow), amino acids, aspic, bone, bone charcoal, bone-meal, bristles,
collagen, down, dried blood, fatty acid derivatives, feathers, fur,
gelatin(e), glycerin(e)/glycerol, hair, hides (leather, suede etc),

hoof & horn meal, oleic acid, oleoic oil, oleostearin, pepsin, proteins (eg elastin, keratin, reticulin), rennet, skins, stearates, stearic acid, stearin(e)

Vegetable, mineral or plant/mineral-derived synthetic forms of the substances above are acceptable, as are microbiologically-fermented substances of plant origin.

NO ANIMAL TESTING

The development and/or manufacture of the product, and where applicable its ingredients, must not involve, or have involved, testing of any sort on animals conducted at the initiative of the manufacturer or on its behalf, or by parties over whom the manufacturer has effective control

ADDITIVES

A food additive alters the properties of a basic foodstuff or mixture of foodstuffs for the purpose of achieving one, or a combination of, the following: aiding the production process, preserving, modifying consumer perception. The majority of additives possess *no* nutritive value.

In terms of cost, number of chemicals employed or quantities used, preservatives account for 1%; colourings, flavourings, flavour enhancers and sweeteners — 88%; and processing aids — 11%.

All the countries of the European Union share a common list of 411 additives. They are preceded with an 'E' to show they have been approved for use within the Union and must be displayed on the labels of all foods containing them. Some additives do not have 'E' numbers and therefore do not have to be declared. These include solvents, used to dilute other additives such as colourings and to extract flavours. Flavourings constitute the largest group of non-'E' additives, totalling 3,700 in the UK alone.

The addition of substances to modify food is by no means a new phenomenon. Salt, for example, has been used as a preservative since *c* 3000BC. However, the sheer number of additives available for use today, the routine and insidious use of animal-derived substances, the known health problems associated with some additives (including eczema, hyperactivity, nausea, allergies, asthma and migraine) — hazards of others that may yet come to light, and the totally unnecessary and morally objectionable requirement to *test new additives on animals*, all provide the animal-free shopper with an incentive to avoid additive-containing products where alternatives are available.

Note: All products appearing in the *Animal-Free Shopper* containing additives listed in the **POSSIBLY** **ANIMAL-DERIVED** category have been judged to be animal-free on the basis of manufacturer/distributor declarations.

ANIMAL-DERIVED ADDITIVES

• **E120** — cochineal • **E542** — edible bone phosphate • **E631** — sodium 5'-inosinate • **E901** — beeswax • **E904** — shellac • **calcium mesoinositol hexaphosphate** • **lactose** • **sperm oil** • **spermaceti**

POSSIBLY ANIMAL-DERIVED

• **E101** — riboflavin, lactoflavin, vitamin B_{12} • **E101a** — riboflavin 5'-phosphate • **E153** *(believed animal-free version only may be used in food)* — carbon black, vegetable carbon • **E270** — lactic acid • **E322** — lecithin • **E325** — sodium lactate • **E326** — potassium lactate • **E327** — calcium lactate • **E422** — glycerol (glycerine) • **E430** *(believed to be no longer permitted in food)* — polyoxyethylene (8) stearate, polyoxyl (8) stearate • **E431** — polyoxyethylene (40) stearate, polyoxyl (40) stearate • **E432** — polyoxyethylene sorbitan monolaurate, polysorbate 20, tween 20 • **E433** — polyoxyethylene sorbitan mono-oleate, polysorbate 80, tween 80 • **E434** — polyoxyethylene sorbitan monopalmitate, polysorbate 40, tween 40 • **E435** — polyoxyethylene sorbitan monostearate, polysorbate 60, tween 60 • **E436** — polyoxyethylene sorbitan tristearate, polysorbate 65, tween 65 • **E470(a)** — sodium, potassium and calcium slats of fatty acids • **E470(b)** — magnesium slats of fatty acids • **E471** — glycerides of fatty acids, glyceryl monostearate, glyceryl distearate • **E472(a)** — acetic acid esters of glycerides of fatty acids, acetoglycerides, glycerol esters • **E472(b)** — lactic acid esters of glycerides of fatty acids, lactylated glycerides, lactoglycerides • **E472(c)** — citric acid esters of glycerides of fatty acids • **E472(d)** — tartaric acid esters of glycerides of fatty acids • **E472(e)** — mono and diacetyltartaric acid esters of glycerides of fatty acids **E472(f)** — mixed acetic and tartaric acid esters of mono- and di-glycerides of fatty acids • **E473** — sucrose esters of fatty acids • **E474** — sucroglycerides • **E475** — polyglycerol esters of fatty acids • **E476** — polyglycerol esters of polycondensed fatty acids of castor oil, polyglycerol polyricinoleate; — polyglycerol esters of dimerized fatty acids of soya bean oil • **E477** — propylene glycol esters of fatty acids; propane-1,2-diol esters of fatty acids • **E478** — lactylated fatty acid esters of gylcerol and propane-1,2-diol • **E479(b)** — thermally oxidized soya bean oil interacted with mono- and di-glycerides of fatty acids • **E481** — sodium stearoyl-2-lactylate •

E482 — calcium stearoyl-2-lactylate • **E483** — stearyl tartrate • **E491** — sorbitan monostearate • **E492** — sorbitan tristearate, span 65 • **E493** — sorbitan monolaurate, span 20 • **E494** — sorbitan mono-oleate, span 80 • **E495** — sorbitan monopalmitate, span 40 • **E570** — fatty acids (including myristic, stearic, palmitic and oleic), butyl stearate • **E572** — magnesium salts of fatty acids (including magnesium stearate); — calcium stearate • **E585** — ferrous lactate • **E627** — guanosine 5'-disodium phosphate, sodium guanylate, disodium guanylate • **E635** — sodium 5'-ribonucleotide • **E640** — glycine and its sodium salt • **E920** — L-cysteine hydrochloride • **E1518** — glyceryl mono-, di- and tri-acetate (triacetin) • **calcium hepatonate • calcium phytate • diacetin • glyceryl • leucine • monoacetin • oxystearin • polygycerol esters of dimerized fatty acids of soya bean oil** • and **any unspecified flavourings**.

VEGAN SOCIETY TRADE MARK

The animal-free marketplace continues to expand as ever-increasing numbers of consumers dispense with animal products for reasons of ethics, health or ecology. Recognizing that it is not always apparent whether a product is entirely animal-free, the Vegan Society promotes a trade mark for use on goods meeting its 'no animal ingredients' and 'no animal testing' criteria *(see page 164)*.

There is a licensing fee for use of the Vegan Society Trade Mark which is assessed on the company's actual/estimated annual revenue. Users are entitled to a 20% discount on display advertising in *The Vegan* magazine.

A 'TM' after the name of a company appearing in the *Animal-Free Shopper* indicates that it is an authorized user of the Trade Mark on *registered* products.

Prospective applicants in the UK are invited to ring 01424 427393 for a free Trade Mark Enquiry Pack.

For a current list of authorized Trade Mark users and their registered products send an SAE marked 'Trade Mark List' to: *The Vegan Society,* Donald Watson House, 7 Battle Road, St Leonards-on-Sea, East Sussex TN37 7AA.

GLOSSARY OF ANIMAL SUBSTANCES

A 'Ω' indicates that non-animal (synthetic, vegetable or plant/mineral-derived) versions/sources by the same name are known to exist.

• **albumen/albumin** — egg white *Use/s:* food binder • **ambergris** — morbid concretion obtained from the intestine of the sperm whale *Use/s:* perfumes • **amino acids**Ω — 'building blocks' of proteins • **amniotic fluid** — fluid surrounding the foetus within the placenta *Use/s:* cosmetics • **anchovy** — small fish of the herring family. Often an ingredient of Worcester sauce and pizza toppings *Use/s:* flavour enhancer • **angora** — fibre obtained from rabbits or goats *Use/s:* clothing • **aspic** — savoury jelly derived from meat and fish *Use/s:* glazing agent • **astrakhan** — skin of still born or very young lambs from a breed originating in Astrakhan, Russia *Use/s:* clothing • **beeswax (E901)**Ω — secreted by bees to produce combs *Use/s:* furniture and floor polishes, candles, cosmetics • **brawn** — boiled meat, ears and tongue of pig *Use/s:* foodstuff • **bristle** — stiff animal hair, usually from pigs *Use/s:* brushes • **calcium mesoinositol hexaphosphate** *Use/s:* baked goods, soft drinks, processed vegetables • **capiz** — shell *Use/s:* lampshades • **carmine/carminic acid (E120)** — red pigment obtained from cochineal *Use/s:* food and drink dyes • **casein**Ω — main protein of milk *Use/s:* cheese making • **cashmere** — fine wool from the cashmere goat and wild goat of Tibet *Use/s:* clothing • **castoreum** — obtained from the anal sex gland of the beaver *Use/s:* fixative in perfumes • **catgut** — dried and twisted intestines of the sheep or horse *Use/s:* stringed musical instruments, surgical stitching • **caviar(e)** — roe of the sturgeon and other fish *Use/s:* a relish • **chitin** — organic base of the hard parts of insects and crustacea eg shrimps, crabs *Use/s:* conditioners and skin care products, thickener and moisturizer in shampoos • **chamois** — soft leather from the skin of the chamois antelope, sheep, goats, deer etc *Use/s:* cleaning cloth • **cholecalciferol** — see **D₃** • **civet**Ω — substance scraped from glands in the anal pouch of the civet cat *Use/s:* fixative in perfumes • **cochineal (E120)** — dye-stuff consisting of the dried bodies of scale insects. Used for making carmine *Use/s:* red food and drink colouring • **cod liver oil** — oil extracted from the liver of cod and related fish *Use/s:* food supplement • **coral** — hard calcareous substance consisting of the continuous skeleton secreted by coelenterate polyps for their support and habitation *Use/s:* ornaments • **collagen** — constituent of connective tissue which yields gelatin(e) on boiling *Use/s:* cosmetics, sausage skins • **D$_3$ (cholecalciferol)** — vitamin derived from lanolin or fish oil *Use/s:* vitamin and food supplements • **down** — underplummage of fowls (especially duck and goose) *Use/s:* filling quilts, pillows, sleeping bags, padded clothing • **dripping** — melted animal fat *Use/s:* frying • **eider down** — small, soft feathers from the breast of the eider duck *Use/s:* filling quilts • **elastin** — protein uniting muscle fibres in meat *Use/s:* moisturizer in cosmetics • **fatty acids**Ω — organic compounds: saturated, polyunsaturated and unsaturated • **feather**Ω — epidermal appendage of a bird *Uses:* fashion accessory, feather dusters • **felt**Ω — cloth made of wool, or of wool and fur or hair *Use/s:* clothing • **gelatin(e)** — jelly obtained by boiling animal tissues (skin, tendons, ligaments etc) or bones *Use/s:* confectionery, biscuits, capsules, jellies, photographic film, match heads • **glycerin(e)/glycerol (E422)**Ω — clear, colourless liquid which may be derived from animal fats, synthesized from propylene or from fermentation of sugars *Use/s:* solvent for flavours, texture improver, humectant • **hide** — animal skin (raw or tanned) *Use/s:* clothing and footwear, clothing accessories, upholstery • **isinglass** — very pure form of gelatin(e) obtained from the air bladders of some freshwater fishes, especially the sturgeon *Use/s:* clarifying alcoholic drinks, jellies • **keratin** — protein found in hair, horns, hoofs and feathers *Use/s:* shampoos and conditioners, fertilizer • **L'cysteine hydrochloride (E920)**Ω — manufactured from animal hair and chicken feathers, or synthetically from coal tar *Use/s:* shampoo, improving agent for white flour • **lactic acid (E270)**Ω — acid produced by the fermentation of milk sugar but also by fermentation in pickles, cocoa and tobacco *Use/s:* acidulant in confectionery, soft drinks, pickles and sauces • **lactose** — milk sugar *Use/s:* tablet filler, sweetener, 'carrier' for flavouring agents — especially in crisps • **lanolin(e)** — fat extracted from sheep's wool *Use/s:* cleaning products, an emollient and emulsifer used in cosmetics — especially lipsticks • **lard** — fat surrounding the stomach and kidneys of the pig, sheep and cattle *Use/s:* culinary • **leather** — tanned hide (mostly from cattle but also sheep, pigs, goats etc) *Use/s:* clothing and footwear, clothing accessories, upholstery •

lecithin (E322)Ω — fatty substance found in nerve tissues, egg yolk, blood and other tissues. Mainly obtained commercially from soyabean, peanut and corn *Use/s:* emulsifier in baked goods and confectionery • **lutein(E161(b))**Ω — substance of deep yellow colour found in egg yolk. Obtained commercially from marigold *Use/s:* food colouring • **mohair** — cloth or yarn made from the hair of the angora goat *Use/s:* clothing • **musk**Ω — substance secreted in a gland or sac by the male musk deer *Use/s:* perfume • **oleic acid**Ω — fatty acid occurring in animal and vegetable fats *Use/s:* soaps, cosmetics, ointments • **oleoic oil** — liquid obtained from pressed tallow *Use/s:* margarines • **oleostearin** — solid obtained from pressed tallow *Use/s:* soap and candle making • **oestrogen**Ω — female sex hormone *Use/s:* cosmetics, body building supplements, hormone creams • **parchment**Ω — skin of the sheep or goat, dressed and prepared for writing etc • **pearl** ('Mother of', or 'cultured') — concretion of layers of pain-dulling *nacre* formed around a foreign particle within the shell of various bivalve molluscs, principally the oyster *Use/s:* jewellery and decorative • **pepsin** — enzyme found in gastric juices *Use/s:* cheese making • **placenta** — organ by which the foetus is attached to the umbilical cord *Use/s:* cosmetics • **progesterone**Ω — sex hormone *Use/s:* hormone creams • **propolis** — bee glue. Used by bees to stop up crevices and fix combs to the hive *Use/s:* toiletries and cosmetics • **rennet**Ω — extract of calf stomach. Contains the enzyme renin which clots milk *Use/s:* cheese making, junkets • **reticulin** — one of the structural elements (together with elastin and collagen) of skeletal muscle • **roe** — eggs obtained from the abdomen of slaughtered female fish *Use/s:* a relish • **royal jelly** — food on which bee larvae are fed and which causes them to develop into queen bees *Use/s:* food supplement • **sable** — fur from the sable marten, a small carnivorous mammal *Use/s:* clothing, artists' brushes • **shellac (E904)** — insect secretion *Use/s:* hair spray, lip sealer, polishes, glazing agent • **silk** — cloth made from the fibre produced by the larvae ('silk worm') of certain bombycine moths, the harvesting of which entails the destruction of the insect *Use/s:* clothing, cosmetics • **sodium 5'-inosinate** — occurs naturally in muscle. Prepared from fish waste *Use/s:* flavour enhancer • **sperm oil** — oil found in the head of various species of whales *Use/s:* candle making • **spermaceti wax** — fatty substance found mainly in the head of the sperm whale, other whales and dolphins *Use/s:*

medicines, candle making, cosmetics • **sponge**Ω — aquatic animal or colony of animals of a 'low order', characterized by a tough elastic skeleton of interlaced fibres *Use/s.* bathing aid • **squalene/squalane**Ω — found in the liver of the shark (and rats) *Use/s:* toiletries and cosmetics • **stearate**Ω — salt of stearic acid *Use/s:* body building supplements • **stearic acid (E570)**Ω — organic acid prepared from stearin • **stearin(e)**Ω — general name for the three glycerids (monostearin, distearin, tristearin). Formed by the combination of stearic acid and glycerin; chiefly applied to tristearin, which is the main constituent of tallow or suet *Use/s:* medicines, skin softener in toiletries and cosmetics • **suede**Ω — kid-, pig- or calf-skin, tanned *Use/s:* clothing and footwear • **suet**Ω — solid fat prepared from the kidneys of cattle and sheep *Use/s:* cooking • **tallow** — hard animal fat, especially that obtained from the parts about the kidneys of ruminating animals *Use/s:* soap and candle making • **testosterone**Ω — male hormone *Use/s:* body building supplements • **urea**Ω — waste nitrogen formed in the liver and excreted by the kidneys *Use/s:* toiletries and cosmetics • **vellum**Ω — fine parchment prepared from the skins of calves, lambs or kids *Use/s:* writing material • **velvet**Ω — fabric made usually of silk but also rayon or nylon *Use/s:* clothing • **whey** — residue from milk after the removal of the casein and most of the fat. By-product of cheese making *Use/s:* margarines, biscuits, crisps, cleaning products • **wool** — the hair forming the fleecy coat of the domesticated sheep (and similar animals) *Use/s:* clothing

ANIMAL-FREE SHOPS

The following entirely animal-free retail outlets are run by vegans and stock a wide range of products:

Hampshire *Time For Change*, 167 Fawcett Rd, Southsea, Hants. 01705 818786 • **Kent** *Earthwise Trading Company*, Indoor Market, 20 St Peter's St, Canterbury, Kent • **Surrey** *Khephra Gift Shop*, 25 Castle St, Kingston-upon-Thames, Surrey KT1 1ST. 0181 547 1485 • **West Midlands** *One Earth Shop*, 54 Allison St, Digbeth, Birmingham. 0121 632 6909 • **Yorkshire** *Evergreen Stores*, 70 Daisy Hill, Dewsbury, W Yorks. 01924 457900

Note: Evergreen Stores offers a 10% discount to full Vegan Society members.

SUGGESTED READING

A '¥' before a title indicates it is available from the Vegan Society. Ring 01424 427393 for current price details or send a SAE marked 'Publications & Merchandise Booklet' to: *The Vegan Society*, Donald Watson House, 7 Battle Rd, St Leonards-on-Sea, E Sussex TN37 7AA.

Note: Many of the titles listed below are not written from an entirely animal-free viewpoint but are included on the basis of their informativeness or practical value. A number of the books are, or may be, no longer in print.

BOOKS

additives

• **Additives — Your Complete Survival Guide** Felicity Lawrence, Century *(1986)* • **Food Additives — Taking the Lid off What We Really Eat** Erik Millstone, Penguin *(1986)* • **The Additives Guide** Christopher Hughes, John Wiley & Sons *(1987)* • **The New E for Additives** Maurice Hanssen, Thorsons *(1987)* • **Understanding Additives** Consumers' Association and Hodder & Stoughton *(1988)*

animal care

• **Dogs & Cats Go Vegetarian** James Peden, Harbingers of a New Age (US) *(1992)*

animal experiments & alternatives

• **Animal Experimentation — The Consensus Changes** Gill Langley, Macmillan Press *(1989)* • **Faith, Hope & Charity** Gill Langley, BUAV *(1990)* • **Health With Humanity** Steve McIvor, BUAV *(1990)* • **Science on Trial: The Human Cost of Animal Experiments** Dr Robert Sharpe, Awareness Books *(1994)* • **Secret Suffering** Sarah Kite, BUAV *(1990)* • **Slaughter of the Innocent** Hans Ruesch,

CEFMR *(1978)* • **The Cruel Deception: The Use of Animals in Medical Research** Robert Sharpe *(1988)* • **¥Why Animal Experiments Must Stop** Vernon Coleman, EMJ *(1994)*

animals and law

• **Animals & Cruelty & Law** Noël Sweeney, Alibi *(1990)*

animal rights/liberation — general

• **¥Animal Liberation** Peter Singer, Thorsons *(1990)* • **¥Animal Liberation: A Graphic Guide** Lori Gruen, Peter Singer and David Hine, Camden Press *(1987)* • **¥Animals, Politics & Morality** Robert Garner, Manchester University Press *(1993)* • **¥Animals' Rights** Henry Salt, Centaur *(1980)* • **Fettered Kingdoms** John Bryant, Fox Press *(1990)* • **Living Without Cruelty** Lorraine Kay, Sidgwick & Johnson *(1990)* • **Political Theory & Animal Rights** Paul Clarke and Andrew Linzey, Pluto Press *(1990)* • **¥The Animal Welfare Handbook** Barry Kew, Fourth Estate *(1993)* • **The Case for Animal Rights** Tom Regan, Routledge *(1988)* • **¥The Dreaded Comparison: Human and Animal Slavery** Marjorie Spiegel, Heretic Books *(1988)* • **The Philosophy of Animal Rights** Tom Regan, Culture & Animals Foundation (US) • **¥The Pocketbook of Animal Facts & Figures** UK Barry Kew, Green Print *(1991)* • **The Struggle for Animal Rights** Tom Regan, ISAR (US) *(1987)* • **Voiceless Victims** Rebecca Hall, Wildwood House *(1984)*

bloodsports

• **Outfoxed** Mike Huskisson *(1983)*

circuses and zoos

• **Beyond the Bars** Virginia McKenna, Will Travers & Jonathon Wray, Thorsons *(1987)* • **The Rose-Tinted Menagerie** William Johnson, Heretic *(1990)*

consumerism

• **The Ethical Consumer Guide to Everyday Shopping** ECRA *(1993)*

cookbooks

• ¥**365 Plus One Vegan Recipes** Leah Leneman, Thorsons *(1993)* •
¥**An Allergy Cookbook (vegetarian edition)** Patricia Carter, Ian
Henry Publications *(1993)* • ¥**Cook Vegan** Richard Youngs, Ash-
grove Press *(1993)* • **Cooking with Sea Vegetables** Peter and
Montse Bradford, Thorsons *(1985)* • ¥**Gourmet Vegan** Heather
Lamont, Gollancz *(1988)* • ¥**Simply Vegan** Debra Wasserman &
Reed Mangels, Vegetarian Resource Group (US) *(1991)* • ¥**The Car-
ing Cook: Cruelty-Free Cooking for Beginners** Janet Hunt, Vegan
Society *(1987)* • ¥**The Single Vegan** Leah Leneman, Thorsons
(1989) • ¥**The Vegan Cookbook** Alan Wakeman and Gordon
Baskerville, Faber & Faber *(1986)* • ¥**The Vegan Health Plan** Aman-
da Sweet, Arlington Books *(1987)* • ¥**The Vegan Kitchen Mate**
David Horton, Vegan Society (NSW) • ¥**Vegan Cooking** Eva Batt,
Thorsons *(1993)*

cosmetics

• **Cover Up — Taking the Lid off the Cosmetics Industry** Penny
Chorlton, Thorsons *(1988)* • **Herbal Cosmetics** Camilla Hepper,
Thorsons *(1987)*

ecology — home

• **Conservation at Home: A Practical Handbook** Michael Allaby,
Unwin *(1988)* • **Home Ecology** Karen Christensen, Arlington
Books *(1989)*

factory farming

• **Assault & Battery** Mark Gold, Pluto Press *(1983)* • **Chicken and
Egg — Who Pays the Price?** Clare Druce, Green Print *(1989)*

gardening

• ¥**Forest Gardening** Robert A de J Hart, Green Books *(1991)* •
Veganic Gardening Kenneth Dalziel O'Brien, Thorsons *(1986)*

land use

• ¥**Beyond Beef — The Rise and Fall of the Cattle Culture** Jeremy Rifkin, Thorsons *(1992)* • **Food: Need, Greed & Myopia** Geoffrey Yates, Earthright Publications *(1986)*

leather & fur

• **Killing for Luxury** Michael Bright, Franklin Watts *(1988)*

non-violence

• **The Non-Violent Revolution — A Comprehensive Guide to Ahimsa** Nathaniel Altman, Element *(1988)*

nutrition & health

• **Alternatives to Drugs** Arabella Melville & Colin Johnson, Fontana *(1987)* • **Dictionary of Nutrition and Food Technology** Arnold Bender, Butterworth & Co *(1982)* • ¥**Foods That Cause You to Lose Weight: The Negative Calorie Effect** Neal Barnard MD, Magni Group (US) *(1992)* • **Holistic First Aid: A Handbook for the Home** Michael Nightingale, Optima *(1988)* • ¥**Pregnancy, Children & the Vegan Diet** Michael Klaper MD, Gentle World (US) *(1987)* • **The Home Herbal** Barbara Griggs, Pan *(1986)* • ¥**Vegan Nutrition** Gill Langley, Vegan Society *(1995)* • ¥**Vegan Nutrition: Pure & Simple** Michael Klaper MD, Gentle World (US) *(1987)*

products — 'traditional' alternatives

• **1,001 Handy Household Hints** Lizzie Evans, Octopus *(1989)*

quotations

• **Fruits of Paradise: A Vegetarian Year Book** Rebecca Hall, Simon & Schuster *(1993)* • ¥**The Extended Circle: A Dictionary of Humane Thought** Jon Wynne-Tyson, Cardinal *(1990)*

theology

• **Animals and Christianity** Andrew Linzey and Tom Regan, SPCK *(1989)* • **Christianity & the Rights of Animals** Andrew Linzey, SPCK *(1987)* • **Replenish the Earth** Lewis Regenstein, SCM *(1991)*

travel

• **München auf Veganen Wegen*** Heidrun Leisenheimer *(1994)* • **¥The Cruelty-Free Guide to London** Alex Bourke & Paul Gaynor *(1994)* • **The Vegan Guide to Amsterdam*** Rochelle Del Gunter & Henk de Jong *(1994)* • **The Vegan Guide to Berlin*** Max Friedman *(1994)* • **The Vegan Guide to New York City*** Max Friedman & Dan Mills *(1994)* • **The Vegan Guide to Paris*** Alex Bourke *(1992)* • **The Vegetarian Travel Guide 1991** Jane Bowler, VSUK *(1990)*
* For details of availability contact the Vegan Society

veganism & vegetarianism

• **¥Abundant Living in the Coming Age of the Tree** Kathleen Jannaway, MCL *(1991)* • **¥Compassion — the Ultimate Ethic** Victoria Moran, American Vegan Society *(1991)* • **¥Food for a Future** Jon Wynne-Tyson, Thorsons *(1988)* • **Living Without Cruelty** Mark Gold, Green Print *(1988)* • **The Sexual Politics of Meat** Carol Adams, Polity Press *(1990)* • **¥The New Why You Don't Need Meat** Peter Cox, Bloomsbury *(1992)* • **¥The Realeat Encyclopedia of Vegetarian Living** Peter Cox, Bloomsbury *(1994)* • **¥Why Vegan?** Kath Clements, GMP *(1994)*

wool

• **Pulling the Wool** Christine Townend, Hale & Iremonger (Aus) *(1985)*

MAGAZINES

• **Arkangel** BCM 9240, London WC1N 3XX • **BBC Vegetarian Good Food** — available from newsagents • **Compassion** BWCC, 57 King Henry's Walk, London N1 4NH • **The Campaigner** NAVS, 261

Goldhawk Road, London W12 9PE • **The Ethical Consumer** ECRA Publishing, 16 Nicholas St, Manchester M1 4EJ • ¥**The Vegan** The Vegan Society, Donald Watson Hse, 7 Battle Rd, St Leonards-on-Sea, E Sussex TN37 7AA • **The Vegetarian** Parkdale, Dunham Rd, Altrincham, Cheshire WA14 4QG • **Turning Point** PO Box 45, Northolt, Middlesex UB5 6SZ • **Vegan Views** 6 Hayes Ave, Bournemouth BH7 7AD • **Viva Active!** *(under 18's)* Viva!, PO Box 212, Crewe CW1 4SD • **Viva Life** Viva! PO Box 212, Crewe, Cheshire CW1 4SD • **Wales Vegan** Montpelier, Llandrindod, Powys, Wales

Note: Many of the organizations listed under **USEFUL ADDRESSES** *(page 187)* produce their own magazines, newsletters etc.

CONTACTS

business

Vegan Business Connection c/o Veggies, 180 Mansfield Rd, Nottingham NG1 3HW. *0115 958 5666*

    Aims to encourage mutual support within the vegan community and lists vegan individuals, as well as companies, providing goods or services suitable for vegans — whether in formal business or not — and well beyond food related services.

families

The Vegan Families Contact List provides a link between parents throughout the UK seeking to raise their children in accordance with vegan principles. To receive a copy of the list, send an SAE marked 'Vegan Families Contact List' to: *The Vegan Society*, Donald Watson House, 7 Battle Road, St Leonards-on-Sea, East Sussex TN37 7AA. To register your family, please send an SAE marked 'Vegan Families Contact List Application'.

organizations — international

• **Australia** *The Vegan Society of Australia*, PO Box 85, Seaford, Victoria 3198, Australia; *The Vegan Society of New South Wales*, PO Box 467, Broadway 2007, NSW, Australia; *Vegan Australasian Network*, PO Box 429, Twantin, Queensland 4565, Australia; *Vegan Society of Queensland*, 36 Hargreaves Rd, West End, Queensland 4101, Australia • **Belgium** *Belgian Vegan Society*, Kapellestraat 66, B 9220 Hamme, Belgium • **Canada** *Canadian Vegans For Animal Rights*, c/o General Delivery, Port Berry, Ontarion, Canada LOB 1NO. (1 91 416 985 3308) **Denmark** *Vegana*, Kirsten Jungsberg, Radmund Steinsalle 45, DK-200, Copenhagen, Frederiksberg, Denmark. (45 31 743 404) • **Finland** *Vegaaniliitto Ry*, PO Box 320 FIN-00151, Helsinki, Finland. (358 0 2963025) • **France** *Société Véganiste de France*, Stéphane Hennion, 12 allée Jacques Becker, 93300 Aubervilliers, France. (33 1 48 33 63 41) • **Germany** *Vegane Offensive Ruhrgebiet*, c/o Langer August ev, Braunschweiger Straße 22, 44145 Dortmund. (49 208 385159) • **Holland** *Dutch Vegan Society*, PO Box 1087, 6801 BB Arnhem, The Netherlands. (31 85 420746) • **Ireland** *Vegan Information Centre* *for Ireland*, Mrs M C Gunn-King, 'Braidujle', 120 Knockan Rd, Bally-cloghan Td, nr Broughshane, Ballymena, N Ireland BT43 7LE • **Italy** *Movimento Vegano Italiano*, Via F.lli di Dio 375, 20099 Sesto San Giovanni, Milano, Italia • **Latvia** *Latvian Vegetarian/Vegan Society*, Lilita Postaza, Stabu Street 18 dz, 15, Riga 226001 Latvia • **Lithuania** *Lithuanian Vegetarian/Vegan Society*, Antakalnio 67-17, Vilnius 232040, Lithunia. (7 0122 741115) • **New Zealand** *New Zealand Vegan Society*, PO Box 26/356, Epsom, Auckland, New Zealand • **Portugal** *Frenta Vegana*, Apdo 75, Torre da Marinha, 2840 Seixal, Portugal • **South Africa** *Vegans in South Africa*, Box 36242, Glosderry 7702, South Africa. (27 021 7979026) • **Spain** *Asociación Vegana Espanola*, Apartado Postal 38.127, 28080 Madrid, Espana • **Sweden** *Swedish Vegan Society*, Klövervägen 6, S-64700, Mariefred, Sweden. (46 159 12467) • **USA** *The American Vegan Society*, PO Box H, Malaga, New Jersey 08328, USA. (609 694 2887); *Vegan Action*, PO Box 4353, Berkeley, CA 94704 USA; *Vegan Association of Conneticut*, 1696 Whitney Ave, Hamden, CT 06517, USA. (1 203 288 9181); *Vegan Network*, 319 Nickuson St, Suite 102, Seattle, WA 98109, USA

Vegans International c/o PO Box 1087, 6801 BB Arnhem, The Netherlands

A network of correspondents who work to promote animal-free lifestyles through a variety of non-violent means. These include: the exchange of information, promoting contact between vegans in different countries, co-ordination of international activities, and helping to establish new vegan organizations in countries where they do not already exist.

UK Co-ordinators: (South) Kerie Ann-Love, 2 Mount Pleasant Rd, London N17 6TS; *(North)* Lynn Baines, Newbigin, 2 Sandy La, Brinscall, nr Chorley, Lancs PR6 8SS.

Note: For a list of international contacts (including individuals) send a SAE marked 'International Contacts' to: *The Vegan Society*, Donald Watson Hse, 7 Battle Rd, St Leonards-on-Sea, E Sussex TN37 7AA.

organizations — local

• **Avon** *Avon Vegans*, Paula Merrifield, Karma Cottage, 3 The Rock, Brislington, Bristol BS4 4PU; *Bristol Vegetarian/Vegan*

Group, 6 Nomis Pk, Congresbury, nr Bristol, Avon BS19 5HB •
Devon *Devon Vegans*, c/o The Old Forge, Throwleigh, Devon EX20
2HS • **E Sussex** *Brighton Vegetarian & Vegan Society*, 14 Terminus
St, Brighton BN1 3PE • **Edinburgh** Edinburgh Vegans, c/o 148(TFR)
Brunton Gdns, Edinburgh EH7 5ET • **Essex** *Colchester Vegetarian
& Vegan Society*, Annette White (01206 263545); Essex SW Vege-
tarian & Vegan Group, Hartley (0181 504 8007) • **Glamorgan** *S
Glamorgan Green Party Vegan & Vegetarian Group*, Chris von Ruh-
land, 4 Dalcross St, Roath, Cardiff CF2 CUB. (01222 463415) •
Gwent *Gwent Vegetarian and Vegan Society*, Chris Sutoris, 10 Duf-
fryn Terrace, Wattsville, Gwent NP1 7QN • **Hampshire** *Portsmouth
Area Vegans*, Chris Tomlinson, Flat 2, 11 Gains Rd, Southsea, Hants
PO4 0PJ • **London** *London Vegans*, Kevin Comer (0171 603 4325)
• **Manchester** *Manchester & District Vegans and Vegetarians*,
Helen (0161 743 1872); Vegan Ecology Group (0161 232 9094) •
Somerset *Wellington & District Vegetarian and Vegan Group*,
Dawn Harries, 17 Foxdown Terrace, Wellington, Somerset TA21
8BL • **S Yorks** *Sheffield Vegan Society*, 130 Pomona St, Sheffield
S11 8JL. (0114 2683865) • **Warwickshire** *Coventry Vegan Society*,
James Kettell, 148 Hillmorton Rd, Wood End, Coventry • **W Mid-
lands** *Wolves Vegan & Veggy Society*, Box V, Students Union,
Wulfruna St, Wolverhampton. (0902 711935) • **W Yorks** *Leeds Veg-
etarian & Vegan Society*, Ian Davison, 41 Hillcourt Dr, Bramley,
Leeds LS13 2AN. (0113 2572760)

organizations — national

Lesbian and Gay Vegan Group Berkeley, 20 Britannia Rd,
Kingswood, Bristol BS15 2BG

Movement for Compassionate Living *(The Vegan Way)*, 47 Highlands Rd, Leatherhead, Surrey KT22 8NQ. *01372 372389*
    Seeks to spread compassionate understanding and to sim-
plify lifestyles by promoting awareness of the connections
between the way we live and the way others suffer, and between
development, consumption and the destruction of the planet.

The Vegan Cyclists' Holiday Club Sue Birchenaugh, *0151 342 5436*
    Aims to organize weekend (and longer) breaks, all ages,
on/off road, accommodation — camping/hostels/caravans.

Vegan Bikers Association 48 Hawkins Hall La, Datchworth, Kneb-worth, Herts SG3 6TE

Aims to promote veganism amongst motorcyclists and set up a fund for the purchase and distribution of alternatives to leather. Publishes *The Long Road*.

Vegan Society Donald Watson House, 7 Battle Rd, St Leonards-on-Sea, E Sussex TN37 7AA. *01424 427393*

An educational charity established in 1944 by a group of vegetarians who had recognized and come to reject the ethical compromises implicit in dairy dependent vegetarianism and consequently decided to renounce the use of *all* animal products.

The Society publishes a quarterly magazine — *The Vegan*, books on animal-free cooking and nutrition, and licenses a trade mark for use on animal-free products. For an Information Pack send two first class stamps.

Vegetarian & Vegan Bodybuilding Sherbourne, 7 Main Drive, Hal-snead Park, Whiston, Prescot, Merseyside L35 3PT

Aims to chart and document members' muscle gains. Enquiry and information service available.

projects

Living Land Housing Co-op 25a Stanley Rd, Whalley Range, Manchester M16 8HS

A veganic growing project. Loans required.

New Shoots PO Box 1229, Clwyd, LL16 5ZA

A small group of vegans aiming to establish a Welsh land-based community based on vegan-permaculture. Loans required.

Organic Growers of Durham Low Walworth Market Garden, Walworth, Darlington, Co Durham DL2 2NA. 01325 362466

Experimental vegan growing project.

Plants for a Future 'The Field', Higher Penpoll, St Veep, nr. Lost-withiel, Cornwall PL22 0NG. 0208 873554 or 873623

An alternative plant project aiming to demonstrate the wide variety of commodities such as fuel, food, fibres, medicines etc. that can be obtained from plants grown in England. Specializes in growing unusual and useful plants.

The Extended Ethic Vegan Village Project PO Box 237, Armidale, New South Wales 2350, Australia

Vegan Community Project 31 Caerau Rd, Caerau, Maesteg, Bridgend, Mid Glamorgan CF34 OPB
     Exists to form a contact network between people who are interested in living in a vegan community and to establish one or more such communities.

Vegan Society Local Contacts

For a list of official Vegan Society Local Contacts send an SAE marked 'Local Contacts' to: *The Vegan Society*, Donald Watson House, 7 Battle Road, St Leonards-on-Sea, East Sussex TN37 7AA.

USEFUL ADDRESSES

Many of the groups listed below have limited funds and therefore would probably appreciate receiving a SAE with your enquiry.

animal experiments & alternatives

• **11th Hour Group** 86 Smithwood Cl, London SW19 6JH. *0181 788 7862* • **Anti Vivisection Agency** 10 Mildred St, Redfield, Bristol BS5 9QR. *01272 553230* • **British Anti-Vivisection Agency** PO Box 82, Kingswood, Bristol BS15 1YF • **British Union for the Abolition of Vivisection** 16a Crane Gro, Islington, London N7 8LB. *0171 700 4888* • **Campaign to End Fraudulent Medical Research** PO Box 302, London N8 9HD • **Campaign For Advancement of Reusch's Exposes (CARE)** 23 Dunster Gdns, London NW6 7NG. *0171 625 5935* • **Christian Anti-Vivisection Society** 15 Dorset Gdns, Brighton, E Sussex BN2 1RL. *01273 699500* • **CIVIS** PO Box 388, London E8 2AL • **Disabled Against Animal Research & Exploitation** PO Box 8, Daventry, Northants NN11 4RQ. *01327 71568* • **Dr Hadwen Trust for Humane Research** 22 Bankcroft, Hitchin, Herts SG5 1JW *01462 436819* • **Doctors in Britain Against Animal Experiments** PO Box 302, London N8 9HD. *0181 340 9813* • **Fund for the Replacement of Animals in Medical Research**, Eastgate Hse, 34 Stoney St, Nottingham NG1 1NB. *0115 9584740* • **Humane Research Trust** Brook Hse, 29 Bramhall Lane South, Bramhall, Stockport, Cheshire SK7 2ND. *0161 439 8041* • **Lord Dowding Fund** Ravenside, 261 Goldhawk Rd, London W12 9PE. *0181 846 9777* • **National Anti Vivisection Society** Ravenside, 261 Goldhawk Rd, London W12 9PE. *0181 846 9777* • **Nurses' Anti-Vivisection Movement** PO Box 32, Matlock, Derbys DE4 3YJ. *01629 824664* • **Quest Cancer Test** Woodbury, Harlow Rd, Roydon, Essex CM19 5HF. *0127979 3671* • **The Cosmetics Industry Coalition for Animal Welfare (CICAW)** 39 Manor Rd, Rusthall, Tunbridge Wells, Kent TN4 8UD. *01892 512413* • **Uncaged** 14 Ridgeway Rd, Sheffield S12 2SS • **Vernon Coleman's Plan 2000** c/o EMJ, Lynmouth, Devon EX35 6EE

bloodsports

• **Action to Abolish the Grand National** PO Box 3152, London E12 5JW • **Anti-Bullfighting Committee** PO Box 175, Liverpool L69 8DY • **Fight Against Animal Cruelty in Europe** 29 Shakespeare St, Southport, Merseyside PR8 5AB. *01704 535922* • **Hunt Saboteurs Association** PO Box 1, Carlton, Nottingham NG4 2JY. *0115 9590357* • **League Against Cruel Sports** 83–87 Union St, London SE1 1SG. *0171 403 6155* • **National Anti-Hunt Campaign** PO Box 66, Stevenage, Herts SG1 2TR. *01438 746372* • **Pisces** PO Box 90, Bristol, Avon. *0117 9441175*

circuses & zoos

• **Born Free Foundation** Cherry Tree Cottage, Coldharbour, Dorking RH5 6HA. *01306 712091* • **Bristol Zoo Action** PO Box 589, Bristol, Avon BS99 1RW. *0117 9610025* • **Captive Animals Protection Society** 163 Marsden Rd, Blackpool, Lancashire FY4 3DT. *01253 765072* • **Circus Network** Leicester Animal Concern, c/o 70 High St, Leicester LE1 5YP. *01533 890767* • **Circus Watch** PO Box 43, Dudley, W Midlands DY3 3DG. *01902 883733*

diet/lifestyle

Fruitarian and Raw Energy Support & Help (FRESH) Harmony Cottage, Cutteridge Farm, Whitestone, Exeter, Devon EX4 2HE • **Movement for Compassionate Living (The Vegan Way)** 47 Highlands Rd, Leatherhead, Surrey KT22 8NQ. *01372 372389* • **Vegan Society** Donald Watson Hse, 7 Battle Rd, St Leonards-on-Sea, E Sussex TN37 7AA. *01424 427393* • **Vegetarian Society** Parkdale, Dunham Rd, Altrincham, Cheshire WA14 4QG. *0161 928 0793* • **Viva!** PO Box 21, Crewe, Cheshire CW1 4SD. *01270 522500*

direct action

• **Animal Liberation Front Press Office** BM 4400, London WC1N 3XX. 0836 310763

factory farming

• **Campaign Against Live Freight** Unit 5, 98 Goldstone Villas, Hove, BN3 3RU. *01273 720401* • **Compassion in World Farming** Charles

Hse, 5a Charles St, Petersfield, Hants GU32 3EH. *01730 264208* •
Farm Animal Welfare Network PO Box 40, Holmfirth, Huddersfield
HD7 1QY. *01484 688650*

fur & leather

• **Beauty Without Cruelty (Charity)** 57 King Henry's Walk, London
N1 4NH. *0171 254 2929* • **Campaign Against Leather and Fur** BM
Box 8889, London WC1N 3XX • **Chinchilla Liberation** PO Box 921,
Caernarfon, Gwynedd LL55 2SQ

general

• **Advocates for Animals** 10 Queensferry St, Edinburgh EH2 4PG.
0131 225 6039 • **Animal Aid** The Old Chapel, Bradford St, Tonbridge, Kent TN9 1AW. *01732 364546* • **Animal Concern
(Scotland)** 62 Old Dumbarton Rd, Glasgow G3 8RE. *0141 334 6014*
• **Animaliberation** PO Box 38, Manchester M60 1NX. *0161 953
4039* • **Animal Rights Bureau** 4 Garden La, Bradford W Yorks BD9
5QJ. *01274 495847* • **Animal Rights Coalition** PO Box 12, Car-
marthen, Dyfed SA33 5YA. *01994 231 559* • **Animals' Contacts
List** Rainbow Centre, 180 Mansfield Rd, Nottingham NG1 3HU.
0115 9585666 **Co-ordinating Animal Welfare** PO Box 589, Bristol
BS99 1RW. *0117 9776261* • **Earthkind** Humane Education Ctre,
Bounds Green Rd, London N22 4EU. *0181 889 1595* • **International Fund for Animal Welfare** Warren Court, Park Rd, Crowborough,
E Sussex TN6 2GA. *01892 663374* • **People for the Ethical Treatment of Animals (Europe)** PO Box 3169, London NW1 2JF. *0171
388 4922* • **Respect for Animals** PO Box 500, Nottingham NG1
3AS. *0115 9525440* • **RSPCA** Causeway, Horsham, W Sussex RH12
1HG. *01403 64181* • **Student Campaign for Animal Rights** Box
155, Manchester M60 1FT. *0161 953 4039* • **Teachers for Animal
Rights** c/o 29 Lynwood Rd, London SW17 8SB • **World Society for
the Protection of Animals** Park Pl, 10 Lawn La, London SW8 1UD

investigation

• **Animal Cruelty Investigation Unit Group** PO Box 8, Halesworth,
Suffolk IP19 OJL • **Animal Liberation Investigation Unit** PO Box
38, Manchester M60 1NX. *0161 953 4039* • **Animal Welfare Investigation Unit** PO Box 589, Bristol, Avon BS99 1RW. *0117 9776261*

marine animals

- **British Divers Marine Life Rescue** Unit 12, Maylan Rd, Earlstrees Ind Est, Corby, Northants NN17 2DR. *01536 201511* • **Campaign Against Dolphinaria** 40 Ormonde Ave, Epsom, Surrey KT19 9EP. *013727 28747* • **Cetacea Defence** PO Box 11, SE District Office, Manchester M18 8GU • **Marine Protection Group** 47 Avon Rd, Bournemouth BH8 8SE • **Shark Protection League** BM LAPL, London WC1N 3XX • **Shellfish Network** Box 66, c/o Greenleaf Bookshop, 82 Colston St, Bristol BS1 5BB. *0117 9425524.*

miscellaneous

- **McLibel Support Campaign** 5 Caledonian Rd, London N1 9DX. *0171 713 1269*

prisoners' support (animal rights)

- **Animal Liberation Front Supporters Group** BCM 1160, London WC1N 3XX

research

- **Vegetarian Economy & Green Agriculture (VEGA)** PO Box 39, Godalming, Surrey GU8 6BT

soya milk

- **British Soya Milk Advisory Service** Plamil Hse, Bowles Well Gdns, Dover Rd, Folkestone, Kent CT19 6PQ. *01303 850588* • **Campaign on Milk Tokens** c/o 24 Hardman St, Liverpool L1 9AX • **Soya Milk Information Bureau** Box 169, Banbury, Oxon OX16 9XE. *01295 277777*

theological

- **Animal Christian Concern** 46 St Margarets Rd, Horsforth, Leeds, W Yorks LS18 5BG • **Anglican Society for the Welfare of Animals** PO Box 54, Tunbridge Wells, Kent TN2 4TX. *01892 525594* • **Catholic Study for the Welfare of Animals** 39 Onslow Gdns, South Woodford, London E18 1ND • **Christian Consultative Council for**

the Welfare of Animals 26 Laburnum Gro, Irwin Pk, The Broadway, Sheppey, Sheerness, Kent ME12 2DE • **Christian Prayer Fellowship for the Protection of Animals** 5 Wemyss Pl, Peebles EH45 8JT Scotland • **Pagan Animal Rights** 23 Highfield South, Rock Ferry, Birkenhead, Merseyside L42 4NA. *0151 645 0485* • **The Custodians** Kent Pl, Lechlade, Glos GL7 3AW • **Quaker Concern for Animals** Webbs Cottage, Saling, Braintree, Essex CM7 5DZ

'Third World'

• **Vegfam** The Sanctuary, Lydford, Devon EX20 4AL. *01822 82203*

wild animals

• **Badger Action Group** PO Box 8, Newquay, Cornwall TR7 1TL. *01637 830897* • **Badger Protection Society** 86 Wentworth Way, Sanderstead, S Croydon, Surrey CR2 9EW. *0181 651 0104* • **British Hedgehog Preservation Society** Knowbury Hse, Knowbury, Ludlow, Shropshire SY8 3LQ. *01584 890287* • **Care for the Wild** 1 Ashfolds, Horsham Rd, Rusper, W Sussex RH12 4QX. *01293 871596* • **Wildlife Advocates** PO Box 4423, Henley-on-Thames, Oxon RG9 1GE

MULTIPLE OUTLET CONTACTS

• **ASDA** Customer Services, ASDA Stores Ltd, Asda House, Southbank, Gt Wilson St, Leeds LS11 5AD. *0113 2435435* • **Body Shop** Watersmead, Littlehampton, W Sussex BN18 9EE. *01903 731500* • **Co-op** Customer Services, PO Box 53, New Century Hse, Manchester M60 4ES *0161 827 5366* • **Gateway** — as for **Somerfield** • **Marks & Spencer** Customer Services, Marks & Spencer, Michael Hse, Baker St, London W1A 1DN. *0171 935 4422* • **Nisa** Customer Services, Nisa Stores, Boverton Rd, Llantwit Major, S Glamorgan CF6 9XZ • **Safeway** Customer Services, Safeway Stores plc, 6 Millington Rd, Hayes, Middlesex UB3 4AY. *0181 848 8744* • **Sainsbury's** Customer Services, J Sainsbury plc, Stamford Hse, Stamford St, London SE1 9LL. *0171 921 6000* • **Somerfield** Customer Services, Somerfield Stores Ltd, Somerfield Hse, Whitchurch La, Bristol BS14 0TJ *0117 9359359* • **Tesco** Customer Services, Tesco Stores Ltd, PO Box 18, Delamare Rd, Cheshunt, Herts EN8 9SL. *01992 632222* • **Waitrose** Customer Services, Waitrose, 171 Victoria St, London SW1. *0171 828 1000*

MAIL ORDER ADDRESSES

ACDO Mallison St, Bolton, Lancs BL1 8PP. *01204 309992* • **Aesop** PO Box 315, N Cambridge, MA 02140-0003, USA. *617 628 8030* • **Ainsworth's** 38 New Cavendish St, London W1M 7LH. *0171 935 5330* • **Alchuringa** The Coach Hse, Derry Ormond Pk, Lampeter, Dyfed SA48 8PA • **Aloe Vera Therapy Centre** PO Box 42, Braunton, N Devon EX33 1YU. *01271 870050* • **Amphora Aromatics** 36 Cotham Hill, Cotham, Bristol, Avon BS6 6LA. *0117 9738310* • **Amyris** PO Box 181 AFS, Harrogate, N Yorks HG2 OLX. *01423 560583* • **Andy Manson** Easterbrook, Hittisleigh, Exeter, Devon EX6 6LR. *01647 24139* • **Animal Aid** The Old Chapel, Bradford St, Tonbridge, Kent TN9 1AW. *01732 364546* • **Aqual Natural** Unit 50, Laurence-Leyland Ind Est, Wellingborough, Northants NN8 1RT. *01933 441818* • **Aqua Source** The Street, Thornace, nr Holt, Norfolk NR25 7AD. *01263 860518* • **Arbonne** Maids Moreton Hse, Buckingham MK18 1SW. *01280 824599* • **Ark** Suite 640–643 Linen Hall, 162–168 Regent St, London W1R 5TB. *0171 439 4567* • **Aromatherapy Products** Newtown Road, Hove, E Sussex BN3 7BA. *01273 325666* **Arrowmed** 59 Winchester Rd, Four Marks, Alton, Hants GU34 5HR. *01420 564300* • **Astonish** Valley Mills, Meanwood Rd, Leeds, W Yorks LS7 2JL. *01132 625206* • **Auro Organic Paint Supplies** Unit 1, Goldstones Fm, Ashdon, Saffron Walden, Essex CB10 2LZ. *01799 584 888* • **Austrian Moor** Whiteladies, Maresfield, E Sussex TN22 2HH. *01825 762 658* • **Avalon Vineyard** E Pennard, Shepton Mallet, Somerset BA4 6UA. *01749 860393* • **Bach Flower Remedies** — as for **Nelsons** • **Barry M** 1 Bittocy Business Ctr, Bittocy Hill, Mill Hill East, London NW7 1BA. *0181 349 2992* • **Baxters** Fochabers, Morayshire IV32 7LD. *01343 820393* • **Bay House Aromatics** 88 St Georges Rd, Brighton, E Sussex BN2 1EE. *01273 601109* • **Beauty Without Cruelty** 37 Avebury Ave, Tonbridge, Kent TN9 1TL. *01732 365291* • **Bermar** 14 Ennerdale Dr, Kings Lynn, Norfolk PE30 3NZ. *01553 673804* • **Berrydales** 5 Lawn Rd, London NW3 2XS. *0171 722 2866* • **Biddenden Vineyards** Little Whatmans, Biddenden, Ashford, Kent TN27 8DH. *01580 291726* • **Bio-D** 22 Alured Garth, Hedon, Hull HU12 8LZ. *01482 897765* • **Bioceuticals** Nutri Hse, 26 Zennor Rd, London SW12 OPS. *0181 675 5664* • **Biorganics** Unit 2, Caxton Pk, Wright St, Old Trafford, Manchester M16 9EW. *0161 872 9813* • **Blackfri-**

ars Bakery Unit 7–9 Blackfriars St, Leicester LE3 5DJ. *01162 622836* • **Blackmores** Unit 7, Poyle Tech Ctr, Willow Rd, Colnbrook, Bucks SL3 OPD. *01753 683815* • **Body Beautiful Products** Unit 1A Black Hall Colliery, Blackhall, Hartlepool, Cleveland TS27 4XX. *01915 871581* • **Body Centre** Units 15–18 Crosshill Ctr, Main St, Crosshill, Lochgelly, Fife KY5 8BJ. *01592 860489* • **Bodyline** Alders Wy Ind Est, Paignton, Devon TQ4 7QL. *01803 555582* • **Bodywise** 14 Lower Crt Rd, Lower Almondsbury, Bristol, Avon BS12 4DX. *01454 615500* • **Bodytreats** 15 Approach Rd, Raynes Pk, London SW20 8BA. 0181 543 7633 • **Bonita** 74 Aggborough Cres, Kidderminster, Worcs DY10 1LG. *01562 822034* • **Borealis** Old Pier Rd, Broadford, Isle of Skye IV49 9AB. *01471 822669* • **BUAV** 16a Grane Gro, Islington, London N7 8LB. *0171 700 4888* • **Burton McCall** 163 Parkington Dr, Leicester LE4 0JP. *01533 340800* • **Cader Idris** Eldon Sq, Dolgellau, Gwynedd LL40 1PS. *01341 422195* • **Camilla Hepper** 51 St Marys St, Wallingford, Oxon OX10 OEY. *01491 26196* • **Carabay** Kylebrough Lan, Moycullen, County Galway, Ireland. *00 353 91 85112* • **Carley** 34–36 St Austells, truro, Cornwall TR1 1SE. *01872 77686* • **Caurnie Soap Co** The Soaperie, Kirkintilloch, Scotland G66 1QZ. *0141 776 1218* • **Chase Organics** Coombelands Hse, Addlestone, Surrey KT15 1HY. *01932 820958* • **Chlorella Health** Butler's Wharf Bus Ctr, 44 Curlew St, London SE1 2ND. *0171 240 4775* • **Coisas Portuguesas** PO Box 283, Lightwater, Surrey GU13 5HW. *01276 451449* • **Community Foods** 19 Forty Hill, Enfield, Middx EN2 9HT. *0181 363 2933* • **Cosmetic House** 29 High St, Poole, Dorset BH15 1AB. *01202 668545* • **Creighton's** Water La, Storrington, W Sussex RH20 3DP. *01903 745611* • **Crimpers** 43 Heath St, Hampstead, London NW3 6UA. *0171 794 2949* • **Culpeper** Hadstock Rd, Linton, Cambridge CB1 6NJ. *01223 894054* • **Daniel Field** 8–12 Broadwick St, London W1V 1FH. *0171 439 8223* • **Davina Health & Fitness** International Hse, Nunnery Dr, Sheffield, S Yorks S2 1TA • **Delta** 14a Clarendon Ave, Leamington Spa, Warks CV32 5PZ. *01926 430222* • **Disos** Disos Bus Ctr, 50 Springfield Rd, Gatley, Cheshire SK8 4PF. *0161 428 7666* • **Dr Hadwen Trust** 22 Bancroft, Hitchin, Herts SG5 1JW. *01462 436819* • **Dolma** 19 Royce Ave, Hucknall, Nottingham NG15 6FU. *0115 9634237* • **Dorchester Chocolates** 14a Poundbury West Ind Est, Dorcester, Dorset DT1 2PG. *01305 264257* • **Doves Farm Foods** Dragonfly Kitchen, Salisbury Rd, Hungerford, Berks RG17 ORF. *01488 684880* • **Dragonfly Foods** Mardle Wy, Buckfastleigh,

Devon TQ11 ONR. *01364 642700* • **Dunkertons** Pembridge, Herefords HR6 9ED. *01544 388653* • **Equal Exchange Trading** 10a Queensferry St, Edinburgh. *0131 220 3484* • **Essentially Celtic** Morfa Clwyd Bus Ctr, Marsh Rd, Rhyl, Clwyd LL18 2AF. *01745 330030* • **Essentially Yours** 366–368 London Rd, Westcliff on Sea, Essex S30 7HZ. *01702 390625* • **Essential Oil Co** Freepost BZ 704 (Dept AS), Basingstoke, Hants RG22 4BR. *01256 337237* • **Ethical Wares** 84 Clyde Wy, Rise Pk, Romford, Essex RM1 4UT. *01708 739293* • **Everfresh Foods** Gatehouse Cl, Aylesbury, Bucks HP19 3DE. *01296 25333* • **Faith** 5 Kays St, Bury BL9 6BU. *0161 764 2555* • **Fantôme** The Elsecar Heritage Ctr, Unit 10, Nasmyth Row, Wath Rd, Elsecar, Barnsley S74 8HJ. *01226 749073* • **Farrow & Humphreys** Wellow Hurst, Wellow, Bath BA2 8PU. *01225 840880* • **Finders International** Winchet Hill, Goudhurst, Kent TN17 1JY. *01580 211055* • **Fleur Aromatherapy** Pembroke Studios, Pembroke Rd, Muswell Hill, London N10 2JE. *0181 444 7424* • **Foodwatch** Natural Path, 9 Corporation St, Taunton, Devon TA1 4AE. *01823 321027* • **G & G Food Supplies** 175 London Rd, East Grinstead, W Sussex RH19 1YY. *01342 312811* • **General Dietary** PO Box 38, Kingston, Surrey KT2 7YP. *0181 3362323* • **Goodness Foods** First Class Health, PO Box 30, Daventry, Northants NN11 4US. *01327 300502* • **Granovita** *(mail order for Vitaslim only)* Ambron Hse, Eastfield Rd, Wellingborough, Northant NN8 1QX. *01933 272440* • **Gramma's** Unit 6 Acorn Ctr, 29 Roebuck Rd, Hainault Ind Est, Essex IG6 3TU. *0181 501 3530* • **Green Shoes** Station Rd, Totnes, Devon TQ9 5HW. *01803 864997* • **Green Things** PO Box 59, Tunbridge Wells, Kent TN3 9PT. *01892 861132* • **G R Lanes** Sisson Rd, Glos GL1 3QB. *01452 524012* • **Hamiltons of Canterbury** Richborough Bus Pk, Ramsgate Rd, Sandwich, Kent CT13 9QT. *01304 617342* • **Happidog** Bridgend Factory, Brownhill La, Longton, Preston Lancs PR4 4SJ. *01772 614952* • **Hartwood Aromatics** Enterprise Hse, Courtaulds Wy, Coventry, West Midlands CV6 5NX. *01203 634931* • **Health Innovations** Unit 10, Riverside Bus Ctr, Brighton Rd, Shoreham, Sussex BN43 6RE. *01273 440177* • **Heartland Products** Box 218, Dakota City, Iowa 50529, USA. *00 515 332 3087* • **Heaven Scent** Herbs Pound Cottage, Pound La, Bridford, Exeter, Devon EX6 7HR. *01363 777754* • **Herbal Force** Church St, Tetbury, Glos GL8 8JG. 01666 505025 • **Hermitage Oils** East Morton, Keighley, W Yorks BD20 5UQ. *01274 565957* • **Highlander** Highlander Hse, Bathgate, West Lothian EH48 2EK. *01506 630778*

• **Hollytrees** 3 Kennet Cl, Ash, nr Aldershot, Hants GU12 6NN. *01252 344010* • **Homecare Products** Broomhill Rd, London SW18 4JQ. *018 871 5027* • **Honesty** 33 Markham Rd, Chesterfield, Derbys S40 1TA. *01246 211269* • **House of Mistry** 15–17 South End Rd, Hampstead Heath, London NW3 2PT. *0171 794 0848* • **Hymosa** Weltech Ctr, Ridgeway, Welwyn Garden City, Herts AL7 2AA. *01707 328118* • **ID Aromatics** 12 New Station St, Leeds, W Yorks LS1 5DL. *01132 424983* • **Inter-Medics** 54 Walsworth Rd, Hitchin, Herts SG4 9TD. *01462 453939* • **James White** Main Rd, Ashbocking, Ipswich, Suffolk IP6 9JS. *01473 890111* • **Janco** 11 Seymour Rd, Hampton Hill, Middx TW12 1DD. *0181 941 8706* • **Janus** Mounts Barn, Shalford Rd, Rayne, Braintree, Essex CM7 5XA. *01376 342111* • **Jerome Russell** 101 Sunnyside Rd, Ilford, Essex IG1 1HY. *0181 478 7771* • **Jessup Marketing** 27 Old Gloucester St, London WC1N 3XX. *01932 854825* • **Julius Roth** Tintagel Hse, Western Rd, Cheltenham Spa, Glos GL50 3RN. *01242 221708* • **Just Wholefoods** Unit 2, Cirencester Bus Est, Love La, Cirencester, Glos GL7 1YG. *01285 651910* • **Katz Go Vegan** Box 161, Vegan Society, Donald Watson Hse, St Leonards on Sea, E Sussex TN37 7AA. *01424 427393* • **Kent Cosmetics** Kent Hse, Harrietsham, Kent ME17 1BW. *01622 859898* • **Khephra Gift Shop** 25 Castle St, Kingston upon Thames, Surrey KT1 1ST. *0181 547 1485* • **Kittywake Perfumes** Cae Citti, Taliaris, Llandeilo, Dyfed SA19 7DP. *01558 685619* • **Kobashi** 50 High St, Ide, Nr Exeter, Devon EX2 9RW. *01392 217628* • **Lance Nicholson** 9 High St, Dulverton, Somerset TA22 9HB. *01398 23409* • **La Riche** PO Box 125, Southend on Sea, Essex SS1 2PJ. *01702 618414* • **Larkhall Green Farm** 225 Putney Bridge Rd, London SW15 2PY. *0181 874 1130* • **LACS** 83–87 Union St, London SE1 1SG. *0171 378 6697* • **Little Green Shop** 16 Gardner St, Brighton BN1 1UP. *01273 571221* • **Little Salked Mill** Little Salkeld Watermill, Penrith, Cumbria CA10 1NN. *01768 881523* • **Macsil** 4 Alma Rd, Rotherham, S Yorks SO60 2HZ. *01709 820840* • **Macsweens** 130 Bruntsfield Pl, Edinburgh EH10 4ES. *0131 229 1216* • **Made To Last** 8 The Crescent, Hyde Pk, Leeds, W Yorks LS6 2NW. *0113 2304983* • **Maharishi Ayur-Ved** Beacon Hse, Willow Walk, Skelmersdale, Lancs LN8 6UR. *01695 51015* • **Markim & Associates** 63 Stayhill Dr, Stalybridge, Cheshire SK15 2TT. *01457 762595* • **Martha Hill** The Old Vicarage, Laxton, Corby, Northants NN17 3AT. *01780 450259* • **Maxim** 4 Allison Rd, London W3 6JE. *0181 993 2528* • **Micheline Arcier** 7 William St, London SW1X 9HL. *0171 235*

3545 • **Montagne Jeunesse** The Old Grain Store, 4 Denne Rd, Horsham, W Sussex RH12 1JE. *01403 272715* • **Morning Foods** North Western Mills, Gresty Rd, Crewe, Cheshire CW2 6HP. *01270 213261* • **Napiers** Forest Bank, Barr, Ayrshire KA26 9TN. *01465 861625* • **Natural Dog Food Co** Audley St, Mossley, Lancs OL5 9HS. *01457 835389* • **Natural Medicina 2000** Dolphin Hse, 16 Hyde Tynings Cl, Eastbourne, E Sussex BN20 7TQ. *01323 647770* • **Nature's Aid** Whiteworth St, Wesham, Kirkham, Preston, Lancs PR4 3AU. *01772 686231* • **Nature's Best** 1 Lamberts Rd, Tunbridge Wells, Kent TN2 3EQ. *01892 534574* • **Nature's Bodycare** Pampas Hse, 6 Hollybush Ave, Herts AL2 3AD. *01727 864041* • **Nature's Naturals** 1 Ashdale Rd, Tonypandy, Mid Glam CF40 1RT. *01443 430239* • **NAVS** 261 Goldhawk Rd, London W12 9PE. *0181 846 9777* • **Neal's Yard Remedies** 5 Golden Cross, Cornmarket St, Oxford OX1 3EU. *01865 245436* • **Nelson & Russell** — as for **Nelsons** • **Nelsons** 73 Duke St, London W1M 6BY. *0171 495 2404* • **New Horizon Aromatics** Horizon Hse, 129 Obelisk Rd, Woolston, Southampton, Hants SO19 9DN. *01703 399664* • **Nirvana** Monks Pond Cottage, Monks Alley, Binfield, Berks RG12 5PA. *01344 360931* • **Norfolk Lavender** Caley Mill, Heacham, Norfolk PE31 7SE. *01485 570384* • **Organic Product Co** 6 Clements Rd, Ilford, Essex IG1 1BA. *0181 478 1062* • **Organic Wine** Co PO Box 81, High Wycombe, Bucks HP13 5QN. *01494 446557* • **Oxfam** Murdock Rd, Bicester, Oxon OX6 7RF. *01865 313444* • **Paul Chaplin** 9 Cwm Business Ctr, Marine St, Cwm Ebbw Vale, Wales NP3 6TB. *01495 371698* • **PETA** PO Box 3169, London NW1 2JF. *0171 388 4922* • **Pharma Nord** Spital Hall, Mitford, Morpeth NE61 3PN. *01670 519989* • **Ploughshares** 2–4 The High St, Glastonbury, Somerset BA6 9DU. *01458 835233* • **Power Health** 10 Central Ave, Airfield Est, Pocklington, York YO4 2NR. *01759 304698* • **Primetime** 4 Somerville Ct, Banbury Bus Pk, Adderbury, Oxon OX17 3NS. *01295 812500* • **Pure Plant** Europa Pk, Stoneclough Rd, Radcliffe, Manchester M26 1GG. *01204 707420* • **Queen Cosmetics** PO Box 52, E Grinstead, W Sussex RH19 4YE. *01342 312739* • **Quest** 8 Venture Wy, Aston Science Pk, Birmingham, West Midlands B7 4AP. *0121 359 0056* • **Respect for Animals** PO Box 500, Nottingham NG1 3AS. *0115 952 5440* • **Rocks Country Wines** New Bath Rd, Twyford, Berks RG10 9RY. *01734 342344* • **Romanda Healthcare** Romanda Hse, Ashley Wk, London NW7 1DU. *0181 346 0784* • **RTR Safety Co** Unit E, Goddard Rd, Whitehouse Ind Est, Ipswich, Suffolk IP1 5NP. *01473 240094* • **Rushall**

Farms The Manor, Upavon, Pewsey, Wilts SN9 6EB. *01980 630264* • **Seabrook** Seabrook Hse, Allerton Rd, Bradford, W Yorks BD15 7QU. *01274 546405* • **Second Skin** Archway 6, Ferry Ct, Ferry La, Widcombe, Bath, Avon BA2 4JW. *01225 481702* • **Sedlescombe Vineyard** Robertsbridge, E Sussex TN32 5SA. *01580 830715* • **Septico** 184 Henwood Rd, Tettenhall, Wolverhampton, W Midlands WV6 8NZ. *01902 752242* • **Shanti** The Herbary, 3–5 Templar Rd, Temple Ewell, Dover, Kent CT16 3DL. *01304 820129* • **Shu Uemura** The Quadrangle, Unit 7, 49 Atlanta St, London SW6 • **Soya Health Foods** Unit 4, Guinness Rd, Trafford Pk, Manchester M17 1SD. *0161 872 0549* • **Sunnyvale** — as for **Everfresh Foods** • **Sunrise** — as for **Soya Health Foods** • **Sunstream** Suite 609, The Chandlery, 50 Westminster Bridge Rd, London SE1 3QY. *0171 721 7551* • **Teresa Munro Aromatherapy** Unit 5, Keeley Hse Bus Ctr, 22–30 Keeley Rd, Croydon, Surrey CR0 1TE. *0181 686 7171* • **The Perfumers Guild** 61 Abbots Rd, Abbots Langley, Herts WD5 0BJ. *01923 260502* • **Thousand Mile Sportswear** Little Broughton Hse, Southam Rd, Banbury, Oxford OX16 7SR. *01295 750606* • **Tisserand** — see **Aromatherapy Products** • **Traquair House Brewery** Traquair Hse, Innerleithen, Peeblesshire EH44 6PW. *01896 830323* • **Trefriw Wells Spa** Trefriw, Gwynedd LL27 0JS. *01492 640057* • **Ultra Glow** 12 St Peters Ct, Colchester CO1 1WD. *01206 576611* • **Union Hemp** 14 South Gallery, Exchange St, Sheffield S2 5TR. *0114 2766234* • **Vegan Candles** 8 Bruntingthorpe Wy, Binley, Coventry CV3 2GD *(SSAE for details)* • **Veganic Garden Supplies** Heath Fm Rd, Worstead, Norfolk NR28 0JB. *01692 404570* • **Vegan Wine Club** 2–5 Old Bond St, Mayfair, London W1X 3TB. *0181 905 5515* • **Vegetarian Hamper Co** 1 Orchard Side, Hunston, nr Chichester, W Sussex PO20 6PQ. *01243 788376* • **Vegetarian Shoes** 12 Gardener St, Brighton, E Sussex BN1 1UP. *01273 691913* • **Vegetarian Society** Parkdale, Dunham Rd, Altrincham, Cheshire WA14 4QG. *0161 928 0793* • **Veggie Jacks** 25 Gardner St, Brighton, E Sussex BN1 1UP. *01273 626498* • **Veggies** 180 Mansfield Rd, Nottingham NG1 3HW. *0115 9585666* • **Vinceremos** 65 Raglan Rd, Leeds, W Yorks LS2 9DZ. *0113 2431691* • **Vintage Roots** Sheeplands Fm, Wargrave Rd, Wargrave, Berks RG10 8DT. *01734 401222* • **VIVA!** PO Box 212, Crewe, Cheshire CW1 4SD. *01270 522500* • **Weider** 10 Windsor Ct, Clarence Dr, Harrogate, N Yorks HG1 2PE • **Weleda** Heanor Rd, Ilkeston, Derbys DE7 8DR. *0115 9309319* • **Well Oiled** Freepost, Plymouth, Devon PL1 1BR. *01752 607381* • **Wholistic Research**

Bright Haven, Robin's La, Lolworth, Cambridge CB3 8HH. *01954 781074* • **Wicken Fen** 36 High St, Wicken, Ely, Cambs CB7 5XR. *01353 723103* • **Woolibacks** 43 Blenheim Rd, Cheadle Hulme, Cheshire SK8 7BD. *0161 485 2557* • **Worlds End Trading** Co 4 Florence Terr, Falmouth, Cornwall TR11 3RR. *01326 316528* • **Xynergy** Lower Elsted, Midhurst, W Sussex GU29 OJT. *01730 813642* • **Your Body** Units 52–54 Milmead Ind Est, Mill Mead Rd, Tottenham, London N17 9QU. *0181 808 2662*

INDEX

THE Vegan SOCIETY

Promoting a diet free from all animal produce for the benefit of people, animals and the environment

MEMBERSHIP APPLICATION

Block letters please

NAME _____

ADDRESS _____

_____ POST CODE _____

PROFESSION/SKILLS _____

SIGNATURE _____

Tick as appropriate:

☐ I am interested in veganism and enclose two first class stamps for an Information Pack

☐ I adhere to a vegan diet and wish to become a Vegan Society member. I undertake to abide by the Society's *Memorandum and Articles of Association* (£2 or may be viewed without charge at the Society's office)

☐ Although not a vegan I support the Society's aims and wish to become a 'Supporter' member

☐ Individual £15   ☐ Family/Joint £20
☐ Unwaged Individual £10   ☐ Unwaged Family/Joint £14
☐ Junior *(under 18)* £8   ☐ Life £250
☐ **Donation**   *Eire and overseas: All applicants must add £5*

I enclose a sterling cheque/PO payable to 'The Vegan Society' for
£_____ (£_____ membership + £_____ donation)

Return to: The Vegan Society, Donald Watson House, 7 Battle Road, St Leonards-on-Sea, East Sussex TN37 7AA United Kingdom

How do I know the course is **right for me?**

☐   **Are you a parent or carer of one or more children aged 0 to 10 years old?**

☐   **Are you expecting your first child?**

☐   **Would you like your family life to be the best it can be?**

If you answered 'yes' to any of those questions, then this course is for you, whether you feel all is going well or you are facing challenges.

While The Parenting Children Course is based on Christian principles, it is designed for parents and carers with or without a Christian faith.

The course is for every type of parenting situation, including parenting on your own, step-parenting and parenting as a couple.

Whatever your situation, the practical tools you learn can help you to improve and strengthen your family life.

What is The Parenting Children Course?

The Parenting Children Course was developed by Nicky and Sila Lee, authors of *The Marriage Book* and *The Parenting Book*. They have been married for over thirty years, have four children and live in London. They started The Parenting Children Course in 1990, and it continues to spread with many courses now running around the world.

Over five weekly sessions (or ten shorter ones) you will discover practical tools to help you:

- **Build** a strong family centred on love
- **Meet** your children's needs
- **Set** effective boundaries
- **Teach** healthy relationships
- **Pass** on the values you hold to be important

What can I **expect** on the course?

A fantastic atmosphere

that is welcoming, encouraging and fun. Courses are run in all kinds of venues – homes, restaurants, cafes (after hours), community halls, churches, nurseries, schools – but wherever your local course is run, you should find a great atmosphere and a friendly welcome.

A delicious meal or snack

– each session begins with something to eat and drink, giving you space to relax and chat to other parents.

Practical talks

that are informative and fun, either played on DVD or given live. They include filmed clips of parents and children sharing their own experiences, street interviews and advice from parenting experts.

Small groups based on the age of your oldest child

so that you can meet other parents/carers who have lots in common with you.

Time to discuss

the challenges you are facing and how to establish long-term strategies for your own family. However, you will not be required to share anything about your family life that you would prefer not to. Every part of the course is optional, including contributing to the small group discussions.

What is the **cost of the course?**

Most courses charge a minimal fee to cover the cost of the meal, course materials and venue (if applicable). Your local course administrator will be able to let you know how much you'll need to pay. Many courses also offer bursaries.

Don't just take our word for it – this is what past guests have said about the course

'We **loved** it and learnt so much.'

'The course was very informative and helped to build my confidence as a parent.'

'It has given me ways to communicate effectively with my kids.'

'It's helped tremendously in many ways, like seeing some of my children's behaviour as just child-like and not losing my cool over it.'

'We don't have children yet but it has prepared us very well for when the baby comes.'